Marriage and Family in India

Marriage and Family in India

Trends and Emerging Challenges

Edited by

JASMEET SANDHU

RAWAT PUBLICATIONS

Jaipur • New Delhi • Bangalore • Guwahati • Kolkata

ISBN 978-81-316-0775-6

Published by
Prem Rawat for **Rawat Publications**
Satyam Apts, Sector 3, Jawahar Nagar, Jaipur 302 004 (India)
Phone: 0141 265 1748 / 7006 Fax: 0141 265 1748
E-mail: info@rawatbooks.com
Website: www.rawatbooks.com

New Delhi Office
4858/24, Ansari Road, Daryaganj, New Delhi 110 002
Phone: 011 2326 3290

Also at *Bangalore, Guwahati* and *Kolkata*

Typeset by Rawat Computers, Jaipur
Printed at Chaman Enterprises, New Delhi

Contents

Section II
Family Formation: Child Bearing

Section III
Emerging Challenges

Preface

Marriage and family have, perhaps, occupied much attention of the sociologists world over because of their universal existence and inevitability. So, the question arises, why write something about marriage and family when so much has already been written about it? Both these institutions have persisted since times immemorial and have withstood the pressures of changing individual and societal needs, changing technologies and changing demography; and have undergone transformation in the process. Every day we come across discussions and debates on how marriages are failing, families are falling apart and values concerning them are changing; in short, how these institutions are withering? It simply means that many questions concerning them rcmain unanswered and need to be looked at from a fresh perspective.

Much is known about changes in marriage and family in the West as these two institutions received a great deal of attention from the social scientists after World War II. But, the same is not the case about the Indian situation. Both these institutions preoccupied the Indian sociologists when sociology gained momentum in India after the establishment of the first Department of Sociology in Bombay University. Caste, marriage and family and village studies dominated the research in initial decades. The interest in family and marriage dwindled during 1950s, 1960s and 1970s (Patel, Tulsi ed., 2005, *The Family in India*, New Delhi: Sage Publications) and the trend continued in 1980s and 1990s also.

Birth rates in India started declining during 1970s and, in conjunction with the decline in death rates, altered the family size, family composition, intergenerational relations, etc. Rise in education, particularly in female education, raised the age at marriage and delayed the process of family formation. Thus, changing marital practices and child bearing patterns reiterated the need to study these institutions. The present volume looks at the changes in marriage and child bearing from a fresh perspective of family formation. It does not address the issues of change in marital practices and in structure, functions or organization of family. All the articles included in the volume have earlier been published in the *Guru Nanak Journal of Sociology* which is being regularly published since 1980. Initially, I was reluctant to take up the task of bringing out this volume because it is very difficult to knit a variety of articles together, which have not been written for the purpose. But, I was able to edit this volume because of my interest in the field of marriage and family and demography. I must confess that I actually enjoyed working on it.

The volume is one in a series of such volumes to be brought out by the faculty of the Department of Sociology, Guru Nanak Dev University, Amritsar, to commemorate the 40 years of establishment of the Department. At the onset, I am extremely thankful to the Vice-Chancellor of Guru Nanak Dev University for allowing us to bring out the series. I would like to thank all the authors/contributors who have written articles for *Guru Nanak Journal of Sociology* from time to time. I am also obliged to my colleagues Prof. Paramjit Singh Judge, Prof. Gurpreet Bal and Dr Neena Rosey Kahlon for their encouragement, suggestions and support. I would like to express my special thanks to my family; my sociologist husband Prof. Ranvinder Singh Sandhu for his critical comments on introduction and my son Mr

Sandeep Singh Sandhu for his overall support in the completion of this work. Discussion with my students in the Family Demography class has been instrumental in the crystallization of ideas, I am thankful to them as well. My thanks are also due to Mr Rajbir Singh who very kindly helped me with computer work. I am also indebted to Mr Antrayami Khandwal for relieving me of my household duties to devote time for the task undertaken. In the end, I take responsibility for any lapses or shortcomings.

Jasmeet Sandhu

Contributors

ARUN KUMAR SHARMA, Professor of Sociology, Indian Institute of Technology, Kanpur.

AMARJIT MAHAJAN, Former Professor, Department of Sociology Punjab University, Chandigarh.

ANUPAM BAHRI, Assistant Professor, P.G. Government College for Girls, Chandigarh.

ANURADHA, Former Student of Sociology, Guru Nanak Dev University, Amritsar.

B.S. NAGI, Former Senior Fellow, Council for Social Development, New Delhi.

DEEP PUNIA, Assistant Professor in Sociology, College of Basic Sciences, HAU, Hissar.

H.D. LAKSHMINARAYANA, Former Professor of Sociology, Bangalore University, Bangalore.

JASMEET SANDHU, Professor and Head, Department of Sociology, Guru Nanak Dev University, Amritsar.

J.P. SINGH, Professor, Department of Sociology, Patna University, Patna.

M.L. SHARMA, Former Dean, Post Graduate Studies, Haryana Agriculture University, Hissar.

P.K.B. NAYAR, Former Professor and Chairman, Centre for Gerontological Studies, Kochuloor, Thiruvananthapuram.

PRABHJOT MALHI, Research Officer, Population Research Centre, Centre for Research in Rural and Industrial Development, Chandigarh.

RANJAY VARDHAN, Assistant Professor in Sociology, Government College for Girls, Chandigarh.

R.K. PUNIA, Professor in Sociology, Haryana Agriculture University, Hissar.

SAVITA THAKUR, Assistant Professor, Population Research Centre, Himachal Pradesh University, Shimla.

SOBHA B. NAYAR, Faculty, Centre for Women's Studies, University of Kerala, Thiruvanathapuram.

SUKHVINDER SINGH, Research Investigator, Population Research Centre, Centre for Research in Rural and Industrial Development, Chandigarh.

SURENDRA K. GUPTA, Member Secretary, Indian Association of Social Sciences Institutions, New Delhi and former Professor, Department of Sociology and Social Anthropology, Punjabi University, Patiala.

V. KALYANI, Former Research Scholar, Department of Anthropology, University of Madras, Chennai.

1

Introduction

JASMEET SANDHU

Marriage and family are the two most basic institutions of society. The statement 'Marriage is rooted in family and not family in marriage' by Westermarck (1971, originally published in 1921), established the relationship between the two as the most intimately connected institutions and set the normative underpinnings for the formation of family. Ever since then both these institutions have undergone change not only as concepts but also in terms of their patterns, practices, forms and significance. Though marriage and family are the most resilient institutions yet both of these have always been changing to accommodate the changing needs and demands of the society but, the changes in the second half of the 20th century have been more marked, challenging and widespread. One of the classic works on family change after World War II has been William J. Goode's *World Revolution and Family Patterns* (1963). He wrote 'whenever economic systems express through industrialization, family patterns change. Extended kinship ties weaken, lineage patterns dissolve and a trend towards some form of conjugal system generally begins to appear, that is, the nuclear family becomes more independent kinship unit' (1963: 8). He predicted that most parts of the world are undergoing a family revolution and in future predominant type of family will be nuclear in structure, made of parents and their unmarried children. However, all his predictions about western and non-western families did not come true but, he still maintained industrialization to be the most pervasive effect on family patterns around the world, weakening family everywhere (Goode 2003: 20). Industrialization and its concomitant changes in the form of urbanization, spread of education, secularization, modernization and participation of married women in work outside the domestic sphere have had profound effect on family formation, family composition, its functions and dynamics. Besides these changes, declines in mortality and fertility in the late 19th and 20th centuries also impacted upon families in the West in a big way. All these changes altered the child bearing patterns, first in the western society and then in the rest of the world. Decline in fertility is one of the important elements responsible for the transformation in the family and its functions and is considered as one of the most profound changes of the era. State policies aimed at reduction of fertility and other legislations concerning marriage and family have also played an important role in lowering fertility and influencing the process of family formation.

Demographic Transitions and Family Change

Four demographic processes bring about change in family formation, family structure, family composition and family dissolution. These are nuptiality, fertility, mortality and migration. The patterns of courtship, marriage, child bearing and family dissolution are the characteristics of social groups: such patterns vary among societies, sub-cultures, and social groups and in time and space and may change over time (Matras 1965). Two types of strategies are at work in family formation, i.e. societal strategies and individual strategies (ibid.). Social strategies include patterns of age at marriage, types and extent of endogamy and patterns of child bearing. The individual strategies include successive decisions concerning dating, courtship, marriage and child bearing, etc. Social strategies can be seen as macro level influences, i.e. constraints and individual strategies as micro level influences, i.e. choices. Bourdieu (2002) pointed out as to how individuals use strategies in arranging marriage of children and he opines that these strategies should not be seen in abstraction as these are part of the complex process of social reproduction through which power and privileges are passed on to new generation. Since family formation takes place in two stages, marriage and child bearing, two aspects of family formation patterns which have greatest impact on family size are age at marriage and efforts to control marital fertility (Matras 1965). In the modern times, a large number of economic, socio-cultural and demographic and technological considerations offer lot of choices to the individuals and play important role in taking decisions concerning marriage and eventually in family formation.

The family change in the last two centuries, world over has been largely brought about by two historical demographic transitions referred to as: First Demographic Transition and Second Demographic Transition. First Demographic Transition, based on the historical experience of the European countries and the United States of America, refers to the transition from high death rates to low death rates and birth rates as a country passes from a pre-industrial stage to a modern stage. Blacker (1947) identified five stages of demographic transition. These are: the high stationary stage, the early expanding stage, the late expanding stage, the low stationary stage and the declining stage. All the populations cross these stages as they pass from high mortality and high fertility to low mortality and low fertility. Declines in mortality and fertility took place in the western countries from 1850 onwards and the developing countries experienced the same after 1920s. During this process, decline in mortality led to the decline in fertility. It is believed that all populations and regions would ultimately follow the same developmental pattern. Fertility control policies were also announced by various developing countries and that hastened the process of fertility decline in such countries. Declines in mortality and fertility were responsible for reduction in the family size, increased life expectancy and aging of the population, etc. in the western countries in the 19th and early 20th centuries and in the developing countries after 1950. During the First Demographic Transition family formation was largely confined to the institution of marriage and contraception played important role in limiting fertility and in reduction in family size. On the other hand reduction in mortality led to increase in life expectancy and aging of the population.

The Second Demographic Transition, whose signs started appearing in 1950s in the western countries, refers to sustained sub replacement fertility, a multitude of living arrangements other than marriage, disconnection between marriage and procreation and no stationary population (Lesthaeghe 2010: 211). This concept was developed by Dirk Van de Kaa and Ron Lesthaeghe in 1986 to explain the changes in western countries after the first transition was complete for which they have been criticized on a number of accounts. But, Lesthaeghe maintains that Second Demographic Transition is not a continuation of the First Demographic Transition. Rather the two transitions have contrasting nuptiality regimes, fertility contrasts and underlying societal contrasts. While the First Demographic Transition was confined to marriage and contraception, Second Demographic Transition occurred due to contraceptive, sexual and gender revolutions leading to rejection of authority and overall normative structures and greater exercise of individuals choices (ibid.). Just as mortality decline provided the 'engine' for the first transition and led to adjustments in fertility; fertility decline is the 'engine' in the second transition (Dirk 2004). As compared to the first transition, the Second Demographic Transition is a very complicated process. Besides the demographic changes it is also affected by changes in culture, social and economic structures and the technology of the societies (ibid.).

Though many Asian countries, including India, have not completed the First Demographic Transition and are at various stages of its completion, yet some signs of Second Demographic Transition have also started emerging particularly in East Asia.

The contraceptive, sexual and gender revolutions which affected the family formation and family demography in the West are also affecting some sections of population in the developing countries. Like First Demographic Transition, Second Demographic Transition is also spreading to other regions and appears to affect populations that have reached high levels of socio-economic development, where contraception is perfect and where the close link between sexuality and procreation no longer exists (Dirk 2008). The findings of the *World Fertility Report 2003*, which is based on the study of fertility, nuptiality and contraceptive use in 192 countries, confirm that family formation and family dynamics in Asia is converging with those in the US or other western countries in many respects.

Change in Asia and India

Asia is a diverse region and there are differences in marriage practices and patterns in East Asia, South-East Asia, South Asia, Central and West Asia. But, marriage behaviour and family life are changing throughout Asia (Choe, Westley and Retherford 2010). Some trends in Asian countries such as late marriage, lower marital fertility and greater participation of women in labour force are similar to the changes that took place in the industrialized countries earlier. However, some aspects of family life in Asia are quite different from those in the West. Fewer Asian couples live together outside marriage, child bearing outside marriage is extremely rare, marriage is generally viewed as a permanent arrangement and divorce rates although rising, are quite low in most Asian countries (ibid.). In South Asia, a few practices like arranged marriages, lower age at marriage and consanguineal marriages still persist and divorce rates are lower (Jones 2010). In fact, all these practices are strategies to maintain parental authority, ensure caste/class endogamy, to avoid dowry and to economize on marriage costs. Quah (2008), while analysing families in Asia, maintains that socio-economic development and concomitant changes in values and attitudes are taking place in Asia but, fundamental aspects of family formation such as the importance of marriage still remain. Marriage still leads to family formation and patterns of family formation are revealed by trends in three aspects: the timing, postponement and prevalence of marriage (ibid.). Lesthaeghe (2010) feels that many populations in East Asia have witnessed increase in mean age at marriage and the marriage revolution that Goode was forecasting in 1960 emerged in full force between 1970 and 2000.

Kaur and Palriwala (2014) recently brought out an edited volume on *Marrying in South Asia*. Various essays reveal the change and continuity in patterns and practices in marriage in Asia. The finding point out that though marriage patterns and practices are changing in Asia, yet, some traditional practices such as child marriages, close kin marriages, polygyny and polyandry continue to exist among different communities in South Asia. These are those practices which are considered as useful individual, familial and societal strategies for family formation under the changing conditions. Unlike the West, in India conjugal families do not dominate anywhere, although, they are more common in urban than in rural areas and parents still play important role in choosing their children's marriage partners (Cherlin 2012). Under the impact of a variety of changes families are becoming smaller, adult children stay with parents for longer time, divorces and remarriages are on the rise and new forms of families such as single parent families, step families and empty nest families are emerging. Family has been going through a great deal of transformation and changes have been taking place through various aspects of people's personal and social lives (Patel 2005). Changes which the western families experienced after 1950s are also being experienced by the families in the East. Three views summarize the changing families in the West. These are: family is deteriorating, family is changing not deteriorating and family is stronger than ever. Changing family has been an important area of research in the West but that has not been the case in India. Many perspectives developed in the West to study family change but two demographic perspectives which dominated research on changing families after 1950 are given below.

Demographic Perspectives on Family Change

Two perspectives developed in the 20th century to study and understand family change from demographic point of view, i.e. the Family Development Perspective and Life Course and Family Change Perspective (Aldous 1990). Family Development Perspective brought the change down to the level of the individual families and replaced the view that families are static entities (ibid.: 572). This perspective used the concept of 'Family Life Cycle'. It is based on the idea that families throughout the world pass through a set of stages. At each stage family has its own dynamics. Basically three stages of family cycle are important – family formation, family growth and family dissolution. Loomis and Hamilton (1936) were the first ones to develop the Family Life Cycle approach to analyse family from the demographic point of view. Later, this concept was further developed by Paul C. Glick in 1947 and 1955. Glick and Parke's (1965) five stages of family life cycle are well accepted. These are:

1. Family formation: First marriage
2. Start of child bearing: Birth of first child
3. End of child bearing: Birth of last child
4. Empty nest: Marriage of last child
5. Family dissolution: Death of one spouse

Later on stages of family life cycle were expanded to 8-stage model by Duvall (1957) and to a 12-stage model by Hohn (1987).When and how these different stages of family life cycle are achieved are important for family, its growth and dissolution. This perspective guided lot of research in the USA and also invited lot of criticism due to increasing complexities of family life cycle.

The Life Course Approach challenged the family development approach and looked at study of family change from a different perspective. Its main focus was on how varying events and their timings in the lives of individuals affected the family in particular historical contexts, i.e. how societal events affect families. This perspective links individual life time, social (family) life time and historical time (Aldous 1990). Both these perspectives had their limitations, were criticized on a number of accounts but family scholars used both these approaches to study changing families. The present analysis of marriage and family in India is based on the family development or family life cycle approach. It must be mentioned here that family life cycle approach gives a partial view of family; yet, it is a significant perspective to grasp family change particularly when fertility has declined and significance of marriage is changing. Further, family life cycle may differ greatly among the rural and urban; the educated and uneducated; the poor, the middle class and the rich and so on.

It is also pertinent to mention here that stages of family life cycle in India, particularly in rural India, are not as clearly demarcated as in the more urbanized, industrialized societies (Mandelbaum 1970). Further, in India, successive stages may overlap, marriage may not immediately lead to a family and child bearing may take place in husband's natal family. Marriage in India is nearly universal, is mostly arranged by the parents/elders at a young age and is considered as a very important event of family life. It was customary to arrange the marriage of girls before they attained puberty. However, that would not lead to an 'effective marriage', i.e. cohabitation and family life. In case of child marriage, marriage would take place in two stages; marriage and *gauna* (consummation of marriage). *Gauna* would take place a few years after the girl's marriage, i.e. after she attains puberty. Collver (1963) compared family cycle in India with that of the United States and found differences in age at marriage, age at the first and last birth and how half of marriages in India end before wife reaches the age of 45 years due to high mortality and the implications of these characteristics for the structure of kinship groups and households. Bloom and Reddy (1986) studied the age pattern of women at marriage, cohabitation and first birth in India. They found that marriage and child bearing continue to be universal but, the timing of marriage and child bearing appear to be undergoing changes. The incidence of child marriages and two stage marriages are on decline. They further concluded that age patterns of marriage in India do not closely resemble western patterns, although age patterns of cohabitation and first birth do. Thus, understanding marriage and family from the perspective of family formation will help us look at these institutions from a fresh perspective.

In India, the process of demographic transition started after 1921 with the decline in the death rates. In other words, it means that up to 1920, India was in the first stage and in 1921 it entered the second stage of demographic transition. Mortality rates started declining in this stage. Unlike the fertility decline in the West, the fertility decline in India, which ensued later, was not just an adjustment to mortality decline but also a consequence of state intervention. Government of India launched a national family planning programme in 1952 and started propagating the two-child family norm. This programme was pursued quite vigorously by the Indian state and India entered the third stage of demographic transition after 1970, i.e. when the birth rates started declining. The process of fertility decline was faster in some states as compared to some other states and this difference has led to the emergence of differences in levels of fertility in the states. The country is expected to reach the fourth stage by 2026 (Premi 2009). Some states in India have already reached the replacement level fertility and others are expected to reach the same in the coming years. As a consequence of these changes, families in India are also changing.

Both marriage and family have been the major research interest with the Indian sociologists. The studies largely focused on the forms and structures of the family as they existed in reality (Patel 2005) as also on the joint family organization, changes in structure and functions (Roy 2000) and on various marriage practices existing in different parts of the country. Singh (in chapter 2 of the present volume) maintains that there are differences of opinion between the sociologists/social anthropologists and demographers on marriage and also family because the former are preoccupied with the qualitative analysis of micro data and the later with the quantitative analysis of macro data. Actually macro level data deal with the generalities and conceal the micro level specificities or variations. But marriage is an area where both are near, Singh opines. As a consequence, marriage and family have not been much studied from the perspective of family demography. Family demography in India is still a low priority research area. Demographic studies of family behaviour add to the knowledge and variations in the structure of family life and throw light on the increasing complexities of household and family patterns (Glick 1988). The socio-economic, demographic and technological changes have brought changes in the reproductive behaviour and the way families are formed. In that context, family demography is an important perspective to analyse family change. How families are being formed these days is an important angle to understand family.

Family formation takes place in two stages, i.e. marriage and procreation or child bearing and in that order. This sequence of marriage leading to child bearing has given normative connotation to the process of family formation. It is no longer a simple process in the contemporary times as a large number of choices are available to the couples concerning marriage and reproduction, within the constraints imposed by the social structures. But, individuals will not limit fertility unless it is advantageous to them and their families and means of controlling fertility are available and are socially acceptable. Lesthaeghe (1980) maintains that most societies have generated arrangements through which reproductive process is regulated and this has been happening since times immemorial.

Keeping all these issues in mind, the present anthology seeks to find answers to some important questions. What kind of changes are taking place in the institution of marriage, the first stage of family life cycle? How important is marriage for the new generations and what are their views concerning various aspects of marriage? What are the ideologies and practices concerning child bearing and family formation? Lastly, what kind of challenges emerge in contemporary times due to the socio-demographic changes which need to be dealt with in Indian families? Here, an effort has been made to understand the changes in the process of family formation in India. The articles cover diverse regions to reflect the diversity in the Indian society. It basically looks at the changes in marriage; the first stage of family formation and changes in fertility; the next stage of family formation and focuses on the changes, choices and preferences which affect the process of family formation. The volume is divided into three thematic sections namely: Family Formation: Marriage, Family Formation: Child Bearing and Emerging Challenges.

Section I

Family Formation: Marriage

The first section focuses on the marriage dimension of family formation. It normatively being the first stage is very significant. There are four articles in this section. In the chapter two, J.P. Singh examines the changing marital practices in India from a multidisciplinary perspective. On the basis of Census and National Family Health Surveys I and II data, he argues that marriage practices in urban India are progressively undergoing process of secularization and variations in marriage practices across castes, communities and regions are disappearing. Two, marriage practices, i.e. child marriage and consanguinity in marriages, which have shown resistance to change, have lost resilience. Although child marriages still exist but incidence has dwindled, age gap between spouses has narrowed and ritual of consummation has disappeared. Dissolution of marriage is infrequent, though no longer it is considered as divine or sacred. B.S. Nagi looks at the trends in child marriages in rural Rajasthan in chapter three. On the basis of an empirical study, he found that although the average age at marriage has risen in India, yet almost all the boys and girls in his sample got married before the legal age of marriage. Further, the child marriages are more prevalent among cultivators and labourers and decline in child marriages is lower in case of females than males. Child marriage is not only a customary practice but is also used by the families as a strategy to cut the marriage costs.

The next two chapters reflect the opinions of young people concerning marriage and family. In chapter four, S.K. Gupta has attempted to portray change in marriage and family through the values and beliefs of the young people in India. This article is based on the evidence drawn from a large number of studies conducted on various communities and in different parts of India. He concludes that young people do not consider marriage as a sacrament or a necessity. Age at marriage is rising and process of and criterion of mate selection has undergone change. Views concerning divorce and widow remarriage have also undergone change. A large number of youth studied by various scholars also favour nuclear family. They express dislike for joint family because it hampers the personality development and creates numerous problems. On the similar lines, D. Punia, R.K. Punia and M.L. Sharma discuss the changing marriage values in the opinions of girl students (Chapter five). They found that traditional values still hold good and girls still consider marriage as sacrament. Education is valued highly for economic independence and for getting a good life partner. Personal characteristics of spouse are rated higher than the social status of family. Age at marriage has increased and girls prefer arranged marriage with their consent. The articles in this section reflect continuity and change in marriage practices in India. The rising age at marriage, the changing criteria of mate selection, changing views on divorce and widow remarriage are particularly important from the point of view of change in the process of family formation in India.

Section II

Family Formation: Child Bearing

Section two of the anthology deals with the child bearing aspect of family formation, i.e. the second stage in the process. It has six articles drawing attention on various aspects of family construction, including fertility norms, preferences and control. H.D. Lakshminarayana brings out the issues and problems of the ideology of small family norm which was propagated by the Indian Government to bring down the birth rates in the country in chapter six. It must be mentioned here that child bearing in India changed largely because of two state interventions. First, the Government of India adopted fertility control policy in 1952 and propagated two-child family norm (*hum do hamare do*) whereas traditionally Indian couples preferred three-four children. Secondly, under the same policy, use of modern contraceptives was promoted and contraceptives were made available through state created health infrastructure. In this chapter, Lakshminarayana discusses the economic aspect of small family on the basis of data collected from 4,232 rural families of handloom weavers in Karnataka state in India. Small family is considered as promoter of economic growth and small family norm is accepted in the interest of the family and nation. In this case, small families have belied the hope of augmenting the economy among this caste group. The weaver families have restricted the economic activity because of their low carrying capacity. Thus, small family unless backed by massive structural amenities and services may become more helpless, more subject to strain, more incompetent and more insecure. In chapter seven, V. Kalyani discusses the effect of age at marriage on fertility. The age at marriage has a significant bearing on family building activity and level of fertility. She found a negative correlation between fertility and age at marriage in a slum in Chennai (Madras) city. Thus, low age at marriage leads the early formation of family and to large families.

Savita Thakur has analysed the changes in fertility preferences and use of contraceptives in Himachal Pradesh in chapter eight. Using data from NFHS-I and NFHS-II she found little change in ideal size and son preference in between the two surveys. The people in Himachal as in other parts of India prefer two children with at least one son in their family. Similarly, the reasons for non-use of family planning are the same in both the surveys, i.e. the desire for more children, particularly more sons. Both these preferences affect the family size and family composition, thus family formation. Similarly, P. Malhi and S. Singh examine the extent of son preference and its impact on desired family size and use of contraception in rural Punjab in the next chapter. A sample survey was conducted on 450 currently married women in their reproductive years. The results indicate that couples' fertility behaviour is strongly determined by the desire to acquire a minimum number of surviving sons. Further, preference for sons also impacts upon the pattern of contraceptive use pattern of the couples. Reproductive ideals and attitudes towards contraceptives among rural poor of Kanpur and Varanasi districts in Uttar Pradesh have been analysed in chapter ten by A.K. Sharma. Generally it is argued that poor have large families because of the economic advantages of children. The present study revealed that poor have large families not because of the economic advantages but because of carelessness, lack of planning, religiosity, illiteracy, etc. Their reproductive goals are undergoing change but, preference for sons and specific desire for sons and daughters make it difficult to implement the ideas. All the articles in this section reflect the changes in norms concerning family size and acceptance of contraception and also point out that values concerning son preference continue to persist and affect family size. How son preference affects the process of family formation is discussed in the next chapter.

Due to technological advancements and medical intervention, family formation is no longer a natural process. Reproductive technologies have been in use for family formation in India since 1980s. Jasmeet Sandhu and Anuradha have studied how a technology is being used for reproduction and gender construction in Punjab. Women have low status in the patriarchal Punjabi society. Begetting sons is the chief role expectation from a married woman. The studied urban women, who did not have sons made use of sex determination tests and female foeticide to beget sons in order to complete their families. Thus, the use of reproductive technology becomes discriminatory and victimizing for the women and helps in formation of individual families and in the construction of gender in the larger society. This section reveals that despite the acceptance of small family norm and modern contraceptives, traditional values guiding family formation and its composition, i.e. son preference continues to persist and continues to influence family formation. That is why modern technologies are being put to use to have the desired family size and composition.

Section III

Emerging Challenges

The demographic changes and the available choices regarding marriage and family formation have led to the rise of newer types of families, such as: single parent families, dual – earner families, step or reconstituted families and empty nest families etc. All these emerging forms of families have numerous challenges for family roles, family relationships and family care. The articles in section three focus on some of these emerging challenges. In chapter 12, P.K.B. Nayar draws attention towards the ageing of the population due to the changing demographic scenario and its implications for old age support. He argues that elderly population is growing faster than the general population, most of the older women are widows and dependency ratio is rising. All these changes have implications for the economic security and health needs of the elderly. Further, it is emphasized that there is need to strengthen the social institutions to give support to the elderly.

In the next chapter, Amarjit Mahajan discusses the problems of the aged in the unorganized sector. On the basis of study of recipients of old age pensions in Haryana state, he concludes that the family in the lower segments of society no more acts as a support system to the aged. So, an alternative support system needs to be evolved for the aging population and increasing number of elderly in the society. Sobha B. Nayar focuses on the specific problems of aged widows who constitute three-fourth of the elderly women in India (chapter 14). Widows enter old age in poverty and with ill health, depend on their children for subsistence and shelter, live without adequate care and medical assistance and spend old age in agony and misery. This is not only the case in poor families but also in many middle class families where the first concern is for the children and male members. Widows' problems are compounded because of discrimination caused by gender, poverty, ill-health and absence of care besides being treated as a widow.

Another issue that has gained significance in the last few decades is the issue of intergenerational relations which also are undergoing change as a consequence of the socio-demographic changes and are challenging the traditional role of family as a care giver. In chapter 15, Anupam Bahri has focused on the changing parental exchange system among elderly and their married children in Chandigarh city. The argument is that patterns of exchange between parents and their adult children vary in frequency, type and quality across the life cycle. The form and frequency of communication and assistance between adult children and ageing parents is influenced by such factors as residential propinquity, social class, sex of the child, ethnicity, age and health of the two generations and the degree of filial responsibility felt by the children. The author concludes that majority of the young old elderly and their married children are interdependent for financial, personal and advisory help which means are both giving and receiving help from each other. On the other hand, the oldest elderly with low education, low economic status and bad health are not in a position to provide help and are only receiving help from children. Further, the elderly who have reciprocal relations with married children enjoy high level of well-being than those who are either independent or dependent.

In the last chapter (16), the problems of single parent families have been discussed. Single parent families are on the rise due to rise in divorces and changing sex norms. Earlier, single households were considered as pathological family forms but such households are a reality and these are providing alternative to the ideal typical nuclear family. Ranjay Vardhan focuses on the problems of single mother/female headed households. Such families suffer from various economic, social, emotional, problems as well as from physical insecurity besides playing the dual role of both man and woman. They never anticipated and prepared for such roles. It is being argued that since single parent families are now a reality in contemporary society, special policies need to be formulated for such families in future.

To conclude, the volume addresses the questions concerning the importance of marriage, the first step towards family formation in Asian cultures and the changes therein. There is change in the opinions of the young people concerning the significance of marriage yet families are formed within the marital unions. Due to the rising age at marriage, family formation is getting delayed. Similarly, due to rising age in child marriages, the gap between marriage and consummation of marriage is reducing which used to be an important stage earlier and also an important strategy to delay family formation. Change can also be observed in the choice of spouses and views concerning divorce and remarriage. Increase in divorces and remarriages will add to the complexity of the family structure and its functioning and also to the formation of step families. Though some changes in marriage practices can be noticed, yet unlike the western societies, the significance of marriage for family formation has not undergone change in India.

Due to governmental policy aimed at reducing fertility, small family norm has been largely accepted. Use of contraceptives has increased. It helps in restricting the family size but, values concerning son preference are showing resilience and influencing the process of family formation. Son preference not only stands in the way of restricting the family size but also leads to the use of available reproduction technologies to have a desired family composition, i.e. at least one son in the family and to the ghastly practice of female foeticide. All these changes are manifesting in newer forms of families and pose fresh challenges for intergenerational relations and family care. As mentioned earlier, after the first transition is complete, Second

Demographic Transition is going to take over. In future, both marriage and family will experience fresh challenges and will undergo further transformation and change. It remains to be seen as to how 'gender and sexual revolutions' will affect family and marriage in the diverse Indian situation.

References

Aldous, Joan, 1990, 'Family Development and the Life Course: Two Perspectives on Family Change', *Journal of Marriage and Family*, 52: 571–583.

Blacker, C.P., 1947, 'Stages of Population Growth', *The Eugenics Review*, 39 (3): 88–101.

Bloom, David E. and P.H. Reddy, 1986, 'Age Pattern of Women at Marriage and Cohabitation and First Birth in India', *Demography*, 23 (4): 599–523.

Bourdieu, Pierre, 2002, 'Pierre Bourdieu on Marriage Strategies', *Population and Development Review*, 28(3): 549–558.

Cherlin, Andrew J., 2012, 'Goode's World Revolution and Family Patterns: Reconsideration at 50 Years', *Population and Development Review*, 38 (4): 577–607.

Choe, Mingakim, Sindney B. Westley and Robert D. Retherford, 2010, *Tradition and Change in Marriage and Family Life: The Future of Population in Asia*, Honolulu: East West Centre.

Collver, Andrew, 1963, 'The Family Cycle in India and the United States', *American Sociological Review*, 28 (1): 86–96.

Dirk, J. Van de Kaa, 2004, 'Is Second Demographic Transition a Useful Research Concept?', in G. Feichtinger (ed.), *Vienna Yearbook of Population Research*, Vienna: Institute of Demography (Assessed on 27.5.2014).

——, 2008, 'Demographic Transitions', *Demography*, Vol. I, The Hague: Netherlands Interdisciplinary Demographic Institute (Assessed on 26.8.2015).

Duvall, E.M., 1957, *Family Development*, Philadelphia: Lippincott.

Glick, Paul C. and Robert Parke, Jr., 1965, 'Approaches to Studying the Life Cycle of Family', *Demography*, 2: 187–202.

Glick, Paul C., 1947, 'The Family Cycle', *American Sociological Review*, 12: 164–174.

——, 1955, 'The Life Cycle of Family', *Marriage and Family Living*, 17: 3–9.

——, 1988, 'Fifty Years of Family Demography: A Record of Social Change', *Journal of Marriage and Family*, 50 (4): 861–873.

Goode, William J., 1963, *World Revolution and Family Patterns*, New York: The Free Press.

——, 2003, 'Family Over the Long Term: A Sociological Commentary', *Journal of Family History*, 28: 15–30.

Hohn, Charlette, 1987, 'The Family Life Cycle: Needed Extensions of the Concept', in John Bongaarts, Thomas K. Burch and Kenneth W. Wachter (eds), *Family Demography: Methods and their Applications*, New York: Oxford University Press.

Jones, Gavin W., 2010, *Changing Marriage Patterns in Asia*, Working Paper Series 131, Asia Research Institute, National University of Singapore, Singapore.

Kaur, Ravinder and Rajani Palriwala, 2014, *Marrying in South Asia: Shifting Concepts, Changing Practices in a Globalizing World*, New Delhi: Orient Blocksman Private Limited.

Lesthaeghe, Ron, 1980, 'On the Social Control of Human Reproduction', *Population and Development Review*, 6 (4): 527–548.

——, 2010, 'The Unfolding Story of the Second Demographic Transition', *Population and Development Review*, 36 (2): 211–251.

Loomis, Charles P. and H.H. Hamilton, 1936, 'Family Life Cycle Analysis', *Social Forces*, 15: 225–231.

Mandelbaum, David, 1970, *The Family in India: Structure and Practice*, New Delhi: Sage Publications.

Matras, Judah, 1965, 'The Social Strategy of Family Formation: Some Variations in Time and Space', *Demography*, 2: 349–362.

Patel, Tulsi (ed.), 2005, *The Family in India: Structure and Practice*, New Delhi: Sage Publications.

Premi, M.K., 2009, *India's Changing Population Profile*, New Delhi: National Book Trust.

Punia, Deep, R.K. Punia and M.L. Sharma, 1987, 'Changing Marriage Values: Opinion of Girl Students', *Guru Nanak Journal of Sociology*, 8 (2): 25–40.

Quah, Stella R., 2008, *Families in Asia: Home and Kin*, London: Routledge.

Roy, P.K., 2000, *The Indian Family: Change and Persistence*, New Delhi: Gyan Publishing House.

Therborn, Goran, 2004, *Between Sex and Power: Family in the World, 1900–2000*, London: Routledge.

Westermarck, Edward, 1971, *The History of Human Marriage*, Vol. I, Fifth Edition, New York: Johnson Reprint Corporation (Originally published by Macmillan and Co., London in 1921).

Section I

Family Formation: Marriage

2

Changing Marital Practices in India

J.P. SINGH

In general, two basic aspects of Indian marriages, the practice of child marriage and consanguinity in marriage, have shown unusual resistance to change for over a long period of time, but they too have lost resilience in the face of new circumstances. They have undergone substantial changes in contemporary period and such changes are much more neat and striking in urban than in rural areas. But the discussion on this subject is not free from difference in opinions because of communication hiatus between sociologists/social anthropologists on the one hand and demographers on the other. The former tend to be preoccupied with qualitative analysis based on micro data, while the later tend to be predisposed to pure statistical treatment of their subject matter based on macro data, despite the fact that there are many similar or common areas of scientific explorations. Marriage is definitely one such area where both the disciplines are nearer rather than divergent from each other. The paper pleads for a conversation across the disciplinary boundary in the Indian context. It aims at explaining certain conspicuous changes relating to marriage practices, particularly relating to urban India, in an inter-disciplinary fashion. The changes that are dealt with may not be typical of urban India alone; rather, some of these changes are also perceptible in rural areas. But they are certainly more conspicuous in urban areas as sources of change first originate there. Cities are a precursor of change. The paper, as said before, sets off a long-overdue dialogue between anthropology/sociology and demography in the Indian context. This paper would show that lots of factual misconstructions have been persisting in Indian sociology due to its closed-door policy towards demography. Such a discussion is an eye opener for those who believe that the Indian society is still largely resilient to change and the changes that have occurred are superficial. As regards the data set, the paper is primarily based on census and the National Family Health Survey (1 and 2) materials. The NFHS-2 is based on a nationally representative sample of 91,196 households and 89,199 ever-married women in the age group of 15–49 years, of which two-thirds are rural ones, covering 25 states of the Indian Union (NFHS-2 1998–99). The National Family Health Survey-2 (1998–99) has no doubt gathered the largest amount of quantitative data so far at the national level; reports released so far have not provided adequate information on issues addressed in the paper. But whatever information could be available, it is very valuable and it demystifies many of the commonly held views concerning nuptial practices in this country.

Evidence from censuses, despite certain inherent limitations, is very useful, authentic and unbiased because such information has not been gathered for any preconceived notion in mind. But the main problem with such data is that they camouflage micro level realities or variations. Census reports provide useful data on the age at marriage by sex and place of residence, divorce and household composition.

Such data are also used in the paper. This paper has also tried to piece together widely scattered survey data in addition to one mentioned above as well as the micro level studies as supplementary evidence to corroborate the arguments regardless of the fact that there is inherent difficulty in drawing credible generalizations from such heterogeneous sources. Here a word of caution is necessary. Generalizations made may hold in a very broad sense, as what is true of one section of society may not be true of others in the same way. Marital practices, in particular, tend to vary from caste to caste and from region to region because of plurality of Indian culture (Trautmann 2003: 1104–1126).

Matrimonial Practices

Rituals relating to traditional Hindu marriage once used to be quite elaborate, have undergone conspicuous changes. In this regard, Srinivas (1977: 125–126) has rightly observed about South India:

> The manner in which wedding ritual has been abbreviated is interesting. Formerly, a full-blown Brahmin wedding would last between five and seven days. Now, however, much of the non-Sanskritic and folk ritual, traditionally the exclusive preserve of women, is being dropped. There is even an increasing tendency to compress Sanskritic ritual into a few hours on a single day.

The prevailing situation in North India is not much different from the above. Countless marriage rituals have been either omitted or abbreviated. Now people are in general found disinclined to adhere to all the rituals laid down for the marriage very minutely. The common people do not have either time or money to observe all the rituals so strictly, and therefore, they have developed liberal attitudes towards them. Priests also do not insist much on their observance. In fact, many priests performing marriage rituals have forgotten the scriptural practices by now. I have watched hundreds of marriage ceremonies, both in towns and villages, being concluded within a couple of hours. In temples the process is faster still. These priests are found to be engrossed in making fast bucks rather than in solemnizing marriage strictly according to the traditional Hindu scriptures. Care, however, is taken that all kinsmen are invited to attend the marriage ceremony. The closest kin are expected to take part in marriage ceremony compulsorily. Other related families should send at least one representative, if they want to keep the kinship bond really alive. They should participate through giving gifts, performing of services or just being present on the occasion. But now family friends and professional colleagues outnumber kinsmen at the time of marriage. This is the real test of one's association or friendship with others (Singh 2004: 157–158).

In the past, the young trusted their parents and watched, with peripheral interest, the matching of horoscopes, the meeting of the families, and lastly the meeting of the two important members of the fixture union. A large percentage of these marriages seemed to work, and if they did not, very few knew about the dissolution of marriage. In conventional families, the wife's subservient attitude curbed her individuality and she tended to take the back seat while the husband devoted his time to his career. Whatever might have been the path which led to a marriage, arranged or otherwise, there were societal pressures and the onus was on the women to keep the marriage together. Expectedly, with the lapse of time, marked changes have occurred in all these affairs of family life. The practice of matching horoscope, however, especially among caste Hindus is still in existence, though educated people do not seem to have so much faith in it. Hindu marriage or *vivah* was once regarded sacrament, ordained and imperative, which every normal man and woman should undergo

With the vast expansion of network of media of mass communication, impact of Hindi cinema and TV serials on Indian marriage practices has become so profound that variations in marriage practices across castes, communities or regions are steadily evaporating into thin air in Indian cities. Heterogeneity in marriage practices is slowly but surely taking a pan-India look. Wedding reception, a purely alien practice, for instance, has emerged as a very widespread and common post-marriage event in urban India. Such events are usually organized either to amass gift or show off one's valued position or both to others. In general marriages are occasions for conspicuous spending. In addition to kinsmen, in order to give expression to family status, all sorts of persons even with ordinary acquaintance such as professional colleagues, members of one's club, well-known caste men, bureaucrats, politicians and even unfriendly neighbours, are invited to attend the marriage ceremony. Care is taken that lots of cars are parked outside the wedding halls. The hospitality is usually on the lavish side. Bride's kin are a little more eager to impress everyone, while the groom's kin and other guests are only too eager to find fault. However, their praise is keenly sought by bride's family. Expenditure on marriage ceremony is one of the prime means of acquiring, demonstrating or validating high status of the family. Temporal assets alone do not automatically bestow higher status. Thus, the Indian marriage practices are progressively undergoing the process of secularization. The Indian society has been highly endogamous. Marriage within the same sub-caste has been followed very strictly. The scheduled tribes are also endogamous, but most of the tribal communities practice clan exogamy (Singh 1997b: 8). The endogamous character of Hindu marriages is changing, though gradually. The traditional role of caste councils of enforcing norms of endogamy has finally evaporated into the thin air. Now the English edition newspapers publish enumerable matrimonial advertisements every Sunday where people are found to be eager to cross the barriers of caste. The people who are well-educated and well-placed in professional career, but a bit over-aged for marriage from the Indian standard, tend to advertise through matrimonial columns of dailies for a suitable mate. An analysis of matrimonial advertisements in a leading English language newspaper in the South India showed that the average age of advertisers was 31 for male and 27 for females. Interestingly, females asking for suitable grooms outnumbered males seeking suitable brides. Such aspirants for nuptial bonds included persons of all major religions, mostly belonging to high educational and occupational brackets (Rao and Sudarsen 1978). A similar fact has been reported about North India by Das (1980).

Marriage alliances materialized through such methods involve invariably long marital distance and are of non-consanguineous types, and sometimes they are inter-caste ones, but rarely inter-community. Civil marriages are on gradual increase. Marriages across sub-castes or *jati* have become a common event in Indian cities. The role of parents in arranged marriages is on gradual decline. The age-old requirement that marriage has to occur within the same *jati* is no longer the cherished value of Hindus. The parents are fully prepared to recognise the nuptial bonds of their sons and daughters across the sub-castes at least. Polygamy, more particularly polygyny, has been one of salient features of Indian family. It has been more popular among Muslims than Hindus. Here it is not suggested that the incidence of polygyny is more common than monogamy. The polygamous males often derived support from age-old scriptures and mythological stories. But mainly those who had no issue from the first wife practiced such marriages. The preference for son has been strong because in a patrilineal society only son can continue the line of the family. Adopted son is no substitute. Sons are needed also because they provide succour to their parents in their old age. This fact has been well explained in some demographic explorations (Mutharayappa et al. 1997). But the practice of polygamy, more particularly among Hindus, is on gradual disappearance with some exception of scheduled castes. Singh (1997b: 7) has reported, 'Two hundred and sixty-five of the scheduled castes (35.2%) allow polygyny'. However, it does not mean that all of them essentially practice polygyny. Enactment of Hindu Marriage and Divorce Act, 1955 and its amendment in 1976 played an important role in this process. With the rise in the level of literacy, the incidence of polygyny has receded even among the Muslims despite the fact that such marriages have got full cultural and legal sanction. The scheduled tribes are somewhat different from others with respect to marriage. While monogamy is the predominant form of marriage, there are a large number of tribes practising sororal polygyny and non-sororal polygyny (Singh 1997b: 8).

These days marriage has become so expensive that it is being arranged or sorted out by some social and cultural organizations. A lot of such organizations have sprung up among different castes and communities separately, which help in matchmaking for marriage either individually or collectively. The *Marwaris, Punjabis* and *Sindhis,* in particular, are quite well-known for such activities in various Indian cities. The parents who are economically hard-pressed contact these organizations to get details of suitable grooms for their daughters readily. The parents of the girls communicate with the parents of prospective grooms for usual enquiries and discussions through 'go-between'. At times such organizations also coordinate meetings of prospective brides and grooms along with their parents. In such meetings, people are introduced one by one to the mass gathering through public address system. Further negotiation and final ceremony of marriage can take place either with the help of such organizations or the parties concerned themselves can conclude the marriage independently at some mutually agreed places. Voluntary organizations also conduct mass marriages annually at a low cost budget. They provide wedding dress for the poor bride and the groom and free feast on the day of mass marriage. Parents take advantage of such non-traditional facilities and conduct marriages in large numbers. Such establishments initially started in temples and big cities and have now spread to small towns. This is true of North and South India alike (Raja 1991; Richard and Sunder Rao 1994: 26). There are some other significant changes in nuptial practices not only in urban areas but also in rural areas. Rules of residence (from matrilocal and bilocal to patrilocal) have changed. The predominant rule of residence is patrilocal, as out of 4,635 communities in the country 4,517 communities follow patrilocal residence for women after marriage and only 42 communities follow patrilocal rules of residence. Rules of divorce have also become quite flexible. In about 596 communities, there has taken place change in the rules of inheritance, while the rules of succession have changed in 186 communities (Singh 1992).

As the status of women is low, the wife is often seen as a full-time assistant rather than a real life-time partner. Or if she works, she may be taken as an additional source of income, but has no special relationship with the members of her new household and thus remains devoid of a support base from other members of joint or extended family. Some 40 per cent of the women are married before the legal age of 18 according to the 2001 census. Illiteracy among women is high, up to 63 per cent in parts of rural areas. As a result they are isolated and often in no position to assert themselves. A recent survey of 10,000 women conducted by India's Health Ministry found that more than half of those interviewed considered violence to be a normal part of married life – the most common cause being the failure to perform domestic duties up to the expectations of their husband's family. The underlying causes for dowry related violence are undoubtedly complex. While the dowry has roots in traditional values system, the reason for prevalence of dowry-related violence, especially death, has comparatively recent origins (Singh 2005: 199–220).

The Practice of Child Marriage

The traditional system of values of Indian society, especially that of Hindus, has been such that it stood for the practice of early as well as universal marriage for females. Child marriage or pre-puberty marriage all through has been an archetypal institution of India. It was prevalent on such a massive scale in India that the mean age at marriage for females was quite low-perhaps the lowest in the world. Historians argue that child-marriage is a 'blessing' of the mediaeval age and it was born from the same compulsions that perpetuated Sati. Child-marriage was possibly not rampant in ancient India.

Table 2.1

Mean age at marriage of females for select states, 1891, 1991 and 1998–99#

States	*1891**	*1991***	*1998–99****
Andhra Pradesh	10.3	16.8	20.3
Assam$	14.6	18.2	23.6
Bihar	11,2	16.9	20.9
Gujarat	NA	19.0	21.1
Haryana	13.2	17.9	21.4
Himachal Pradesh	NA	18.1	23.7
Karnataka	14.1	18.0	21.5
Kerala	NA	19.8	22.7
Madhya Pradesh	12.7	16.6	20.9
Maharashtra	NA	17.9	21.3
Orissa	11.2	18.0	22.8
Punjab	13.2	19.7	23.2
Rajasthan	13.0	16.7	19.9
Tamil Nadu	NA	19.1	21.7
Uttar Pradesh	12.3	17.3	21.5
West Bengal	11.2	17.2	22.4
India	12.5	18.5	21.5

Sources: Agarwala (1977: 95); Census of India (1998: 56–60).

Note: The age at marriage for 1891 is based on census synthetic cohort. The age at marriage here and elsewhere refers to the singulate mean age at marriage.

Certain states are missing in the table because the 1891 data relating to marriage for those states could not be available. While certain new states, which were in existence at the time of 1991 census and the NFHS-2 (1998–99), have been excluded from this table for the purpose of offering a comparative view of the rise in the age at marriage over period of a century.

* The age at marriage has been worked out for the total population for want of data classified by rural and urban areas.

** The age at marriage refers to that of urban areas only.

*** The age at marriage refers to that of urban areas of undivided states of Bihar, Madhya Pradesh and Uttar Pradesh.

$ Here Assam includes the whole of North-Eastern region, except in case of 1998–99.

With respect to the practice of pre-puberty marriages, India has been a unique country in the world. In India during the 1860s, marriage meant girls below 8 or 9 years old getting married. Socio-religious reform movements such as the *Brahmo Samaj* and the *Arya Samaj* did pioneering work against the practice of child marriage. At the instance of some social reformers like Raja Ram Mohun Roy, Malabari and Ishwar Chandra Vidyasagar, the British took several legislative measures to enhance the age at marriage. Late in the 1860s some success was met when the Indian Penal Code prohibited intercourse with a wife who had not reached 10 years of age. Nevertheless, it wasn't until 1880 that child marriage as a problem became a public issue, which led to a national level debate on the Age of Consent Bill in British India. While the British India was still debating the bill relating to age at marriage, it was reported through media that a child wife of 11 years old, named Phulmani, died when her husband raped her. More than 500 women doctors sent a memorandum to the Viceroy requesting him to stop marriage of girls below 14 years of age. The resulting bill compromised at 12 years old. According to the Agarwala's (1962) estimate, the mean age at marriage for females in India during 1891–1901 was 12.5 years.

The mean age at marriage, stated as above, was reported to be quite low in 19th century and so also in earlier days. The mean age at marriage for females was about 13 years between 1901 and 1931 censuses and it did not differ much by community. Until that time almost all communities, barring Christians, had a nearly similar age at marriage. The age at marriage for Christians was 3 to 4 years higher than that of other communities. Of all the legal measures, the Child Marriage Restraints Act, 1929, happened to be the most effective one. But quite expectedly changes occurred at a snail's pace. Changes in the age at marriage really became conspicuous during the post-Independence era, that is, during the period onward 1950. The Act was further amended in 1978 wherein boys' marriage age was raised to 21 and girls' age to 18 years. On the whole, the state level census information for the last one hundred years has revealed a clear rise in the age at marriage for girls. During 1891-1991 the age at marriage increased by 4 to 7 years in different parts of the country. Data from NFHS-2 has shown further increase in the age at marriage from 18.5 years to 21.5 years at the national level. Such states as Punjab, Himachal Pradesh and those of the North-Eastern region have recorded a mean age at marriage of more than 23 years for females in towns (see Table 2.1). The recent National Family Health Survey-3 has revealed the highest median age at marriage among Jain women, followed by Christian women and Sikh women. Hindu and Muslim women have the lowest median age at first marriage (NFHS-3 2005-06: 165).

Table 2.2

Singulate mean age at marriage of females by religion in India

Religion/Community	*1901*	*1931*	*1991*	
	Total	*Total*	*Total*	*Urban*
Hindu	12.8	12.3	17.6	18.4
Muslim	13.7	12.7	17.5	18.1
Christian	17.2	17.2	20.1	20.6
Sikh	14.4	15.2	19.8	19.9
Jain	13.4	13.5	19.1	19.5

Sources: Agarwala (1977: 98); Census of India (1998: 56).

Here it is not suggested that the practice of child marriage has now disappeared from the Indian scene. Doubtless, a large number of child marriages do still take place every year. Child marriages during the annual *Akha Teej* festival in Rajasthan are a notable example, but such practice of child marriage is really more an exception than a rule even in educationally or economically underdeveloped regions. Rise in the age at marriage surely suggests substantial decline in the incidence of child marriage. It is much less frequent now than ever before. The NFHS-1 data has clearly shown that only 6.5 per cent of the girls in the 15–19 years age group were married by age 15 in urban areas. However, this percentage was recorded larger in rural areas (21%) (Das and Dey 1998: 96).

When the age at marriage of females is viewed in terms of level of literacy, it appears that in urban areas it climbs from 17.5 years to 21.8 years, depending upon the level of education. The spread of modern education, especially among females, in addition to some other factors, has played a significant part in the rise of age at marriage. There is evidence of a positive association between age at marriage and education of female. The mean age at marriage for females rises with the level of education in the following order: illiterate 17.5 years, literate below middle 18 years, middle below matriculation 18.7 years, matriculation but below graduation 20 years and graduate and above 21.8 years in case of urban areas (see Table 2.3). Similarly in a study of the State of Uttar Pradesh based on the 1961 and 1971 census data, Srivastava (1983: 59–73) demonstrated that there was a positive relationship between the levels of education and urbanization on the one hand and age at marriage on the other. With the increase in the level of female education and urbanization, the incidence of child marriage dwindled and this relationship was found statistically highly significant. The recent National Family Health Survey-3 has also borne out steady increase in age at marriage with increasing education (NFHS-3 2005-06: 165–166).

Table 2.3

Mean age at marriage of female by education in urban India in 1991

Level of education	*1991*
Illiterate	17. 5
Literate, but below middle	18.1
Middle, but below matriculation	18.7
Matriculation, but below graduate	20.0
Graduate and above	21.8

Source: Census of India (1998: 62).

This suggests that for the sake of education and professional career, girls prefer to delay their marriage – hopefully with the consent of and encouragement from their parents. It seems that parents of such girls do not intend to marry their daughters at an early age to help them pursue higher education without any interruption, even though education is an expensive affair and there is no return from education and consequent employment of their daughters. Parents are now able to appreciate and recognise the value of education in the life of their daughters. It seems that most educated parents are disinclined to see their daughters as dependant housewives of their sons-in-law.

In urban areas, the difference in age at marriage by sex varies from 4 to 5 years in most parts of the country and it is higher by one more year in urban South India. A similar trend is also noticeable in rural parts of the country. The main reason for this fact is possibly that the need for marrying off a grown-up son is not quite as urgently felt as that of marrying a daughter. This is partly because there is not the same spur of fear about his unspoken sexuality and in part because the status and reputation of his family do not suffer so much if he remains unmarried for a long time. Yet another important reason is that many parents or the boys themselves delay their marriage for want of proper employment and desired amount of dowry. In case of South India, consanguinity in marriage could be yet another reason for a greater difference in the age at marriage between male and female. Yet another important development is the age gap between the spouses, which used to be much higher in South than North India, has appreciably narrowed down. But it is still higher from the Western standard, since the age gap between the spouses is five years in case of North and seven years in case of South India (Caldwell, Reddy and Caldwell 1982: 689–727). Sex differentials in the age at marriage would shrink still further with the rise in the age at marriage. For instance, the average age at first marriage in the United States in 1994 was 24.5 for women and 26.7 for men (Riley 1997: 12).

With the rise in age at marriage the post-nuptial ritual of consummation, locally called *gauna* in Hindi (wrongly transliterated as second marriage in Indian English), has virtually disappeared from the urban scene. Those who still believe in it perform *gauna* in conjunction with the ritual of marriage. In the past, when there was a practice of child marriage, the gap between marriage and *gauna* used to vary from three to six years, depending on the age at marriage of females. The lower the age at marriage, the longer was the time gap between age at marriage and consummation ceremony (Singh 2004).

Consanguineous Marriage

The practice of consanguineous marriage has been another notable feature of a large segment of the Indian society since long. Through the ages the system of cross-cousin and cross-uncle niece marriages has been the most favoured kind of marriage in South India. The most desirable mate for a man has been his own sister's daughter or mother's brother's daughter (Driver and Driver 1988; Nair 1978: 121, 131). However, such marriages have remained tabooed among a large majority of Hindus in North India. The Hindu Marriage Act 1955 prohibits marriage among close relatives – called *sapinda* marriage. The *sapinda* relationship extends as far as the third generation in the line of mother and the fifth in the line of father. In North India only Muslims, certain scheduled castes and scheduled tribes tend to practice consanguineous marriages.

Singh (1997b: 8–9) has reported that most of the tribal groups practice consanguinity of both types such as marriage with the father's sister's daughter, the mother's brother's daughter and the elder sister's daughter. As many as 359 scheduled tribes (56.4%) allow marriage with the mother's brother's daughter and 259 with the father's sister's daughter in India. Of these, 84 tribes also permit an uncle-niece alliance. Such consanguineous marriages are reported from all tribal areas in South, Central and North-East India. The incidence of such marriages is much less in the North-West. Marriage with parallel cousins is practiced among 23 tribes. Contrary to the general belief, Singh (1997b: 8–9) has provided evidence to argue that the incidence of cross-cousin marriages is far more widespread than was earlier believed. In addition to sororate and levirate marriages of both types – senior and junior – tribes are also unique in their institution of polyandry of the fraternal type. But those tribes who have migrated to urban areas or those who are under constant influence of city life do not strictly follow the traditional kind of marriage practices. According to the 1991 census, of the total population of 65 million, about 8 per cent of the scheduled tribes are settled in urban areas. Both National Family Health Surveys (1 and 2) data have clearly shown that there has been appreciable decline in consanguineous marriage, more particularly in Dravidian India. At the national level, nearly 15 per cent of ever-married women have married blood relatives.

In Tamil Nadu and in some parts of Karnataka and coastal Andhra Pradesh only 25–50 per cent of the marriages are of the consanguineous type, and on the west coast consanguineous marriages were less frequent and accounted for only 10 to 20 per cent of all marriages. In the rest of India, consanguineous marriages are extremely rare, generally as low as two per cent (Bhat and Zavier 1999: 3021–3024). These percentages are bound to be still lower in urban areas. A study conducted by Richard and Sunder Rao (1994: 17) in Tamil Nadu has clearly borne out that consanguineous marriages have declined and the rate of decline is much greater in urban than rural areas. Conversely, the data also imply that non-consanguineous marriages have increased quite markedly and the amount of increase is still much greater in urban areas (see Table 2.4).

It is also evident from the census materials that parallel cousin marriages have been in retreat among the Muslims as well. However, marriage between relatives is diminishing because the increasing socio-economic and educational heterogeneity in the community has provided a wider social spectrum to obtain a suitably matched spouse. In addition, increasing interest in dowry has also adversely affected the practice of consanguineous marriage (Caldwell, Reddy and Caldwell 1983: 343–361).

Table 2.4

Distribution of marriages in per cent among blood-related persons by place of residence

Types of marriage	*1969–70*		*1982–87*	
Rural/Urban	*Rural*		*Urban*	
1. Consanguineous	46.9	29.1	35.6	25.1
(a) Uncle-niece	15.8	6.6	9.5	4.8
(b) First cousin	24.8	17.5	20.6	15.4
(c) Beyond first cousin	6.3	5.0	5.5	4.9
2. Non-consanguineous	53.1	70.9	64.4	74.9
N=	11,628	8,998	2,758	1,049

Source: Rao and Inbaraj (1977); Richard and Sunder Rao (1994).

Note: Based on the studies conducted in Vellore town and rural areas of the K.V. Kuppam Block of North Arcot District in Tamil Nadu during 1969–70 and 1982–1987.

Dissolution of Marriage

There has been a significant change in the views and attitudes towards marriage in the recent past. Marriage is no longer held to be a 'divine match' or a 'sacred union'. Now it is more like a transfer of a female from one family to another, or from one kinship group to another. Marriage is no longer sanctified as it was believed in the past, and is viewed only as a bonding and nurturing of a life-long relationship and friendship. The rather flippant and superficial reasons given by many women and men to break a marriage may not portend well for the future. Indian marriages are still largely resilient and lasting, whereas in many developed countries they seem to break up for seemingly trivial reasons. Marriage is very fragile there. One in every four or five marriages breaks up despite more space and freedom in the

West. The longevity of marriage in most developed countries ranges on an average from five to seven years.

Where gender roles are defined it is easier to conform to a pattern, but with the, inevitable emancipation of women, her economic independence, Western influences and new value systems, imbibed from peer groups or passed on by her parents, marriage in Indian metropolises has assumed a new face. Marriage counsellors, formerly pooh-poohed at, have today assumed a lot of importance in guiding couples through stormy seas and averting the imminent pain of divorce. Today in cities, there is disenchantment with the system of arranged marriages in a large number of cases.

The Indian family is faced with a new kind of social and psychological constraints. The women, however, tend to be more concerned about their marriage than men and in case of a problem they are expected to go for counselling. They are expected to take lead to resolve conflicts and when they give up the effort, the marriage is generally over. The men feel that the expectations of the women are immense, and they cannot please them however hard they may try, despite a sizeable contribution to the family. They are under pressure to improve financial contribution, share in raising the children and provide emotional support to the wives. With tremendous pressure at work, the men confront emotional exhaustion. The simpler role of husbands in the past has now been replaced with a more complex role. 'But the emotional needs of a woman are different: she wants a soul-mate, someone who can understand her needs, someone who is caring and one who will take care of her when she is unduly stressed' (Singh 2004: 155).

Dissolution of marriage, like many other societies of both developed and developing world, has been quite uncommon and infrequent in India. Marriage was taken as a life-long union for the couple. Hindu marriage was taken as a sacrament rather than a contract between the couples to live in a social union so long as it is cordially feasible. Even in the event of frequent mental and physical torture the most Indian women try to continue their marriages. Remarriage of divorced or separated women are quite difficult. Morality relating to sex is so highly valued that every male wants to marry a virgin girl only. In the past, Hindus demanded pre-nuptial chastity on the part of both, but now it is by and large limited to females only. In fact, both boys and girls try to know secretly about each other's pre-marital sex life. Virginity is regarded as the girls' greatest virtue and symbol of respectability. To the surprise of many, a married woman is described as a 'second-hand-stuff' – an expression covertly pejorative of women. Under the circumstances remarriage of women is so difficult that annulment of marriage is a very hard choice or option. It is obvious from the census data that the divorced and separated women had never constituted even one per cent of the total women at any age between 15 and 49 years during the 1961-2001 census. The NFH Surveys have also recorded that the divorced and separated women constituted merely one per cent of the total married women in the age group of 15–49. The given statistics, however, may not hold so strongly in case of metropolitan cities about which there are uniform reporting of rise in the incidence of divorce.

It is generally stated that in India there has been so much emphasis on gender equality without adequate supporting changes that the relationship between wife and husband has become more tense now than before, despite the fact that the level of education, family income and rationality has improved. The incidence of divorce rate even in a country like India, with different norms of sustenance and forbearance is reported to have increased in some metropolises. A Chennai based legal practitioner, Sheila Jayaprakash, once reported that till 1988 only one civil court was earmarked for divorcees under the Hindu Marriage Act. Today, three Family Courts work overtime to deal with petitions from all religious groups (Radhakrishanan, 1999: 37). So, one can readily imagine how much the incidence of divorce has gone up. While divorce has already been in practice both among scheduled castes and scheduled tribes, the incidence of divorce in recent years is reported to be on retreat among the scheduled castes (Singh 1997a). In this respect the tribal communities have been more liberal than others. Divorce is permitted in 93 per cent of the tribal communities as also the remarriage of widow (609 tribes, 96%). Either party can seek divorce (Singh 1997b: 8).

The incidence of widow remarriage is similarly much higher than the Indian sociologists and social anthropologists have ever believed. Based on the census data, Bhat and Kanbargi (1984: 9) have estimated that about one-third of the ever-widowed women are currently remarried. This proportion is bound to be still higher in the case of urban areas. This is certainly a very startling demographic fact for most Indian sociologists and anthropologists. Since long they have been arguing that Indian society is so tradition-bound that widow remarriage has been a rare event, ignoring the fact that remarriage of young widows has never been uncommon among low castes and tribal population. The statistics provide clinching evidence that the Indian value system, with respect to widow remarriage, has experienced tremendous changes with the rise in education and level of development. In today's shifting values and changing times, there is less reliance on marriage as a definer of sex and living arrangements throughout life. There are a greater number of extra-marital relationships, including open gay and lesbian relationships, a delay in the age at marriage, higher rates of marital disruption and more egalitarian gender-role attitudes among men and women where norms and values have been totally restructured. High divorce rates, inter alia, connote that marriage is an institution on the rocks or is considered so important that people are no longer able to put up with the kinds of dissatisfaction and empty-shell marriages previous generation tolerated. High rates of remarriage similarly mean that people are sacrificing their marriages because of unsatisfactory relationships. Or they can also be interpreted to mean that the strain of living in modem society drive people into marriage but makes hard to sustain.

Conclusion

Rise in the age at marriage of females from 12.5 years in 1891 to about 22 years in 1998–99 or passing of child marriages, higher incidence of civil marriages, dwindling of consanguineous marriage, rise in divorce and remarriage of widow, shrinking of kinship ties, especially in urban India, are concrete and clinching evidence to suggest a whole range of changes in the institution of marriage and so also in the family system – its structure, functions, core values and regulative norms and the position of women within family (Trautmann 2003: 1104–1126; Singh 2004: 129–166). Changes that have occurred under the new circumstances in contemporary India are irreversible. With the rise in the level of education, more particularly of females, urbanization, rising spirit of individualism, modernization, increasing occupational differentiations with greater social mobility and search for new social identity far-reaching changes have occurred in practices relating to marriage and cognate demographic processes. Rising material aspirations of life has indirectly exacerbated dowry practices despite being declared illegal. Since dowry has become a status symbol, it is not going to disappear or dissipate so readily in near future. All the changes that have occurred have been the consequence of interplay of various factors and forces and these changes have come through the multiple heterogenetic and orthogenetic sources.

All the changes that have surfaced are not pre-planned, intended or functional. Some of these changes are certainly unintended and dysfunctional not only for the family system but also for the society in general – increase in dowry and divorce, for example. Social change seldom occurs in planned and intended manner. Therefore, what has happened or is happening is not unusual. However, this fact is recognized that what is dysfunctional from one angle may be functional from another. Divorce, separation or even dowry is not necessarily dysfunctional from all angles in all cases. This becomes obvious when, being free from value orientation, one seeks to delve deeper into certain changes and their consequences which have taken shape in Indian society.

References

Agarwala, S.N., 1962, *Age at Marriage in India*, Allahabad: Kitab Mahal Pvt. Ltd.

——, 1977, *India's Population Problems*, New Delhi: Tata McGraw-Hill.

Bhat, P.N. Mari and Francis Zavier, 1999, 'Findings of National Family Health Survey', *Economic and Political Weekly*, XXXIV (42–43): 3008–3032.

Bhat, P.N. Mari and R. Kanbargi, 1984, 'Estimating the Incidence of Widow Re-Marriages in India from Census Data', *Population Studies*, 38 (1): 89–103.

Census of India, 1991, *Final Population Totals: Brief Analysis of Primary Census Abstract, India*, Series I, Paper 2, New Delhi: Registrar General and Census Commissioner.

——, 1998, *The State Profile 1991, India*, New Delhi: Registrar General and Census Commissioner.

Caldwell, John C., P.H. Reddy and P. Caldwell, 1982, 'The Causes of Demographic Change in Rural South India: A Micro Approach', *Population and Development Review*, 8 (4): 689–727.

——, 1983, 'The Causes of Marriage Change in South India', *Population Studies*, 37 (3): 343–361.

Das, M., 1980, 'Matrimonial Advertisements: An Examination of its Social Significance in Mate Selection in Modern India', *Man in India*, 60: 187–203.

Das, N.P. and Devamoni Dey, 1998, 'Female Age at Marriage in India: Trends and Determinants', *Demography India*, 27 (1): 91-115.

Driver, E.D. and A.E. Driver, 1988, 'Social and Demographic Correlates of Consanguineous Marriages of South India', *Journal of Comparative Family Studies*, 19: 229–244.

Mutharayappa, R. et al., 1997, *Son Preference and its Effect on Fertility in India*, NFHS Subject Reports No. 3, Mumbai: International Institute for Population Sciences.

Nair, P.T., 1978, *Marriage and Dowry in India*, Calcutta: Minerva Associates.

National Family Health Survey-1, 1992–93, *India: Introductory Report*, Mumbai: International Institute for Population Sciences.

National Family Health Survey-2, 1998–99, *India: Introductory Report*, Mumbai: International Institute for Population Sciences.

National Family Health Survey-3, 2005–06, *India*, Vol. I, Mumbai: International Institute for Population Sciences.

Radhakrishanan, S., 1999, 'Marriage in Crisis', *The Hindu* (Sunday Magazine), September: 37–39.

Raja, M.K.D., 1991, 'Cult of Mass Marriages', *Indian Perspectives*, 4: 35–37.

Rao, P.S.S. and S.G. Inbaraj, 1977, 'Inbreeding in Tamil Nadu, South India', *Social Biology*, 24: 281–288.

Rao, P.V. and V. Sudarsen, 1978, 'Continuity and Change in Marital Choices: A Note on Matrimonial Advertisements in South India', *Social Action*, 28: 50–61.

Richard, I. and P.S.S. Sunder Rao, 1994, 'Changes in Consanguinity and Age at Marriage', *Demography India*, 23 (1): 15–28.

Riley, Nancy E., 1997, 'Gender, Power and Population Change', *Population Bulletin*, 52 (1).

Singh, J.P., 2005, 'Dowry in India: A Search for New Social Identity', *The Eastern Anthropologist*, 58(2): 199–220.

Singh, J.P., 2004, 'The Contemporary Indian Family', in Bert N. Adams and Jan Trost (eds), *Handbook of World Families* (29–166), California: Sage Publications.

Singh, K.S., 1992, *People of India: An Introduction*, Calcutta: Anthropological Survey of India.

——, 1997a, *The Scheduled Castes (People of India, Vol. II)*, New Delhi: Oxford University Press.

——, 1997b, *The Scheduled Tribes (People of India, Vol. III)*, New Delhi: Oxford University Press.

Srinivas, M.N., 1977, *Social Change in Modern India*, New Delhi: Orient Longman Ltd.

Srivastava, J.N., 1983, 'Socio-economic Determinants of Child Marriage in Uttar Pradesh', *Demography India*, 12 (1): 59–73.

Trautmann, Thomas R., 2003, 'Patterns of Marriage', in Veena Das (ed.), *The Oxford Indian Companion to Sociology and Anthropology* (1104–1126), Vols I & II, New Delhi: Oxford University Press.

3

Trends in Age at Marriage

B.S. NAGI

The study of age at marriage has acquired importance because it is one of the determinants of fertility. It is also one of the features of economic and social development. More generally, Matras (1965) has formulated a 'typology' of marriage and fertility patterns consisting of early or late marriage with controlled or uncontrolled fertility.

Average age at marriage for females in India in 1971 was 17.1 years. During 1986–87 it was estimated at 18.30 years. It has changed only slowly since 1921 when it was 13.89 years, rising to 15.83 years in 1961. For males, the 1971 figure was 22.5 years. Analysis of the effect of alterations in the age at marriage is made difficult by the fact that early marriages are usually not consummated for years – indeed a separate ceremony *gauna* is celebrated when cohabitation begins (Cassen 1979).

The Government and the intellectuals agree that a rise in the age at marriage is desirable. Opinions, however, vary on the impact of social change which could help in raising the age at marriage.

What determines the age at marriage? Agarwala (1965) observed the distinct regional differentials in India, with the South having the highest and the North and West having the lowest age at marriage. There are also differentials by religion and caste but they conform to some extent to the regional patterns. Thus Hindus, who tend to marry youngest of the main religious groups, marry later in states where the average age at marriage is higher. Urban men and women marry later than rural as do the educated relatively to the less educated (Gulati 1969; Kale 1969; Das Gupta 1974).

Raising the age at marriage could have a significant effect, but it is hard to believe that legislations would be effective enough to have any significant impact on age at marriage. It is, therefore, relevant to examine various aspects connected with the question of age at marriage.

Study Design

Rajasthan state was selected for the study because child marriages are more prevalent in Rajasthan as compared to other states in India. For an in-depth study, three districts, namely Udaipur, Bhilwara and Chittorgarh, were selected purposively keeping in mind convenience of contact and communication for data collection. From the three sampled districts, four villages, two from Udaipur and one each from Chittorgarh and Bhilwara, were selected. Keeping in view the convenience in data collection, these villages were again selected purposively. The villages from the same districts were selected to gauge differences both within the same district as well as across the districts. From Chittorgarh and Bhilwara districts, the villages of Gopal Nagar and Raila were selected, respectively. From Udaipur two villages were selected, namely, Kuraj and Rao Madra.

After selecting the villages, 50 households from each village were randomly selected. Each village was first divided into five zones, i.e. South, North, East, West and Centre and from each of these zones, 10 households were selected. A semi-structured schedule was designed to collect the requisite information.

An attempt has been made here to analyse the age at marriage of the children who got married last in the sample households, their sex-wise and village-wise distribution, and the relationship of age at marriage with present age, education and occupation.

Children who got Married Last and Age at Marriage

There are 22 households where no child marriage has taken place. The meaning of child marriage according to the respondents understanding is the marriage of girls before puberty. But the analysis of households data shows that almost all the marriages in the 200 households were performed before the legal age of marriage. So the distinction is being made here between the child marriage and the legal age of marriage. Here, child marriage means the marriage of a boy or a girl before the age of 15 years. It is a general practice or tradition in India that the age of the married girl should be lower than that of her husband.

Respondents were asked to mention the age at marriage of boys and girls who were married last in their families. Table 3.1 shows the percentage distribution of 178 marriages which look place in the family by the age at marriage. The table shows a different trend for boys and girls as far as the age at marriage is concerned. There are 23 per cent of the families in which the boys got married before the age of 11 years as compared to as many as 51 per cent girls. The difference of percentage might be due to the reason explained earlier that the girls are mostly younger to the boys at the time of marriage. But all the boys got married before the legal age of marriage which is 21 years and almost all the girls (98.3%) also got married below the legal age of marriage which is 18 years The table also reveals that there are 69.1 per cent families in which the boys who got married last are below the age of 16 years, whereas there are 86.5 per cent of the families in which the girls got married last are below the age of 16 years. The pattern of child marriage is quite visible, that is, most of the boys and girls got married at lower age but it is more so in the case of girls.

Table 3.1

Distribution of respondents by sex and age at marriage of children in the family who were married last

Sex	*Age at marriage*				
	1–10 yrs	*11–15 yrs*	*16–17 yrs*	*18–20 yrs*	*Total*
Male	41 (23.0)	82 (46.1)	21 (11.8)	34 (19.1)	178 (100.0)
Female	91 (51.1)	63 (35.4)	21 (11.8)	3 (1.7)	178 (100.0)

(Figures in parentheses are percentages)

Children who got Married Last and Age at Marriage (by Village)

The distribution of boys and girls who got married last is presented village-wise and by their age at marriage in Table 3.2. The table makes it very clear that in about 80 per cent of the families in Raila village in Bhilwara district the females who got married last are below the age of 11 years. The percentages of such families in Gopal Nagar village of Chittorgarh district and Kuraj village of Udaipur district are 56 and 48.9, respectively. But there are only 8.6 per cent families in Rao Madra village of Udaipur in which the females got married last are below 11 years of age. The table also indicates that families in which the males and females got married last in lower age groups are less in Rao Madra village whereas in other villages such families are more. Kuraj village and Rao Madra villages are both in the Udaipur district but the pattern of child marriage is different in both these villages, i.e. the incidence of child marriage is more in lower age groups in Kuraj village, whereas it is more in the higher age groups in Rao Madra village. The trend of child marriages is more or less the same for both males and females in Gopal Nagar and Kuraj villages, that is, in the age groups 1–10 years and 11–15 years, respectively. But the trend is different in Raila village. In this village, there are more families in which the males and females got married last are below the age of 11 years. Here, the percentage for males is 54.2 and for females it is 79.2.

Table 3.2

Distribution of the households in which the male and female got married last by village and age at marriage

Village		*Age at marriage*				
		1–10 yrs	*11–15 yrs*	*16–17 yrs*	*18–20 yrs*	*Total*
1. Gopal Nagar	M	7 (14.0)	30 (60.0)	7 (14.0)	6 (12.0)	50 (100.0)
	F	28	20	1	1	50
		(56.0)	(40.0)	(2.0)	(2.0)	(100.0)
2. Kuraj	M	7	32	4	2	45
		(15.5)	(71.1)	(8.9)	(4.4)	(100.0)
	F	22	21	2	—	45
		(48.9)	(46.7)	(4.4)	—	(100.0)
3. Rao Madra	M	1	3	8	23	35
		(2.8)	(8.6)	(22.9)	(65.7)	(100.0)
	F	3	14	16	2	35
		(8.6)	(40.0)	(45.7)	(5.7)	(100.0)
4. Raila	M	26	17	2	3	48
		(54.2)	(35.4)	(4.2)	(6.2)	(100.0)
	F	38	8	2	—	48
		(79.2)	(16.7)	(4.2)	—	(100.0)

(Figures in parentheses are percentages).

It is quite clear from Table 3.2 that most of the males and females got married last are in the lower age groups in Raila village. It is also quite clear that all males and about 96 per cent of females got married last are below the legal age of marriage in all the four villages.

Age at Marriage and Present Age

In all, there are 1258 members in 200 households; 59 per cent of them are males and 41 per cent are females. The number of married males and females are 352 and 387, respectively. The trend of marriages for males and females can be observed from Table 3.3. The data in Table 3.3 reveal that there are 66 male members who got married below the age of 10 years and out of this, 47 per cent are now above 35 years of age and 27.3 per cent are in the age group of 20 to 34 years. There are 118 male members who got married when they were in the age group of 10–14 years. Out of these, 74.6 per cent are now above 19 years of age. The table also reveals that except for 15 females and 6 males almost all the married members got married below the legal age of marriage irrespective of their present age. It is also clear from the table that from the present period to more than 35 years back, the males and females are getting married in their childhood. This trend gets supported from the fact that most of the respondents have also mentioned that child marriage has become, more or less, a custom and they have to follow this custom. When we study the percentage of members getting married before 10 years in different age cohorts, we find that it declines from 47 to 27, 14 and 12 from older ones to younger ones as far as males are concerned and from 36 to 31, 27 and 5 as far as females are concerned. But over the years the decline of child marriage is lower in the case of females than males.

Table 3.3 also reveals that 78.6 per cent of the married female members got married when they were below 15 years of age. This trend supports the respondents point of view when they say that most of the girls got married as soon as they achieved puberty. There are 147 married female members who got married when they were even below 10 years of age. Out of this, 24.8 per cent are at present above 34 years of age and 55.4 per cent are at present in the age group 20–34 years. Even those females, who are at present above 20 years of age got married in their childhood. It is, thus, once again reiterated that it has become customary to get the marriages of the boys and girls performed in their childhood.

Table 3.3

Distribution of married male and female members by age at marriage and present age

Age at marriage		*Present age*				
		0–9 yrs	*10–19 yrs*	*20–34 yrs*	*35+ yrs*	*Total*
		1	2	3	4	5
0–9	M	8	9	18	31	66
Years		(12.1)	(13.6)	(27.3)	(47.0)	(100.0)
	F	8	40	46	53	147
		(5.4)	(27.2)	(31.3)	(36.1)	(100.0)
10–14	M	—	30	51	37	118
years		—	(25.4)	(43.2)	(31. 4)	(100.0)
	F	—	31	87	39	157
		—	(19.7)	(55.4)	(24.8)	(100.0)
15–17	M	—	6	46	40	92
years		—	(6.5)	(50.0)	(43.5)	(100.0)
	F	—	12	37	19	68
		—	(17.6)	(54.4)	(27.9)	(100.0)
18–20	M	—	—	37	33	70
years		—	—	(52.9)	(47.1)	(100.0)
	F	—	—	9	6	15
		—	—	(60.0)	(40.0)	(100.0)
21 +	M	—	—	2	4	6
year		—	—	(33.3)	(66.7)	(100.0)
	F	—	—	—	—	—
Total	M	8	45	154	145	352
		(2.3)	(12.8)	(43.8)	(41.1)	(100.0)
	F	8	83	179	117	387
		(2.1)	(21.4)	(46.3)	(30.2)	(100.0)

(Figures in parentheses are percentages) M = Male, F = Female

Age at Marriage and Education

In rural areas, it is problematic especially for the girls to continue their education after marriage. Since marriages are performed in the early childhood, the children, especially the girls, either remain illiterate or drop out of schools very early. By the time girls complete their primary education they are already above 10 to 14 years which, in all probability, is the age of their marriage. Therefore, those who get married before achieving the age of I0 years generally remain illiterate or below primary level and those who get married after I0 years of age, are able to complete just their primary education. Such trend is reflected from the data presented in Table 3.4.

Table 3.4

Distribution of married household members by age at marriage and education

Age at marriage		*Illiterate*	*Primary*	*Middle*	*High school and above*	*Total*
0–9 years	M	43	23	—	—	66
		(65.2)	(34.8)			(100.0)
	F	129	18	—	—	147
		(87.8)	(12.2)			(100.0)
10–14 years	M	42	38	15	23	118
		(35.6)	(32.2)	(12.7)	(19.5)	(100.0)
	F	125	24	8	—	157
		(79.6)	(15.3)	(5.1)		(100.0)
15–17 years	M	27	38	9	18	92
		(29.3)	(41.3)	(9.8)	(19.6)	(100.0)
	F	44	18	3	3	68
		(64.7)	(26.5)	(4.4)	(4.4)	(100.0)
18–20 years	M	26	12	8	24	70
		(37.2)	(17.1)	(11 4)	(34.3)	(100.0)
	F	7	5	2	1	15
		(46.7)	(33.3)	(13.3)	(6.7)	(100.0)
21 + year	M	3	—	—	3	6
		(50.0)			(50.0)	(100.0)
	F	—	—	—	—	—
Total	M	141	111	32	8	352
		(40.1)	(31.5)	(9.1)	(19.3)	(100.0)
	F	305	65	13	4	387
		(78.8)	(16.8)	(3.4)	(1.0)	(100.0)

(Figures in parentheses are percentages). M = Male, F = Female.

Table 3.4 reveals that there are only four married females who have studied up to high school and above. One of them got married in the age group of 18 to 20 years while three of them got married in the age group of 15 to 17 years. It means these girls might have got married after completing their education. About 80 per cent of the married females are illiterate. In the case of married male members, 40.1 per cent of them are illiterate and 31.5 per cent of them have completed their primary level education. There are 28.4 per cent married male members whose level of education is up to middle and above. The Pearsonian correlation between education and the age at marriage of married members has been computed. The coefficient of correlation between these two is .34 which is significant and it means that late marriage will lead to higher education if not the vice-versa.

Age at Marriage and Occupation

The distribution of married male and female members by their age at marriage and present occupation is given in Table 3.5. Table 3.5 reveals that 66 married male members got married at the age of 0–9 years. At the time of marriage, the children below 10 years of age cannot decide about their occupations but certain occupations mentioned in the table are family occupations, like labourers, business, etc. Out of 66 married males, 42.4 per cent are in the cultivation and 18.2 per cent are labourers. In other words, it may be said that cultivator and labour class have more child marriages than members from other occupations. Similarly, there are 118 married males who got married when they were 10 to 14 years of age. Out of these, 31.5 per cent are labourers and 16.6 per cent are doing cultivation. There are 17.8 per cent who are engaged in business. It may be concluded from the table that the children who get married at an early age may not think of any independent occupation of their own at the time of marriage but are generally forced to choose occupation of their elders when they grow up. The trend that seems to be emerging from the table is that lack of occupational mobility is one of the causes of child marriages.

Table 3.5

Distribution of married male and female household members by age at marriage and occupation

Age at marriage		Occupation categories						
		No occupation	Labourer	Artisan	Cultivation	Business	Service	Total
		0	1	2	3	4	5	
0–9 Years	M	19 (28.9)	12 (18.2)	1 (1.5)	28 (42.4)	3 (4.5)	3 (4.5)	66 (100.0)
	F	110 (74.8)	31 (21.1)	—	6 (4.1)	—	—	147 (100.0)
10–14 years	M	23 (19.5)	30 (25.4)	10 (8.5)	22 (18.6)	21 (17.8)	12 (10.2)	118 (100.0)
	F	133 (84.7)	14 (8.9)	—	9 (5.7)	—	1 (0.6)	157 (100.0)
15–17 years	M	1 (1.1)	29 (31.5)	17 (18.5)	10 (10.9)	14 (15.2)	10 (10.8)	92 (100.0)
	F	36 (52.9)	18 (26.5)	—	12 (17.7)	—	2 (2.9)	68 (100.0)
18–20 years	M	4 (5.7)	17 (24.3)	3 (4.3)	17 (24.3)	6 (8.6)	23 (32.8)	70 (100.0)
	F	10 (66.7)	1 (6.6)	—	4 (26.7)	—	—	15 (100.0)
21 + year	M	—	—	—	3 (50.0)	3 (50.0)	—	6 (100.0)
	F	—	—	—	—	—	—	—
Total	M	58 (16.5)	88 (25.0)	31 (8.8)	80 (22.7)	47 (13.4)	48 (13.6)	352 (100.0)
	F	289 (74.7)	64 (16.7)	—	31 (8.0)	—	3 (0.8)	387 (100.0)

(Figures in parentheses are percentages). M = Male, F = Female

The table also reveals that 74.7 per cent of the female members either do the household work or they do not do any work. But in those families where the women work as labourers, the girls who get married at any early age may also later turn to do the labourer's job. Same is the case with cultivation. In those families where the women do the cultivation, the girls who get married at an early age are likely to become cultivators later in their lives. And thus, no definite pattern can be observed for females because the table does not show any causal relationship between age at marriage and occupation pursued by the married female members.

Conclusion

In rural areas covered under this study, almost all the boys and girls got married before the legal age at marriage. Majority of the boys (69%) and girls (86%) got married before the age of 16 years. There were greater village-wise variations in case of marriages below the age of 11 years. From the present period to more than 35 years back, the males and females have been getting married in childhood. Child marriage has become more or less a custom but over the years the decline of child marriage is lower in case of females than males. The trend of child marriages has been a major cause of girls' illiteracy or lower level of education. It is also evident that child marriages are widely prevalent among cultivators and labourers. Dependency on elders and lack of independent occupational aspirations or occupational mobility further hampers the efforts of limiting child marriages.

References

Agarwala, S.N., 1965, 'Effect of a Rise in Female Marriage Age on Birth Rate in India', Paper Presented at United Nations World Population Conference, Belgrade.

Cassen, R.H., 1979, *India: Population, Economy, Society,* Delhi: Macmillan.

Das Gupta, M., 1974, *Factors Affecting Age at Marriage in India,* London School of Economics (Unpublished).

Gulati, S.C., 1969, 'Impact of Literacy, Urbanization and Sex Ratio on Age and Marriage in India', *Artha Vijnana,* 11 (4): 85–92.

Kale, B.D., 1969, 'Contours of Female Education and Age at Marriage in Urban India: A District Level Study', *Journal of the Institute of Economic Research, Dharwal,* 4 (2): 34–50.

Matras, J., 1965, 'The Social Strategy of Family Formation: Some Variations in Time and Space', *Demography,* 2: 349–362.

4

Young People

Their Values and Beliefs Concerning Marriage and Family in India

SURENDRA K. GUPTA

Many research studies have been conducted to determine the extent to which institutions of marriage and the family in India have undergone change by examining the influence of industrialization, urbanization, modernization and increasing educational and occupational facilities. These forces have not only affected the age at marriage and familial relations, but also the process of mate selection as well as the attitude, values and beliefs concerning other aspects of marriage and the family, especially of the young people. In this paper, an attempt has been made to present young peoples' values and beliefs concerning marriage and the family on the basis of available studies. Major trends emerging from the discussion have also been highlighted.

The paper has four sections dealing with the values and beliefs concerning marriage, values and beliefs concerning the family, major trends and evaluation and suggestions for further research. In each section, first an attempt has been made to discuss the traditional views and then the changes have been described.

Values and Beliefs Concerning Marriage

Marriage as a Necessity

Traditionally, marriage among Hindus was considered a social duty towards the family and the community and it was necessary for a Hindu, both male and female, to obtain a partner through marriage for the fulfillment of one's religious duties i.e. *dharma*. This was essential for the attainment of *moksha* (final liberation) which is the ultimate aim of all Hindus in order to free herself or himself from the bonds of a chain of links of births in the past and in the future. For Hindu females, marriage had a special significance because this was the only sacrament performed for a woman.

Gradually, a change is coming especially in the attitude of young females. Now, some of them do not consider marriage as a necessity. They have already started looking for an alternative to marriage. Suitable career, creative arts, social service and philanthropic activities were frequently mentioned as the alternate by the young females (Blumberg and Dwaraki 1980; Kumari 1978).

Traditional girls (Ghadially and Kazi 1980) and rural youth (Kumari 1978) still consider marriage as a social obligation which must be fulfilled. The most important benefit of marriage cited by these people is that it provides opportunities for procreation and child rearing, followed by companionship. About one-third of the respondents regard it as a means to sexual gratification, whereas few think that marriage provides protection and comforts of life, shelter and food. More or less similar views were expressed by the women studied by Blumberg and Dwaraki (1980) and by the college students, both male and female, studied by Ghadially and Kazi (1980). Parsi women expect companionship and emotional satisfaction from the spouse. (Billimoria 1991).

Age at Marriage

Pre-puberty marriage especially in case of females was the dominant pattern in traditional India. Parents preferred to transfer their responsibility of a daughter to her husband as early as possible. They wanted to marry a daughter before she attained maturity and questioned their decision. It was generally, the Brahman caste which set the pattern followed by other castes. Since pre-puberty, marriage was the norm among Brahmans it became popular among other castes also. Virginity was not accorded high priority, but gradually became a status symbol of higher castes, which also affected the age of marriage.

Other factors which affected the age at marriage were caste endogamy and village exogamy. Caste factor narrowed down the choice of selection of a spouse which made the competition tough; people preferred to marry their daughters at the first opportunity. Early marriage also enhanced the social prestige of the family. Gradually, the marriage at puberty became very popular and '... the practice became so compelling that a departure from it was a matter of social disapproval and even of social disgrace' (Kapadia 1990: 145–146). Lower castes went a step ahead by contracting marriages even before the birth of a child. Marriages were fixed when the children were in the womb.

Due to the efforts of social reformers, the average age at marriage for boys and girls has risen over the last 100 or so years. In 1860, a law was passed by which marriage below 10 years of age was declared as rape and persons violating this law were liable to punishment including imprisonment for life. Following this, various state governments also introduced their own laws to control the age at marriage. In 1929, the British Government passed the Child Marriage Restraint Act restricting the age at marriage to 18 for males and 14 years for females. The Hindu Marriage Act of 1955 passed in independent India accepted 15 as the minimum age of marriage for a girl. This Act was amended in 1978 which restricted the minimum ages at marriages for boys and girls at 21 and 18 years, respectively.

Though the age at marriage has shown upward trend in independent India, but it has remained much below the age prescribed by the 1978 Act, especially in the case of females. The analysis of census data concerning age at marriage shows that the mean age at marriage for males has increased from 21.39 years in 1961 to 22.24 years in 1971 and to 23.10 years in 1981. The corresponding figures for females are 16.10 years in 1961 to 17.23 in 1971 and to 18.41 years in 1981 (cf. Goyal 1988: 67). In rural India, the mean age at marriage for females and males increased from 15.69 in 1961 to 17.81, in 1981 and 20.80 in 1961 to 22.42 in 1981, respectively. The corresponding figures for urban India are 23.53 in 1961 to 24.82 in 1981 for males and 17.92 in 1961 to 20.14 in 1981 for females.

Religion wise the highest age at marriage is among Christians followed by Muslims and Hindus. In 1972, the mean age at marriage for males and females among Christians was 25.2 and 18.8, respectively. Among Muslims the mean age at marriage was 23.1 for males and 16.5 for females and it was 22.0 for males and 16.3 for females among Hindus (cf. Goyal 1988: 37).

According to 1981 census data, the age at marriage of about two-third of the ever married females of urban Christians was more than 18 years whereas among Hindus and Muslims highest number of such females were married between 14–17 years of age. The same trend has been observed among rural females.

Empirical studies have been conducted among young people in different parts of the country to ascertain their attitude and views regarding the suitable age of marriage for males and females. Most of the students in B.V. Shah's (1964) study conducted in Gujarat colleges have suggested 24 to 26 as the appropriate age of marriage. They expected to complete their studies and also settle in life by this time. There were some married students in his sample whose average age at marriage was about 20.9 years which was much below the age at marriage suggested by these students. The university students in Mathew's study (1966: 47) favoured 22 to 24 as the most suitable age of marriage for females. Goldstein's sample (1972: 93) regarded 20 to 25 years as the most appropriate age for marriage. The females in Blumberg and Dwaraki's (1980: 83) study also preferred 21 to 24 as the suitable age of marriage.

The college students studied by Rao and Rao (1982) preferred 25 years or earlier as the ideal age of marriage for a boy and 21 years or earlier for girls. The female students subscribed 22 years or later as the ideal age of marriage for themselves. Rao and Rao found that father's education and income affect students' choice for early marriage.

Haryana girls (Punia, Punia and Sharma, 1987) favoured 18 to 21 years as the appropriate age of marriage for girls, and 21 to 25 for boys. Chaudhary's (1988a: 105) young women also suggested 22 to 25 years as the suitable age of marriage.

Most of the studies referred above have suggested 20 to 25 as the ideal age of marriage for boys as well as for girls. However, slight deviation from this trend has been reported by Patel (1982). Average age of marriage for boys and girls preferred by his sample was 17.82 for boys and 16.89 for girls.

Among Muslims, there was no fixed age of marriage for girls, but like Hindus they were married before they attained puberty. Even Prophet Mohammed married a child wife. Muslim girls have also shown signs of change, especially the educated females. Indu Menon (1981), in her study among Kerala Muslim women, found that 58 per cent of the females were married between 15–19 years of age and only one-third of the women were married below 15 years. However, majority of these women would like to marry their daughters between l6 and 21 years. Menon observed that educated females preferred higher age of marriage for their daughters. Muslim girls of Patna studied by Ashrafi (1992) considered 21–25 years as the ideal age of marriage for boys and girls, though majority of them were married between 16–20 years. Ashrafi also pointed out that education is positively related to age of marriage.

Selection in Marriage

The selection in marriage has been discussed under three categories: (a) Field of selection; (b) Party to selection; and (c) Criteria for selection.

Field of Selection

Hindu society is divided into a number of castes and sub-castes. Sub-castes have been further divided into what is called *gotra*. Caste and sub-caste are endogamous units whereas *gotra* is an exogamous unit. One is supposed to marry within same caste and sub-caste but outside *gotra*. Marriages between persons related to each other within certain generations on father's side (four generations) and certain generations on mother's side (three generations) are also prohibited. This aspect of exogamy is called *sapinda* exogamy. Among some communities marriage with particular relatives was more or less obligatory. For instance, cross-cousin marriage has been a characteristic feature among the Telugus, the Kannadigas and the Tamilians. In North India, according to Kapadia (1990), it has been found among Yadavas and Pandavas. The Hindu Marriage Act of 1955 has allowed cross-cousin marriage to continue as a local custom, but has prohibited marriage between uncle and niece.

Among Muslims, marriage with a father's brother's daughter, who is called *bintaam,* the first wife, was more or less obligatory. It was considered an insult and in a certain measure an offence, to refuse to accept one's father's brother's daughter in marriage. The Sunnis and the Shias, the two broad sections of Muslims, follow endogamous rules at least in theory.

Changes have been observed in intra-caste and intra religious marriages. Das (1978a, 1978b) conducted a study to find out the pattern of touchable and untouchable inter-caste as well as Christian and non-Christian inter-religious marriages. The predominant pattern of inter-caste marriages according to Das is a low caste male of high achievement marrying a high caste female of low achievement. The minor trend is marriage between high caste male of low achievement and low caste female of high achievement. Among Christian and non-Christian marriages, Das found non-Christian male marrying very often Christian females.

Fifty per cent of the students in Gangrade's (1975) study in Delhi University approved of inter-religious marriages. The number of males who approved this form of marriage is more than the girls. Sixty-three per cent of the students also approved of inter-caste marriages. Again males are more liberal than females. Same has been observed by Prasad and Usha (1990) in their study among the postgraduate students of Osmania University. They also found that Scheduled Castes and Scheduled Tribe students are more inclined towards inter-caste marriages than the students of backward and forward castes. Muslim and Hindu students are more rigid in their attitude than Christians.

Fifty six per cent of the college girls of Patna University (Chaudhary 1988b) showed positive attitude towards inter-caste marriages, but disapproved inter-religious marriages. College girls in Haryana (Punia, Punia and Sharma 1987) preferred intra-religious and intra caste marriages.

Syrian Christians (Kurian 1961) are divided into various sub-groups depending on their Church denominations and each group practices endogamy, though they are not very rigid. Generally, Syrian Christians do not like to marry other Christians but there are no water tight separations.

Party to Selection

Arranged marriages was the norm followed in traditional India. Marriages were fixed by the parents without consulting the boy and the girl. Love between husband and wife was supposed to be the result of marriage rather than a prelude to it. Gradually, a change is coming in the process of mate selection.

Now, the number of young people who regard marriage as a personal affair of an individual and the parties involved must be consulted before final decision, is gradually increasing. Following trends can be noticed:

(i) Traditional form of marriage where parents select the mates without consulting the boy and the girl.

(ii) Where parents finalize marriage only after consulting the parties involved.

(iii) Parties select their own partners and then take approval of the parents.

(iv) Parties select their own partners without taking approval of the parents.

The predominant pattern preferred by the young people is the second category where parents select the mates with the approval of the boy and the girl. This view has been found in many studies conducted among college students by Shah (1964), Shah (1975), Kumari (1978), Fonseca (1980), Rao and Rao (1982), Punia, Punia and Sharma (1987), and Chaudhary (1988a). The students in Shah's study (1964) have exerted that if parents strongly disapprove of any proposal children would drop that proposal and similarly if the boy disapproves of any proposal, the parents would not force him. More females than males will depend on their parents for selection (Shah 1975). Majority of the girls studied by Punia, Punia and Sharma (1987) and Pratima Chaudhary (1988a) emphasized that they would like to meet their partners before finalization of their marriage. Educated girls feel that they are in a better position to judge the candidates presented by their parents than the uneducated (Blumberg and Dwaraki 1980).

Majority of the boys and girls now want more freedom in selecting their future partners. A large number of students studied by Rao and Rao (1982) expressed their desire to get to know the future partners before marriage. About 50 per cent of the sample of Bombay college students of Fonseca (1980) would like to have only symbolic communication before marriage and another 40 per cent (including females) considered desirable to have 'emotive reactive behaviour' including physical union before marriage.

Only one-fourth of the girls in Chaudhary's (1988b) study were against love marriage, whereas 60 per cent favoured it. Similar views were expressed by 17 per cent of the youth included in Kumari's (1978) study.

Though the number of youth who would prefer to select their own spouse is increasing, the majority of them would like to have the approval of their parents before finalization of marriages.

Syrian Christians also followed the practice of arranged marriage, but with the spread of education mutual compatibles of the boy and girl play significant role. They get an opportunity to meet each other and '... thus get to know something about each other personalities, though actual courting is almost unknown even among the educated people' (Kurian 1961: 65). In 65 per cent of the cases studied by Kurian the marriages were arranged by parents with consent of the respondents and in about one-fourth cases choice was made by the respondents with consent of the parents. Only seven per cent of the parents arranged marriages of their wards without consulting them.

Like Hindus, among Muslims also the marriages were arranged by the parents without consulting the parties concerned. While of late, the Muslim males have gained some freedom to choose the spouse, but still Muslim females have little say. Only one-fourth of the Muslim females in Menon's (1981) study expressed their views before their marriages were finalized. Educated females are given more liberty than the uneducated. Roy's (1979) findings are also more or less similar. She studied Muslim women of Delhi and Lucknow. Roy reported that in her study 22 per cent of the females were consulted before fixing their marriages.

A large number of Muslim girls in Ashrafi's (1992) study did not specify but evaded the question when they were asked 'would you like to give freedom to your daughter in selecting her spouse'. Their response was 'depends on circumstances', but it appears that they were not against giving a free hand to the girl in selecting her spouse. Only 18 per cent of the Muslim females in Menon's study will have no objection if their daughters select their own spouse provided other conditions are agreeable to them; 82 per cent will never approve of it.

Among Parsis, generally the marriage is based on love or friendship. The parties concerned take their own decisions which are generally accepted by the parents. Even in those cases where parents take the decision, the consent of the boy and the girl is a must (Billimoria 1991: 105). They would prefer to have courtship before marriage so that they can understand each other better. Very few females were in favour of indulging in sex before marriage.

Now the matrimonial advertisements in the newspaper columns are frequently used by all categories of people to select a mate for their wards. In this they specify their own particulars and also mention the qualities and characteristics required in the spouse. The Sunday issue of, *The Times of India,* dated 23 August 1992, went a step ahead when they published photographs of two match seekers along with their other particulars. One advertisement gave the following particulars below the photograph 'A suitable match for handsome Punjabi *Khatri* boy 23/I67, own house, car with good running business, NRI preferred. Well settled family'.

Other advertisement was from an Indian who had acquired Canadian citizenship and was on a short visit to India. The advertisement contained his photograph and the following particulars. 'Mr Amit Manharlal Parekh, B. Chem. (U.D.C.T. Bombay) is M.A. Sc. in Polymer (University of Toronto-Canada) Jain, S/o Prominent Well established Businessman Mr Manharlal Parekh, 25/5–11, Fair Handsome, Canadian citizen on short visit to India, qualified, fair, beautiful, Doctor, B. Pharm. Engineer, C.A., girl willing to settle in America or Canada only criteria'.

Both these advertisements have given their age, caste and occupation. While one mentioned about owning a car and house, the other emphasized on settling in Canada or America. One specified that girls merit is the only consideration, while the other preferred an NRI girl.

Criteria for Selection

Since a marriage among Hindus was regarded as an alliance between two families, the family background and reputation of the boy and the girl were the main considerations. Other considerations in selecting a mate were: (i) no history of persons suffering from incurable diseases, and (ii) the standard of living (cf. Kapadia 1990: 137). Physical beauty and educational qualifications took secondary place. These characteristics can come handy to reduce the amount of dowry. Despite the fact that selections were made by the parents, very often marriages proved to be successful.

Now different criteria are followed in selecting a spouse. Some scholars have covered this aspect in their studies of youth to find out their views. Health, beauty and charm were given the top priority by the youth included in Kumari's (1978) sample. Personal qualities occupied second position and educational attainment was ranked third. When S. Kumari enquired about the ideal choice, majority gave preference to educational attainment followed by qualities of heart and personal qualities. Family history and character of the girl still get top priority among the rural youth (Karanth 1981; Gandhi 1983). Girls have emphasized more on personal characteristics of the future partner (Punia and others 1987). Even girls from rural areas gave emphasis to the qualifications of the future spouse (Chahil 1972).

Muslim girls in Ashrafi's study (1992) would give priority to 'employment of the boy' and his academic achievement while selecting a spouse. Lineage or caste, and the physique and character were given secondary place.

An ideal spouse according to majority of the Parsi females should be loving and understanding and affectionate (Billimoria 1991). A few gave emphasis on his education and qualification. When asked about the qualities they wanted in their spouse, majority preferred him to be understanding and accommodating.

Dowry System

Traditionally, all parents used to give 'gifts' in cash or ornaments to their daughters at the time of marriage. These were regarded as symbol of affection and love and were given voluntarily. But in the 20th century people have started demanding dowry from bride's family and gradually it became a prestige issue. Dowry system has helped some families to raise their socio-economic status. Rao and Rao (1982) consider it as a positive factor in raising age at marriage, because very often lower and middle class families have to wait till they find a suitable match for their wards which also suit their purse. It has also contributed to the bankruptcy of some parents. In 1961, Dowry Prohibition Act was passed making it as a punishable offence, but it has not been enforced due to many problems. Still dowry plays significant role in many marriages, though young people's attitude shows gradual change.

Nearly two-third of the youth studied by Kumari (1978) are against the dowry system. Urban youth are more opposed to this practice as compared to rural youth. Rao and Rao (1982) have observed that dowry expectation increases with higher education. They found higher dowry expectations among high socio-economic status students, medical majors, non-Hindus and urbanites. Father's education and income significantly affected students' attitude toward dowry. They also found a contradiction between the values of the youth and the normative orientation of the adults towards dowry.

Some girls are against the dowry system and do not consider it as a necessity for marriage (Punia, Punia and Sharma 1987), whereas there are others who consider that dowry is a must (Goldstein 1972). A large number of girls studied by Chaudhary (1988a) consider dowry as a social evil. Majority of them want that the giver as well as the receiver both should be punished. These girls have also given some suggestions to check harassment of brides who bring less dowry. The measures suggested are: (a) the strict enforcement of Dowry Prohibition Act; (b) the masses should be made aware of its evil consequences by mass media; (c) by giving employment and economic independence to girls; (d) boys and girls should raise voice against it; (e) girls should be bold enough to refuse to marry those who demand dowry; and (i) by providing higher education to girls.

One major trend noticed by Goldstein (1972) is that the girls who are working or seeking employment reported very often that their families do not expect to give or receive dowry. In other words, it may mean that the income from these earning women will take the place of dowry.

Dowry system has equally affected the Muslims and the Christians. Majority of the Muslim females in Menon's (1981) study emphasized that they have to give dowry for their daughter's marriage, though 50 per cent of these females considered it as undesirable. In Ashrafi's (1992) study, 89 per cent of the Muslim girls are against dowry. They suggested that the youth should be educated against it and supporters of dowry should be boycotted.

Syrian Christians also believe in dowry system. About 82 per cent of the respondents studied by Kurian (1961) accepted dowry in their own marriage and majority expected to get better match for their daughter if dowry is paid. About 40 per cent consider it a way of settling property claims of daughters. Majority of such people hail from rural areas.

Divorce and Widow Remarriage

Since Hindu marriage is accompanied by certain sacred rites, it is regarded as a sacrament and is, therefore, irrevocable. It cannot be dissolved at the will of either party. The husband and wife '... are bound to each other until the death of either of them; and the wife is supposed to be bound to her husband even after his death' (Kapadia 1990: 168).

In a traditional Hindu marriage, a woman is supposed to merge her individuality with that of her husband and his satisfaction was her main motto. However, she was allowed to have second husband if her husband became ascetic or is absent from home for a long time. According to sacred texts, a Hindu widow is supposed to remain chaste and was not allowed to remarry.

A male is allowed to have a second wife if the first dies issueless or did not give birth to a male child, which is a must for a Hindu not only for continuation of the family line but to save father from going to hell. Without a male progeny a man cannot perform his *dharma* and is, therefore, permitted to have a second wife.

The attitude of educated women towards divorce is changing. Now they have started asserting their right to divorce their husbands and favour dissolution of marriage (Kapadia 1990; Kapur 1978). The educated women in Kapur's sample (1978: 155–156) emphasized that a divorced woman could marry again at any age and stage of her life, provided she feels its necessity and also availability of a person of her choice.

Young women studied by Chaudhary (1988a) felt that the right of divorce for women is a healthy development. Very few young females considered it an unhealthy development. Those who favoured it regard divorce as a solution to save a woman from a life of torture, and it may help her to develop her personality. Not all people consider divorce as a healthy development. Gangrade (1975), in his study, found that about two-third students were against it.

Muslim tradition favours widow remarriage, but in practice it is not so. Muslim females favoured the remarriage of young widows and widows who had no children from the first marriage (Menon 1981; Ashrafi 1992).

Mohammendan Law permits the husband to divorce his wife without assigning any reasons. A Muslim woman is not given such freedom. If she wants to marry again after *talaq* (divorce) she has to wait for three menstrual periods. Among Muslims, *mehr* or dower, which is a sum of money or other property which the wife is entitled to receive from the husband, is considered to be the fundamental right of a woman. 'Mehr is a tool against exploitation of the fairer sex and a security against adversity. It is also a check against sudden divorce' (Ashrafi 1992: 56). About 41 per cent of the females in Ashrafi's study (1992) said that they would press their husband to pay maintenance, whereas other 35 per cent stated that they will forego it and will try to get a job.

Majority of the Parsi women are not in favour of divorce. Almost all the respondents stated that widows' remarriage should be freely permitted (Billimoria 1991).

Values and Beliefs Concerning Family

Sacramental marriage and the joint family, the two pillars of Hindu society, have shown signs of cracking in the independent India. However, the process has been accelerated in the past two-three decades with the enactment of new laws giving women equal status to men and overall improvement in education and mass media. These developmental activities have considerably affected the attitude, values and beliefs of the young people. In this section, the views of young people concerning family have been discussed.

Many studies have shown that women, especially the educated women, feel suffocated in the joint family system and, therefore, prefer living in the nuclear family (Gore 1968; Ross 1961). Even the young college going girls favour nuclear family (Chaudhary 1988a). They dislike the joint family system because it impedes the development of their personality and creates difficulties in the proper care of children and their education. About three-fourth of the students in Haribhai Patel's study (1982) prefer small sized families with two or three children. Youth in Kumari's (1978) study have also expressed similar views. Fifty per cent of the youth in her sample would prefer to have only two sons and another 55 per cent wanted only one daughter. About two-third of the students in Rao and Rao (1982) sample favour nuclear family.

This change in the attitude of young people towards joint family was also found in 1960s and 1970s. Quite a big chunk of students in Shah's (1964) study did not like the system due to quarrels in the family system, while others consider that it thwarts the development of individuality. Even those students who preferred joint family system did not favour living in very large joint families which includes uncles, aunts and their dependents. Their concept of joint family means living with parents, themselves and their children, their married brothers and their dependents and their unmarried brothers and sisters.

Stuers (1975), while studying the attitude of Jaipur Girl students towards family life, found that post-graduate girls were more pronouncedly against the joint family, whereas the younger girls were nearly as strongly for it. Both have their own reasons for their preference.

A large number of Syrian Christians, both rural and urban, preferred to live in nuclear family consisting of their husbands and children only (Kurian 1961: 55).

Majority of the Parsi women, both married and unmarried, did not want more than one or two children, thus Parsi women also favouring small family norm (Billimoria 1991).

Major Trends

On the basis of the preceding presentation, major trends observed among young people concerning their values and beliefs towards marriage and the family are summarized in this section:

1. Attitude of young people towards marriage as a necessity is gradually changing. There are a few females who have started looking for an alternative to marriage. Some of them give more weightage to their career, while a few others would like to devote their life to creative arts, or in social service and philanthropic activities. Though the number of such females is not very large but certainly a new trend is emerging in their thinking process.
2. Mean age at marriage as recorded in various censuses and the attitude of young people reflect upward trend. A large number of young people would an prefer to marry between 20–25 years of age. Both, male and female, have expressed this opinion. Young generation from rural areas is also showing signs of change and education is emerging as a major factor affecting change. The highest age at marriage is among Christians followed by Muslims and Hindus.

3. Young people's attitude towards inter-caste and inter-religious marriages is changing. Majority of the girls are against inter-religious marriages but are favourably inclined towards inter-caste marriages. Boys are more open to both kinds of marriages. Muslims and Hindu students are more rigid and traditional as compared to Christians. The scheduled caste and scheduled tribe students are more willing towards inter-caste marriages than the backward and forward caste students.

   The predominant pattern of touchable and untouchable inter-caste marriage is a low caste male of high achievement marrying a high caste female of low achievement. The minor trend is where high caste male of low achievement marrying a low caste female of high achievement. Among Christian and non-Christian marriages, the trend is marriage between a non-Christian male with a Christian female.

4. Parents are gradually giving more laxity to their wards in the selection of mate. Though in majority of the cases, marriages are still arranged by the parents; but the opinion of the parties involved are always kept in mind. Quite a few youth want to select their own mate but with the approval of the parents. Among Muslims, parallel cousin marriage is no more obligatory.

   Attitude of youth towards love marriage is also changing. Even girls are not against it; however, they would not finalize the marriage till their parents approve the proposal.

5. Though 'dating' is not yet a common practice in India, but a large number of youth expressed their desire to get to know the future partners before marriage. Some would prefer to have symbolic communication before marriage, whereas there are others who favoured more close contact, including physical union.

   Christians and Parsis are more inclined to know their future partners before marriage as compared to Hindus and Muslims. Muslim girls are more rigid and traditional in this matter though education has brought some change in their attitude.

6. Selection of mates through matrimonial advertisement in various newspapers and magazines is gaining momentum. Publication of photograph along with other particulars is a new trend seen recently.
7. Rural youth still give preference to family background and character of the girl while selecting a mate. Girls from rural as well as urban areas but more emphasis on the personal characteristic and qualification of the future spouse. Mutual compatibility of the boy and girl significantly affect the decision-making process among Christians and Parsis. Muslim girls gave priority to academic achievement and 'employment of the boy'. Majority of the Parsi women would like to have an 'understanding and accommodating' husband.
8. It is significant that a large number of youth are against dowry system. Urban youth are more opposed to dowry as compared to rural youth. There is a contradiction between the values of the youth and the normative orientation of the adults towards dowry system.

   Almost all the girls in various studies were against the dowry. Girls should refuse to marry dowry seekers was one of the measure suggested by them. Some suggested to provide more educational and occupational opportunities for girls. Muslims girls also opposed the dowry system. They want youth to be educated against dowry and supporters of dowry should be boycotted.
9. Attitude of educated women towards divorce is also changing. Young women consider the right to divorce for women as a healthy development. It saves a woman from a life of torture and may help her in personality development.

   Muslim females favoured remarriage of young widows and widows who had no children from the first marriage. Some Muslim women would press their husbands to pay maintenance after divorce, whereas there are others who are ready to forego it and would prefer to have a job.

   Parsi women are against divorce but in favour of widow remarriage.

10. Quite a large number of youth studied by various scholars have favoured nuclear family system. Many studies have shown that educated women feel suffocated in the joint family. They dislike the joint family system because it hampers their personality development and also create problems in the proper care of children and their education.

Evaluation and Suggestions for Further Research

Most of the opinion surveys available on this theme were conducted in 1960s and 1970s. Very few studies have been conducted on the attitude and belief of youth concerning marriage and the family in 1980s and 1990s.

Majority of the studies available have covered only some aspects of marriage and the family. No study has included all aspects of marriage and the family. Not much information is available on some aspects such as criteria for mate selection and youth's attitude towards dowry, divorce, widow remarriage and the family system.

Very few studies of Muslim and Christian youths are available and that too of females only. Rural youth are also under represented. Same is the case with the youth belonging to scheduled castes and scheduled tribes.

It may be better if a cross-section of youth, both male and female, representing all the major religious groups with rural and urban background, is selected for any study to be conducted in the future. This study should cover all aspects of marriage and the family. Ideally speaking, such studies should be undertaken in different regions of the country. To start with, one region may be selected depending on the convenience of the researcher

References

Ali, Zeenat Shaukat, 1987, *Marriage and Divorce in Islam*, Bombay: Jaico Publishing.

Ashrafi, Talat Ara, 1992, *Muslim Women in Changing Perspective*, New Delhi: Commonwealth Publishers.

Billimoria, H.M., 1991, *Attitude of Parsi Women to Marriage*, Bombay: Himalaya Publishing House.

Blumberg, Rhoda Lois and Leela Dwaraki, 1980, *India's Educated Women: Options and Constraints*, Delhi: Hindustan Publishing Corporation.

Chahil, Renu, 1972, 'Rural Elite: Between Tradition and Modernity', in *Indian Family in the Change and Challenge of the Seventies* (84–91), New Delhi: Sterling Publishers.

Chaudhary, Pratima K., 1988a, *Changing Values Among Young Women*, Delhi: Amar Prakashan.

——, 1988b, 'College Girls on Inter-Caste and Love Marriages', *Social Welfare*, 35 (6): 27–28.

Das, Man Singh, 1978a, 'Touchable-Untouchable Intercaste Marriage', in Man Singh Das and Panos D. Bardis (eds), *Family in Asia* (88–98), New Delhi: Vikas.

——, 1978b, 'Christian and Non-Christian Inter-Religious Marriages', in Man Singh Das and Panos D. Bardis (eds), *Family in Asia* (98–108), New Delhi: Vikas.

Devadoss, T.S., 1979, *Hindu Family and Marriage*, Madras: University of Madras.

Dhagamvar, Vasudha, 1987, *Women and Divorce*, Bombay: Somaiya Publications.

Fonseca, Mabel, 1980, *Family and Marriage in India*, Jaipur: Sachin Publications.

Gandhi, P.K., 1983, *Rural Youth in Urban India*, Delhi: Seema Publications.

Gangrade, K.D., 1975, *Crisis of Values: A Study in Generation Gap*, New Delhi: Chetana Publications.

Ghadially, Rehana and Khalid Ahmed Kazi, 1980, 'Sex-Role Attitudes, Marriage and Career Among College Men and Women', *Indian Journal of Social Work*, 40 (4): 441–447.

Goldstein, Rhoda L., 1972, *Indian Women in Transition: A Bangalore Case Study*, New Jersey: Scarecrow Press.

Gore, M.S., 1968, *Urbanisation and Family Change*, Bombay: Popular Prakashan.

Government of India, 1988, *Census of India 1981, India*, Part VI A & B, Series I (Fertility Tables).

Goyal, R.P., 1988, *Marriage Age in India*, Delhi: B.R. Publishing Corporation.

Kapadia, K.M., 1990, *Marriage and Family in India*, Bombay: Oxford University Press (Third Edition, Twelfth Print).

Kapur, Promilla, 1978, 'Women in Modern India', in Man Singh Das and Panos D. Bardis (eds), *Family in Asia* (108–147), New Delhi: Vikas Publishing House.

Karanth, G.K., 1981, *Rural Youth*, Delhi: Concept Publishing House.

Kumari, Sudarshan, 1978, *Aspirations of Indian Youth*, Varanasi: Chaukhambha Orientation.

Kurian, George, 1961, *The Indian Family in Transition: A Case Study of Kerala Syrian Christians*, The Hague: Mouton and Co.

Mahajan, Amarjit, 1968, 'A Study of Attitude of Women Students Towards Mate-Selection', *Journal of Family Welfare*, 12: 1–4.

Masland, B.B. and D. Brass, 1991, 'Careers, Marriage and Children: Are Women Changing their Minds', in Chetna Kalbagh (ed.), *Women and Development* (291–303), Vol. 1, New Delhi: Discovery Publishing House.

Mathew, A., 1966, 'Expectations of College Students Regarding their Marriage', *Journal of Family Welfare*, 12: 46–52.

Menon, M. Indu, 1981, *Status of Muslim Women in India*, New Delhi: Uppal Publishing House.

Patel, Haribhai G., 1982, 'Attitude of Urban Student Youth to Age at Marriage and Family Size', *Journal of Family Welfare*, 28 (3): 58–62.

Prabhu, P.H., 1954, *Hindu Social Organization*, Bombay: Popular Prakashan.

Prasad, P. and M. Usha, 1990, 'Students Attitude Towards Inter-Caste Marriage', *Social Welfare*, 36 (12): 12–22.

Punia, Deep, R.K. Punia and M.L. Sharma, 1987, 'Changing Marriage Values: Opinion of Girl Students', *Guru Nanak Journal of Sociology*, 8 (2): 25–40.

Rao, V.V. Prakasa and V. Nandini Rao, 1982, *Marriage, Family and Women in India*, New Delhi: Heritage Publishers.

Ross, A.D., 1961, *Hindu Family in its Urban Setting*, Toronto: University of Toronto Press.

Roy, Shibani, 1979, *Status of Muslim Women in North India*, Delhi: B.R. Publishing Company.

Shah, B.V., 1964, *Social Change and College Students of Gujarat*, Baroda: The Maharaja Sayajirao University of Baroda.

Shah, Vimal P.Z., 1975, 'Mate Selection: Theories and Educated Hindu Youth's Attitude Towards Mate Selection', in Dhirendra Narain (ed.), *Explorations in the Family and Other Essays* (288–304), Bombay: Thacker and Co. Ltd.

Sharma, R.D., 1989, *India Youth and the Small Family Norm*, New Delhi: National Book Organization.

Stuers, Cora Vreede, 1975, 'Attitude of Jaipur Girl Students Towards Family Life', in Dhirendra Narain (ed.), *Explorations in the Family and Other Essays* (151–162), Bombay: Thacker and Co. Ltd.

5

Changing Marriage Values

Opinion of Girl Students

DEEP PUNIA, R.K. PUNIA AND M.L. SHARMA

Institution of marriage has existed throughout the history of human civilization and all societies consider married life the most desirable type of existence of adults. Since Vedic period (4000–1000 B.C.), marriage has been a ritual of sacramental union and an indispensable, irrevocable and indissoluble event of Hindu life (Prabhu 1961; Kapadia 1966; Kapur 1973). It is the religious and social obligation on parents to marry their children at appropriate age in accordance with community customs and traditions, and of children to obey their parents.

Mate selection is the first, important preliminary step towards the establishment of marriage relationship and has never been a matter of entirely free choice. In every community, culture lays down formal or informal or both rules which govern, regulate, allow, prohibit or make certain relationships as preferential or obligatory. In mate selection, several aspects are being considered. Besides the general rules, proscriptive, prescriptive and preferential (Kapadia 1966; Ross 1967; Prabhu 1961; Goode 1963; O'Malley 1970), parents of the spouse consider economic status and general reputation of the family, the dowry and the effect of alliance on the property, physical appearance and education of the partner. The traditional normative system did not provide any opportunity of participation to prospective spouses in the decision-making process of their own marriages (Prabhu 1961; O'Malley 1934; Townsend 1913). In certain communities even parents of' the spouses did not know each other before the actual marriage as the family *Brahmin* and *Nai* settled all matters (Townsend 1913).

Dowry used to be essentially a gift provided by rich and royal families as a symbol of affection and love. It was not a financial burden on parents and an obstacle in marriage. Since the medieval period, dowry demands increased in many communities and unfortunately, by the turn of the century, it has increased to the extent of becoming a very rigid custom. The newly emerging phenomenon is that progressive professionalism, lucrative appointments and prospective economic position of youth have made the boy more eligible and attractive. The problem is more grave among educated and urbanized communities (Hooja 1969).

Since Independence, the social institutions in India are undergoing gradual changes and modifications. Though family is the most conservative institution, only next to religion, yet it is not untouched by the forces of change. Weakening of the conviction of sacrament of marriage started from the third decade of the 20th century (Hate 1980, 1947; Merchant 1935; Desai 1945) and trend of valuing 'personal concept of marriage' might have taken some shapes. Rules of endogamy have undergone changes (Ghurye 1950; Kapadia 1966;, Kapur 1973; Gore 1961). Some researchers are of the view that aspects of mate selection have shown some flexibility in providing opportunities to spouses to give their consent (Ross 1967; Kapadia 1966; Gore 1968; Kapur 1973; Rao and Rao 1982; Jyoti 1983) whereas others argue that there is no significant change and Indian family system maintains its basic character adhering to traditional pattern of life (Kurian 1961; Vatuk 1972). Analysing both the sides of dowry system, it was felt as a burden on bride's family and Dowry Prohibition Act of 1961 was passed in which dowry is an offense. Opening of new vistas for women in education, employment, politics and other important fields of life, it is expected that the attitude of young people towards this system is changing (Kapadia 1966; Dumont 1959; Gore 1968' Vatuk 1972).

In the present study, an attempt has been made to know the opinion of college girl students who are at the threshold of married life, about marriage, mate selection and dowry with an assumption that this younger generation is more receptive towards change. Moreover, these students were getting education in home science and exposed to different normative patterns of behaviour.

Methodology

The present study was conducted on all the 130 pre-final and final year unmarried students of B.Sc. Home Science of academic session 1981–82 at Haryana Agricultural University, Hisar. This group was purposively selected because a large majority of students enter married life after completion of this programme and, also attain physical, mental and social maturity to give valid and reliable response to such matters. A questionnaire containing questions pertaining to research objectives of the study was devised, pre-tested and finalized. This pre-tested, semi-structured questionnaire was administered to all the students.

Data from filled in questionnaires was tabulated in a master table. Frequency and percentages were calculated and two way frequency tables with familial background factors were prepared and chi-square analysis was done to discern the association between the attributes. In order to ascertain the exact order of choice of qualities in choosing a mate, choices were assigned one to 10 scores in ascending order of choice. For each quality the frequency of order of choice and score assigned was multiplied and the product was added, which yielded the total scores of the specific quality. Inferences are drawn with simple statistical analysis and content analysis of open ended questions.

Findings and Discussion

Contextual matrix of respondents: Majority of the girl students are from Hindu religion (92.3%) followed by Sikh (5.4%) and *Bishnoi* (2.3%). Among the different caste groups, *Khatri* and *Arora* constituted 55.4 per cent of respondents followed by *Jat* (22.3%), *Bania* (85%), *Brahmin* (62%), *Ahir* (3.8%) scheduled castes (2.3%) and *Rajput* (1.5%). Pre-eminently girls are from urban areas (63.8%) and service families. Only 30 per cent of the girls are from farming families.

Family is of nuclear type in 69.2 per cent of the cases. In majority of the families (61.5%), highest education in the family is graduation or post-graduation and in no case less than matriculation. At least one family member in each family is working outside the residential place of family. Mothers of 24 per cent of the respondents are illiterate. Thus, a majority of the students is from upper caste urban families with substantially high educational status.

Mate Selection

Mate selection is an important aspect of the institution of marriage (Karlson 1962). In Hindu society, mate selection is generated by the rules of endogamy, exogamy and preferential mating (Kapadia 1966; Prabhu 1961). The selection of suitable partner is the duty of parents and they apportion the socio-economic background of the family (Burgess and Locke 1950; Ross 1961; Winch 1963). In the present study, students were asked to give their opinion about the age, education, job and qualities of their prospective partners.

Age and Education of the Mate: Somewhat older age is preferred by 77.7 per cent of the students and in no case a younger mate is preferred. Similarly, none of the students wanted to have a mate less educated than her. About half of the students (49.2%) prefer to have a mate above post-graduation, followed by post-graduation (45%) and graduation (5.8%).

Rao (1969) also reported that women prefer to have partners with slightly higher qualifications and higher age. Similar are the findings of Hallen (1963), Raheja (1978), Jain (1980) and Rao and

Rao (1982). Invariably, male superiority and seniority in age is observed in other countries (Saroukhani 1981).

Preferred Job of the Mate: The most preferred job of the mate is 'professional civil services' in government departments (like engineering, medical, excise-taxation, etc.) as 33.8 per cent students accorded first preference, followed by 'defence services' (30.8%), 'Indian Administrative Services' (19.2%), 'educational services' (7.7%), 'private professional services' (6.2%) and 'business and trade' (2.3%). The second preference is also in congruence with the first preference (Table 5.1).

Table 5.1

Preferred job of mate

Sr. no.	*Job*	*Preference*		
		I	*II*	*III*
1.	Professional services in a government department	44 (33.8)	41 (31.5)	21 (16.2)
2.	Defence services	40 (30.8)	31 (23.8)	24 (18.5)
3.	Indian administrative executive service	25 (19.2)	18 (13.8)	16 (12.3)
4.	Educational services	10 (7.7)	9 (7.9)	23 (17.7)
5.	Private professions	8 (6.2)	11 (8.5)	21 (16.2)
6.	Business and trade (own)	3 (2.3)	11 (8.7)	12 (17.7)
7.	Political career	0 (0)	4 (3.1)	5 (3.3)
8.	Unspecified	0 (0)	5 (3.8)	8 (6.2)
	Total	130	130	130

Figures in parenthesis denote percentages.

Upreti's (1966) analysis confirms the present findings as women prefer professional qualifications such as engineers, doctors, government executives, etc. which is in agreement with the reporting of Rao (1969), Bayti (1970), Mohan and Kumar (1970) and Jain (1980).

Attributes in Choosing a Mate: As show in Table 5.2, the highest importance is bestowed to the 'educational level of the mate' (1,030) followed by 'moral character' (982), 'physical handsomeness' (921), 'nature of job' (723), 'income of mate' (526), 'honesty and devotion of mate' (504), 'present social status of family' (458), 'total family wealth' (436) and 'traditional social status of the mate's family' (279).

Raheja (1978) found a large majority of boys (72%) and girls (68%) expressing the need to consider family background but not to the extent mentioned by Burgess and Locke (1950: 400) for 'oriental countries, namely China, India, Japan, Korea and Philippines, where all decisions are made by parents and elders.' Reputation of the family is given first preference among familial attributes by the first and the second generations of Sikhs, and moral character of the spouse by the first and the economic independence of spouse by the second generation (Jyoti 1983), which in many respects are similar to Hindus. Girls considered socio-economic status, education and profession of parents and relations among family members for better adjustment in new home. But in the present study, girl students have ignored the family background and grant intrinsic worth to the personal qualities of mate. Khan and Yunus (1977) have lodged a similar report.

Education and moral character of the prospective partner are being given more weightage as compared to the physical appearance which was given highest weightage in the studies by Shah (1975) and Jain (1980). Kadetotad (1979) found good physique and Kapadia (1966) that the spouse did not suffer from any disease and is not deformed, as the main consideration in mate selection. Thus, education is becoming more important for the educated girls.

Significant discernable change is that the most valued basis of traditional mate selection, i.e. traditional social status of the family, is being rated as the lowest and the personal characteristics of the mate are being given the highest importance. Thus, it is obvious that the educated younger generation is becoming more individualistic, personalized, independent, and alien to the traditional norms of mate selection.

Marriage

Aims of Hindu marriage are *dharma* (religious obligations towards the family, community and society), *praja* (progeny as social obligation towards society) and *rati* (pleasure as individual sexual gratification). Marriage is primarily for religious functions and *vivah* (marriage) is *sarira sanskaras* (sacramental rites sanctifying the body) through each of which every man and woman passes at appropriate age (Prabhu 1961: 149). This traditional value about marriage might be changing. Therefore, the students were asked to give their opinions about marriage in their communities and families.

Opinion about Marriage: A majority of the students consider marriage as a sacred union of boy and girl, in their community (84.6%), in their family (86.9%) and in their own opinion (87.7%). Except one, all students want to marry at an appropriate age and stage of life. They feel that life is incomplete without marriage. Jain (1980) also reported that 95.5 per cent of the respondents were in favour of getting married.

It may be inferred that traditional values about marriage hold good and the changes are marginal. At community, family and personal level, marriage is considered to be a sacrament, and obligatory. Relatively lower percentage (55%) of the students considering marriage a sacrament in the study conducted by Jain (1980) in the same locale is primarily because of post-graduate (30%) and doctorate (20%) students in her sample who are more exposed to westernization, urbanization, secular education and other such forces of change. It can be said that higher education makes an individual more secular.

Opinion about Appropriate Age of Marriage: The age of marriage in India varies from time to time, region to region, religion to religion, caste to caste and even according to convenience of the families (Ross 1961). Early marriage has been a distinctive feature of the Indian society (Karve 1965) and in this particular region, custom of marrying a girl even just after birth existed. Students were asked to give their opinion about most appropriate age of marriage for girl and for boy, and age at which they would like to get married.

Table 5.2

Order of preference of qualities in choosing a mate

Sr. no.	*Quality*	*Scores*	*Order*
1.	Educational level	1,030	I
2.	Moral character	982	II
3.	Physical handsomeness	921	III
4.	Nature of job	723	IV
5.	Income/earnings	526	V
6.	Honesty and devotion	504	VI
7.	Present social status of family	491	VII
8.	Sociability	1,458	VIII
9.	Family wealth	436	IX
10.	Traditional social status of family	279	X

Note: Maximum possible score is 1,300.

None of the students is of the opinion that a girl be married before the age of 18 which is the minimum age for marriage according to the prevailing law. A majority (56.2%) of them are of the opinion that the most appropriate age for marriage for a girl is from 18–21 years followed by 22–25 years (43.1%) and above 25 years (0.8%). Appropriate age for marriage for a boy is a little higher, as 76.2 per cent consider 21 to 25 years as the most appropriate age followed by above 25 years of age. They desire to marry before the age of 25 years, except 2.3 per cent girls who are willing to marry after 25 years.

Among the different familial background factors, main occupation of the family is significantly associated ($X^2 = 8.6921$ with 2 degrees of freedom, $C = 0.2491$) at 0.01 level of probability with appropriate age for marriage. A majority (59%) of the girl students from agriculture and rural occupations prefer below 21 years as the most appropriate age whereas a majority (69%)

of the students from non-agricultural occupations approve age above 21 years.

While analysing matrimonial advertisements, Anand (1965) and Upreti (1967) found most of the spouses above standard age. Rao (1969) found majority of women between 19 to 25 years. Rao and Rao (1982) reported similar results with a little difference that here the girls like to marry at a little early age and that might be because of more rural environment and custom of marrying girls at a very early age (Townsend 1913). Thus, there is a general trend of increase in women's age at marriage. Even studies by Kapadia (1966), Gore (1968) and Jyoti (1983) also assert the increasing age at marriage. In the present context, education is the major factor (Ross 1961; Gore 1968; Bhatnagar 1972; Rao and Rao 1982; Jyoti 1983).

When to marry: None of the students is willing to marry before completion of their present course of studies. Only 13.1 per cent are willing to marry after completion of the present course and 25.4 per cent intend to do so after obtaining their post-graduation degree. About one-third of the students (31.5%) want to marry immediately after getting a job and about one-fifth (19.2%) after some years of service.

About a half of the girls are willing to take up jobs before marriage. None of the familial background factors is associated with the stage of marriage which clearly shows that irrespective of family factors, educated girls like to go for service.

Type of Marriage Liked Most and Reasons: There can be three forms of marriage, i.e. (i) where the marriage proposal is entirely in the hands of the parents and guardians, (ii) where the marriage proposal is with the consent of the spouses and, (iii) the selection of spouse is entirely the business of the boy and girl concerned but arranged by the parents.

To discern the change in traditional type of arranged marriage, the students were asked to give their opinions along with their reasons for the same. Their responses are summarized in Table 5.3.

Arranged marriage with consent of spouses (60%) is liked most and rationality of parents (53.5%) is the basis of liking. Only 10 per cent of the students like arranged marriage without the consent of spouses and the main reason is the traditional right (66.7%) of the parents. About one-third of the girls give higher weightage to choosing spouses by themselves. They are not willing to break their relations (50%) with their parents after marriage but give higher weightage to their choice which is a stage of ambivalence. Similar ambivalence towards the traditional type of marriage was indicated by Kapur (1973) among educated working women, Cormack (1961), Shah (1961) and Mathew (1966) among unmarried university and college students.

Family background factors like main occupation of the family, family type and educational status of family are not associated significantly with preferred type of marriage arrangements. Shah (1961), Anand (1965), Mahajan (1965), Hallen (1963), Khan and Yunus (1977), Raheja (1978), Kadetotad (1979), Jain (1980) and Rao and Rao (1982) have also reported that a majority of the students, especially girl students, want to select their partners with the consent of their parents as that would be a rational selection in maintaining good relations after marriage. In the present study, relatively more weightage is given to personal selection and involvement in mate selection process as compared to earlier studies and observations by Burgess and Locke (1950) about oriental countries, including India.

Thus, it may be concluded that students would choose their partners and ask the parents to arrange their marriage. Dominant role of parents is likely to become recessive in future, irrespective of differences in the family background. Though students consider themselves more independent and rational in mate selection, yet they feel it better to persuade their parents to arrange marriage rather than to go against their wishes. This seems to be the most transitory phase in the institution of family.

Table 5.3

Types of marriage liked most and reason for liking

Sr. no.	*Type of marriage*	*Reasons for liking*			*Total*
		Parents have right on child (traditional)	*Parents are more judicious (rational)*	*For maintaining relations after marriage (social)*	
1.	Arranged by parents without consent of spouses	8 (66.7)	3 (25)	1 (8.3)	12 (10)
2.	Arranged by parents with the consent of spouses	12 (15.5)	45 (58.5)	20 (26)	77 (60)
3.	Choice by spouses and then arranged by parents	7 (17)	13 (33)	21 (50)	41 (30)
	Total	27	61	42	130

Figures in parentheses denote percentages.

Willingness to See the Prospective Partner: According to traditions, the prospective mates were not allowed to see each other. It used to be a social offence. The girl students were asked to know their willingness to see their prospective mates, directly or indirectly.

All the girl students would like to see their prospective mate before the finalization of their marriage (engagement). They would like to see their partners directly (72%) and talk to them in the absence of their parents. The main purpose of seeing directly and talking is not to have any misunderstanding and making some assessment about the partners. The main purpose of seeing indirectly (28%) is to have a look at them.

Shah (1961), Kannan (1963), Mathew (1966), Khan and Yunus (1977) and Raheja (1978) also reported much willingness to see the prospective partner before marriage for gaining better understanding and to make a better choice which was not allowed in the past.

Endogamy and Exogamy: Throughout the world, communities prescribe certain groups to marry and others not to marry.

Religion and caste have been the main endogroups of marriage and sub-caste the exogroup as per Indian customs and traditions. Students were asked about their likings of different groups in this regard.

The students overwhelmingly (95.5%) like endogamous marriage to religion and caste (90.8%). Most preferred spatial territory is own country (69.2%) followed by state (20.8%) and district (6–9%).

Endogamous quality of mate selection is primarily because of more familiarity with the group which helps them in making adjustments in a new environment. Jain (1980) also reported the same for preferring similar culture and tradition. Gore (1968) found about 10 per cent respondents in favour of inter-caste marriage in a metropolitan city. Shah (1961) reported a little more deviation (35) in the matter of caste and religious exogamy. Rao and Rao (1982) found preference of 22 per cent of their female students for caste exogamy and 14 per cent for religious exogamy which is a little higher than the present study. Kannan (1963), Mathew (1966), Rao (1969) and Ramu and Weike (1971) also reported caste consideration of much importance in mate selection while analysing matrimonial advertisements which are generally of well educated, well placed and modern people. Jain (1980) reported 69.23 and 53.85 per cent girls giving no importance to religion and caste endogamy, respectively which is primarily because of postgraduate and doctorate girl students who might be secular than these under-graduates. Even linguistic endogamy is also practiced (Jyoti 1983) among Sikhs which might be for better cultural adjustment of the spouses.

In the present study, family background does not bring significant differences in their liking for inter-caste marriage. The liking is lesser because the environment of the city and the university in which they are living is conservative. Moreover all the students are from under-graduate classes coming to this place only after their school leaving examination (Matriculation).

Dowry

Opinion about dowry: Dowry is a part of presents given to girls during the time of marriage, but this custom became so rigid and undesirable that society recognized it as a social evil. In 1961, the Dowry Prohibition Act was passed and in Haryana the revised version of the act is Haryana Dowry Prohibition (Amendment) Act 1976. Hooja (1969) found that higher education of the girl increased the amount of dowry and instead of discouraging it, encouraged it. Therefore, students were asked to give their likings and opinions about this aspect.

Dowry is being considered 'an unnecessary burden on parents', by 74.6 per cent of students whereas 14.6 per cent students are of the opinion that dowry is a 'kind of help to newly wedded couples to establish their new home'. Dowry as 'a sign of prestige' is the opinion of only 3.4 per cent and as 'a share of parental property' in case of 3.8 per cent students. Dowry as 'a compensation for the lack of any quality in girl' (23%) and 'a mean for getting good match' (1.5%) are also mentioned by a small fraction of the students.

Jain (1980) reported that 'a majority of the girls (60.60%) consider dowry as a social evil and 36.33 per cent as a burden on girls'. In their study, Rao and Rao (1982) found dowry an important consideration in settling marriages and a burden on females' parents.

Opinion about Giving Dowry: None of the students is of the opinion that dowry must be given; whereas 33.8 per cent are of the opinion that dowry should not be given at all. However, a majority (60.8%) of the students feel that dowry is not necessary and only a few (5.4%) feel it necessary.

Jain (1980) found 84.61 per cent of the girls against dowry. Rao and Rao (1982) reported one-fifth of the students in favour of dowry and an equal number in favour of its continuity. Thus, the students do not feel dowry a must but also do not hesitate in favouring it which is a revelation of the continuity of dowry in the Indian social system. Acceptance of dowry: If parents can afford, majority (67%) of the students are in favour of acceptance of dowry. The percentage of the respondents of the opinion that 'if parents could afford dowry then they must accept it' (18.5%) is more than those of the opinion 'should not accept at all' (15.4%) It is obvious that the girl students are ready to accept dowry if parents can afford. The notion of social evil seems to be full of hypocrisy and dowry will continue, but may change dimensions. Similar conclusions can be drawn from analysis of data presented by Rao and Rao (1982).

Form of Dowry: Dowry in kind is preferred by 56.9 per cent of the respondents followed by both kind and cash (40%) and cash alone (3.1%).

Jain (1980) reported a majority of girls in favour of giving dowry both in kind and cash where the latter goes to parents and the former to wedded couple. Thus, the students desire dowry not only for themselves but also for their in-laws.

Amount of Dowry: Amount of dowry is increasing in the opinion of 68.5 per cent students and decreasing in the opinion of only 13.8 per cent. Amount of dowry is increasing primarily because of higher demands from grooms having lucrative jobs.

Rao and Rao (1982) reported higher expectations of dowry from engineers and medicos than those who have devoted more years to education. The study further reports that even if a girl is equally educated, boys expect dowry.

Anti-Dowry Regulations: Anti-dowry regulations are 'very helpful' in the opinion of 37.7 per cent, 'helpful' in the opinion of 35.4 per cent and 'not helpful' in the opinion of 26.9 per cent. As a whole, the awareness about anti-dowry regulations is very poor among the students. Legislations are only on paper. Hallen (1963), Chatterjee, Singh and Yadava (1971) and Jammu (1976) also reported poor knowledge about anti-dowry regulations among the masses.

Conclusion

1. A majority of the girl students come of families with higher caste, income and education.
2. A majority of the girls consider marriage a sacramental union of the two persons and families. Irrevocable and indissoluble character of the Hindu marriage would help in maintaining cordial relations and the problem of divorce may not become much grave in the near future.
3. The age of marriage is increasing which would not only decrease the growth rate of population but also the nutritional drainage, death at delivery and other problems related to child and early marriage.
4. Education is highly valued for economic independence and for getting a good life partner. It may affect the dowry system adversely at least among the lower and the middle class families. There is an urgent need to explore possibilities of gainful employment of these graduates before a syndrome of economic dependency develops among them.
5. Girls feel it their right to see the prospective spouse and expect their involvement in decision-making process which was denied to them. In future the opinion of girls would be more important than that of parents.
6. Girls prefer to marry the boys with remunerative jobs having public image. It may provide greater opportunities for dowry seekers from those jobs, or rich parents may buy these jobs for their would-be sons-in-law.
7. An educated girl bestows much importance on the education of a boy. An increase in the education of a girl would increase the general level of literacy and education in the society.
8. Girls still consider the moral character an important aspect of personality of the boys. Individual characters are replacing the traditional ascribed status of family.
9. Education is more important than the family background as far as the opinion and liking about marriage, mate selection and dowry is considered.
10. Ambivalent behaviour dominates in respect of liking for type of marriage. The trend is towards liberalization and decrease in the authority of the family.

11. Dowry is perceived as a social problem by girls. They do not like dowry explicitly but accept it implicitly.
12. Dowry cannot be eradicated from our social system. Middle class families, the reformist class, can ameliorate the problem by educating their girls, finding employment and marrying them off in the families of equal status.
13. Anti-dowry regulations are not much effective but with the spread of education these may become effective to some extent.

References

Anand, K., 1965, 'Attitude of Punjab University Women Students Towards Marriage and Family', *The Indian Journal of Social Work,* 26: 86–90.

Bayti, Jamna Lal, 1970, 'Matrimonial Advertisements: An Analysis', *Journal of Family Welfare,* 17: 48–57.

Bhatnagar, G.S., 1972, *Education and Social Change,* Calcutta: The Minerva Associates.

Burgess, E.W. and H.J. Locke, 1950, *The Family,* New York: American Book Co.

Chatterjee, B.B., S.S. Singh and D.R. Yadava, 1971, *Impact of Social Legislation on Social Change,* Calcutta: The Minerva Associates.

Cormarck, Margret, 1961, *She Who Rides a Peacock,* New York: Praeger.

Desai, G.B., 1945, *Gujarati Women in Modern Life,* Unpublished Master's Dissertation, University of Bombay, Bombay.

Dumont, L., 1959, 'Dowry in Hindu Marriage', *The Economic and Political Weekly,* 11: 519–520.

Ghurye, G.S., 1950, *Caste and Family in India,* Bombay: Popular Prakashan.

Goode, William J., 1963, *World Revolution and Family Patterns,* London: Free Press of Glencoe.

Gore, M.S., 1961, *The Impact of Industrialisation and Urbanization on the Aggarwal Family in Delhi Area,* Unpublished Ph.D. Dissertation, Columbia University.

——, 1968, *Urbanization and Family Change,* Bombay: Popular Prakashan.

Hallen, G.C., 1963, 'Dowry: A Social Evil', *Indian Sociological Bulletin,* 13: 1–7.

Hate, C.A., 1947, *The Social Position of Hindu Women*, School of Economics & Sociology, Bombay University, Bombay.

——, 1980, *The Socio-Economic Conditions of Educated Women in Bombay City*, School of Economics & Sociology, Bombay University, Bombay.

Hooja, S.L., 1969, *Dowry System in India*, Delhi: Asia Press.

Jain, Manjusha, 1980, *Socio-Economic Factors Affecting Mate Selection*, Unpublished M.Sc. Thesis of Haryana Agricultural University, Hisar.

Jammu, P.S., 1976, *The Problem of Dowry in Punjab*, Patiala: Punjabi University, Department of Sociology and Social Anthropology.

Jyoti, S.K., 1983, *Marriage Practices of the Sikhs: A Study of Inter-Generational Differences*, New Delhi: Deep and Deep Publications.

Kadetotad, N.K., 1979, 'The Attitude of Postgraduate Students Towards Choice of Partners', Paper Presented in the Section of Anthropology and Archeology at the 67th Session of Indian Science Congress.

Kannan, C.T., 1963, *Inter-Caste and Inter-Community Marriages in India*, Bombay: Allied Publishers.

Kapadia, K.K., 1966, *Marriage and Family in India*, Bombay: Oxford University Press.

Kapur, P., 1973, *Love, Marriage and Sex*, New Delhi: Vikas Publishing House.

Karlson, G., 1962, 'Mate Selection', *International Journal of Comparative Psychology*, 3: 91.

Karve, Irawati, 1965, *Kinship Organization in India*, Bombay: Asia Publishing House.

Khan, Shaheen and Mohammad Yunus, 1977, 'Changing Attitudes of Girl Students Towards Marriage', *Social Welfare*, 24: 16–17.

Kurian, G., 1961, *The Indian Family in Transition: A Case Study of Kerala Syrian Christians*, The Hague: Mouton and Co.

Mahajan, A., 1965, 'A Study of Attitudes of Women Students Towards Mate Selection', *Journal of Family Welfare*, 12: 46.

Mathew, A., 1966, 'Expectations of College Students regarding Their Marriage', *Journal of Family Welfare*, 12(3): 46–52.

Merchant, K.T., 1935, *Views on Marriage and Family*, Madras: B.G. Paul and Company.

Mohan, J. and A. Kumar, 1970, 'Study of Preference for Husband's Profession', *Recent Trends in Education*, 1: 38–39.

O'Malley, L.S.S., 1934, *India's Social Heritage*, New Delhi: Vikas Publishing House.

Prabhu, P.H., 1961, *Hindu Social Organization*, Bombay: Popular Prakashan.

Raheja, S., 1978, *Opinion of M.S. University Students Regarding the Selection of the Marriage Partner*, Unpublished Master's Dissertation, Faculty of Social Welfare, M.S. University of Baroda, Baroda.

Ramu, C.R. and P.D. Weike, 1971, 'Marriage in India: Contemporary Analysis of Matrimonial Advertisements', *Man in India*, 51: 111–120.

Rao, B.S.S., 1969, 'A Study on Matrimonial Advertisements', *Indian Journal of Social Work*, 29: 279–387.

Rao, V.V. Prakasa and V. Nandini Rao, 1982, *Marriage, the Family and Women in India*, New Delhi: Heritage Publishers.

Ross, Aileen D., 1961, *The Hindu Family in its Urban Setting*, Oxford: University of Toronto Press.

Saroukhani, Bagher, 1981, 'Age Gap in Marriage: A Study in Contemporary Iran', *International Journal of Sociology of the Family*, 11(1): 87–98.

Shah, B., 1961, 'Gujarati College Students and Selection of Bride', *Sociological Bulletin*, 11: 121–140 (March-September).

Shah, V.P., 1975, 'Mate Selection: Theories and Educated HinduYouths Attitudes Towards Mate Selection', in D. Narain (ed.) *Explorations in the Family and Others Essays*, Bombay: Thacker and Company, 255–304.

Townsend, C.A.H., 1913, *Customary Law of Hisar District*, Vol. 25, Lahore: Punjab Government Press.

Upreti, H.C., 1967, 'Matrimonial Advertisements: Brief Sociological Analysis', *The Journal of Family Welfare*, 14: 33–43.

Vatuk, S., 1972, *Kinship and Urbanization*, Berkeley: The University of California Press.

Winch, Robert F., 1963, *The Modern Family*, New Delhi: Holt, Rinehart and Winston.

Section II

Family Formation: Child Bearing

6

The Ideology of Small Family

H.D. LAKSHMINARAYANA

The rapid increase of population without corresponding development in the economy has been a cause of great anxiety in the developing countries. Therefore, an active policy is pursued to regulate family in terms of its size, by preventing the number of children born to a couple. This policy is characterized as Family Planning Programme (FPP). This programme is founded on certain assumptions with regard to the notion of 'family' and the 'desired type of family'.

India is one of the leading and pioneering countries in the Third World in launching the family planning programme systematically and on a sizeable scale (Desai 1980: 4). During the Third Five Year Plan, a call for three-child family was given by the Family Planning Committee headed by Dhanvanthi Ram Rau (Mamoria 1965: 231–232). Later, the working group on population policy set up by the Planning Commission also recommended the long-term demographic goal of reducing the net reproduction rate to one by 1996 from the present level of 1.67. The implications of this are that the average size of the family would be reduced from 4.2 children to 2.3 children (Government of India 1981). There is also a presumption underlying Government FPP that a small family is a happy family (Desai 1980) and people are persuaded to accept the small family norm.

As in India, in most of the countries people are being motivated to desire smaller families or to penalize those who have large families (Stamper 1977: 64). For instance, in the early 1970s Pakistan launched a scheme to provide life insurance to couples with no more than two children. Singapore launched the National Family Planning and Population Programme soon after independence and the small family norm was actively promoted through slogans like 'plan your family small', and disincentive measures were introduced to persuade couples to plan for a '2 child family' irrespective of the child's sex (Shanthakumar 1983: 171). And recently, it is all too well known that China has launched the programme of single child family.

The small family is much favoured and has become a synonym with economic growth. One of the arguments in favour of small family is that it enables families to save and ensures better future to the members of the family. It also appears that the governments hold the view that 'Small Family Norm' is ethically, economically and from the point of view of long-term national interest of economic and social development superior to 'Large Family Norm' (Desai 1980: 175).

Another argument of the population experts in favour of small family is its cost benefit. The argument was presented by Robert McNamara of the World Bank. He formulated that the cost of a child bearing would be $660 and that of avoiding it would be $6 only. But a number of scholars have pointed out the fallacy of cost benefit argument in favour of 'small family happy family' norm as formula for the poor in Third World countries. According to them poor people find large family more essential for their survival, security and 'old age insurance', and even income augmentation (Desai 1980). In their critique of government's plea of cost-benefit, and logic underlying cost-benefit analysis, Rangarajan and Satia (1976: 1161) point out that the benefit of an additional child will depend upon the income level of the family. The higher the income level, the less will be the need for social security and, therefore, the less will be the utility of the benefit of additional children and, therefore, family size shrinks. Similarly, the amount of consumption of the additional children will also be higher at higher income level of the family. On the contrary, parents at low level of income do not expect to incur larger additional cost for raising their children to work in the farm and in their house as in the case of artisan. It is also pointed out that the size of the family is by and large inversely related to the income. According to Mamdani (1976: 114), the wage earners and small farmers want large family as children are viewed as a source of labour power, as an insurance against old age. So too is the case of the artisans employed in domestic industries who value children as economic assets (ibid.).

Thus, while planners and population experts make a strong plea to limit the size of the family to promote economic growth, the critics of the small family think that economic security and/or stability is conducive to control the size of the family. It is even argued that until people are better off, are educated, can look forward realistically to security in old age without a large family to support them, and above all can expect most of their children to survive, they will have no reason to limit the number of their offspring. Samir Amin (1976) argues that having large families in an impoverished capitalist country is a form of economic rationality, and large families are often the best or only means of social security and 'old age pension' in a neo-colonial situation.

In the light of the above debate, it is worth examining the problem from a wider perspective, granting that small family norm is widely accepted and small family is widely prevailing, it is necessary to know the economic aspect of the small family in terms of its income, levels of education, dependency ratio and its economic activity.

The present analysis is based on a part of the data collected from 4,232 rural families of the *kurubina setty* caste, handloom weavers in Karnataka. Data in Table 6.1 indicate the number of families of different size. Of the 4,232 families, 60.20 per cent are small families having six members and less. Of the small families, nearly 26 per cent have three members, and the rest four–six members. The large number of small families is a welcome feature, since it is held as conducive for the progress and prosperity of the nation at large. Given this position, one shall look at the other aspects of the small family.

Table 6.1

Number of families by size

Size	*Number*	*Per cent*
Small (1–6)	2,548	60.20
Medium (7–11)	1,425	33.68
Large (12 & above)	259	6.12
Total	4,232	100.00

Family Size and Occupation

A small family is a compact unit and can be well managed to ensure better lifestyle and better life-change to its members. But its advantage confines only to the rearing of limited number of children by providing them with better facilities. Beyond this, as an economic unit, the small family is not quite competent to venture into more gainful activities to improve its economy, for lack of supporting hands in the family. A perusal of the occupational pattern among families will make this point clear. Table 6.2 presents data about the distribution of families in relation to the number of occupations. There are families which follow one occupation only, such as weaving/agriculture/business/service/skilled or unskilled work, and there are families which follow two occupations or more. It is clear from the table that small families are invariably following one occupation (96.78%) whereas more than one occupations (2–3) are mostly followed by large-size families (30.50%) and also to some extent medium-size families (12.42%). The constraints on the small family to venture into more occupations is quite understandable. But the point is that due to their small size many a times some of the most lucrative economic activities may have to be foregone. With the result, the small family though endowed with talent, may have an economic set back. This can be seen from the levels of income vis-à-vis the family size.

Table 6.2

Family size by number of occupations

Family size	*No. of occupations*		
	One	*Two*	*Total*
Small	2,466 (63.32) 96.78	82 (24.26) 3.21	2,548
Medium	1,248 (32 04) 87.57	177 (52.36) 12.42	1,425
Large	180 (4.62) 69.49	79 (23.37) 30.50	259
	3,894	338	4,232

Family Size and Income

There is no gainsaying that smaller the family lesser the burden and greater the scope for economic progress. But how far does this hold good in a country where the mode of production, whether agriculture or weaving, is still archaic and labour intensive, and every member in the family is looked upon as an asset is a moot question. Because, large families are more beneficial to carry more economic activities as they could depend on their own labour. They are found to be advantageous in labour intensive tasks like agriculture, sericulture, weaving or mercantile enterprises. As said earlier, small families are unable to follow more number of economic activities and are forced to forego the gains of such activities. This directly impinges on their income. A perusal of the level of income among families of different size makes this point clear. Table 6.3 shows data about the differential levels of income. Out of 4,232 families, about 74 per cent are below poverty line, i.e. having an income of rupees

3,500 or less per annum. Among small families, about 83 per cent are below poverty line. Income-wise, among families which are below poverty line, small families constitute more than two-third (67.87%). It is, thus, evident that the small family which is considered to be desirable for economic progress is itself in a quandary. And though small families are over-whelming, they are overwhelmingly below poverty line.

Table 6.3

Family size and income

Family size	*Income*				
	Below ₹ 3,500	*₹ 3,501 to ₹ 5,000*	*₹ 5,001 to ₹ 10,000*	*Above ₹ 10,000*	*Total*
Small (1–6)	2,118 (83.12) 67.87	215 (8.43) 40.41	176 (6. 9) 39.11	39 (1.53) 30.46	2,548 60.20
Medium (7–11)	927 (65.05) 29.69	252 (17.68) 47.36	191 (13.40) 42.44	55 (3.85) 42.96	1,425 33.67
Large (12 & above)	77 (29.72) 2.44	65 (25.09) 12.21	83 (32.04) 18.44	34 (13.12) 26.56	259 6.12
Total	3,122 (73.78)	532 (12.58)	450 (10.64)	34 (0.80)	4,232

Family Size and Dependency

It is generally held that high dependency ratio is not conducive to the growth of economy, as it will offset the gains obtained by the country's development efforts, because the higher the dependency ratio, the greater the burden on society. To overcome this, small family is held to be beneficial as it will have fewer members to be cared for and, hence, less burdensome. But contrary to this, in the present study we had the small families that are burdened. Table 6.4 shows that small families have about 40 per cent dependents of the total dependents, and on an average a little more than three dependents per family. The dependency ratio in small family works out to be 1:2 which is slightly less than in the other two and nearly one-third of the small families have one-two dependents and two-third have three–five dependents. Though one cannot visualize and much less advocate 'dependency free family' or 'zero dependency family', the amount of burden on the small family cannot be ignored. It neutralizes the economic gains. This can be further amplified by examining the level of income and dependency.

Table 6.4

Family size and dependency

Family size	*No. of families*	*No. of dependents*	*Average no. of dependents per family*
Small (1–6)	2,546 (60.20)	7,948 (40.05)	3.1
Medium (7–11)	1,425 (33.68)	8,846 (44.58)	6.2
Large (12 & above)	259 (6.12)	3,048 (15.36)	117
Total	4,232	19,842	4.6

Family Size, Income and Dependency

From the foregoing it is now evident that the small family instead of ensuring economic betterment has belied the hope. The pace of economic development depends on the diversion of resources from consumption to uses that raise future output. A population with a high ratio of dependents to producers consumes more of a given output and devotes less to investment (Coak and Hoover 1955: 333). Under this condition even a small family may arrest the pace of economic development. To understand this more fully, we may look at family size, income and dependency. Table 6.5 shows that the rate of dependency is inversely related to size and income. Among the total dependents, one-third are found in small families which are also below poverty line. And among the dependents in small families, more than 82 per cent are found in families which are below poverty line. Further, among families which are below poverty line, nearly 50 per cent of the dependents are found in small families. These figures corroborate that small families are impoverished and overburdened.

Family Size and Levels of Education

Small family is considered to be endowed with better means to provide more education to its members. But from Table 6.6, we find that though the average education is more or less same irrespective of the size of the family, the percentage of small families is relatively more in the low level education. This low level education is the result of low income and high dependency ratio in the small family.

Table 6.5

Percentage of dependents by family size and income

	No. of dependents in different income groups				
Income family size	*Below ₹ 3,500*	*₹ 3,501 to ₹ 5,000*	*₹ 5,001 to ₹ 10,000*	*Above ₹ 10,000*	*Total*
Small (1–6)	6.555 (82.47) 49.26	675 (8.49) 24.24	597 (7.51) 21.79	121 (1.52) 11.94	7,948 40.05
Medium (7–11)	5,883 (66–50) 44.21	1401 (15.83) 50.32	1,217 (13.75) 44.43	345 (3.90) 34.05	8,84,64 4.58
Large (12 & above)	868 (28.47) 6.52	708 (23.22) 22.43	925 (30.36) 35.77	547 (17.94) 54.00	3,04,81 5.35
Total	13,306 67.05	2,784 14.03	2,739 13.80	1,013 5.10	19,842

Table 6.6

Family size and levels of education

Family size	*Level of education*			
	Low	*Medium*	*High*	*Total*
Small	1,901 (74.60) 61.02	603 (23.66) 57.21	44 (1.72) 69.84	2,548
Medium	1,023 (71.78) 32.84	385 (27.01) 36.52	17 (1.19) 26.98	1,425
Large	191 (73.74) 6.13	66 (25.48) 6.26	02 (0.77) 3.17	259
Total	3,115	1,054	63	4,232

Conclusion

The foregoing analysis of the families among weavers shows that small families, in spite of their large number, have belied the hope of augmenting the economy. They have restricted the economic activities because of their low carrying capacity. They are saddled with more dependents and, hence, their economic condition is poor. And these, in turn, have affected the chances of better education to their members. It appears, as Desai (1980: 178) holds that there is a naive unsubstantiated assumption that smallness of size will enable the families automatically to save, which may provide an assurance for better future. The argument of saving propagated in favour of small family should take into account the possibility of income creations by the family. And the cost-benefit of the small family acquires rationality only after the family has crossed certain economic educational and cultural threshold. To sum up, small family unless backed by massive structural amenities and services may become more helpless, more subject to strain, more incompetent and more insecure. The concept of small family should not be considered in isolation, because family is not a discrete entity, but an integral part of the wider system. As such the quality of life in the family is influenced by the wider system rather than by the size of the family alone.

References

Amin, Samir, 1976, 'Population and Development', *Socialist Revolution*, 6 (1), January–March: 70–79.

Coak, J. Ansley and M. Edger Hoover, 1955, *Development in Low Income Countries: A Case Study of India's Prospects*, New Jersey: Princeton University Press, p. 333.

Desai, A.R., 1980, *Urban Family and Family Planning in India*, Bombay: Popular Prakashan Pvt. Ltd., p. 4.

Government of India, 1981, 'Sixth Five Year Plan', Planning Commission, p. 376.

Mamdani, M., 1976, 'The Ideology of Population Control', *Economic and Political Weekly*, XI (31–33), August: 114.

Mamoria, C.B., 1965, *Population and Family Planning in India*, Allahabad: Kitab Mahal Pvt. Ltd., pp. 23–132.

Rangarajan, C. and J.K. Satia, 1976, 'Population Policy and Redistribution of Income', *Economic and Political Weekly*, XI (31–33), August: 1161.

Shanthakumar, G., 1983, 'Population Policy: Singapore's Experience', in Vatsala Narain and C.P. Prakasam (eds), *Population Policy Perspectives in Developing Countries*, Bombay: Himalayan Publishing House, p. 171.

Stamper, B. Maxwell, 1977, *Population and Planning in Developing Nations*, New York: The Population Council, p. 64.

7

Effect of Age at Marriage on Fertility

A Study in Madras City

V. KALYANI

The study of age at marriage has acquired importance because it is one of the determinants of fertility. The analysis of nuptiality and associated factors has recently become an important branch of demographic studies. This is because, it is now more and more realized that age at marriage has an important bearing on family building activity and the level of fertility. Age at marriage can significantly affect the population growth of a country, particularly a non-contraceptive using country. It is often felt that the enhancement of age at marriage leads to a reduction in fertility. As a social institution, universality of marriage was recognized in the history of nuptiality of India. Malthus (1798), in his thesis on population, stated that delay in marriage is a major preventive check of moral restraint on the growth of population. Age at marriage, a strong point in the reproductive process, is traditionally low in many developing countries as compared to developed countries. Several of the earlier studies broadly explained a few important determinants of fertility behaviour (Kurup and George 1965; Zachariah 1983).

In the developed world as a whole, age at marriage is high and fertility is low, but the picture is not the same in the developing countries. Age at marriage has risen in East Asia and in a few countries of South–East Asia and this might have contributed to the overall decline in birth rates in these countries. However, Indonesia and countries belonging to the Indian subcontinent still have lower age at marriage and this provides a partial explanation of high birth rates in those nations (Population reports 1985).

The inverse association between age at marriage and fertility has been depicted in various studies, namely; Agarwala (1966), Karkal (1965), Raman (1973), Goyal (1974) and UN (1961). Raising the age at marriage for women beyond 20 years has been viewed to cause a reduction in fertility of about 15 to 30 per cent by Talwar (1967). Das (1969) claimed, on the basis of an empirical study, that women marrying between 20 and 24 have similar fertility to those marrying before the age of 20. Cassen (1978: 53) also pointed to a negative association between age at marriage and fertility. Empirical evidence on age at marriage by Gulati (1969) and Das Gupta (1974) clearly shows that age at marriage is higher in urban areas than rural and educated men and women marry later than uneducated ones.

Socio-economic development, particularly improvement in women's education, provision of increased employment opportunities for women and raising their status, can contribute to a higher age at marriage. In Kerala, where literacy level has increased as high as 70 per cent (1981 census), the mean age at marriage has also correspondingly increased. Age at marriage forms an important variable that generally regulates fertility. A number of studies affirm that age at marriage is positively associated with socio-economic development and, thus, it becomes extremely difficult to assess its direct effect on fertility.

Methodology

The aim of the study is to ascertain the major determinants of fertility behaviour. More specifically, my discussion here is about age at marriage and its direct and indirect influence on fertility behaviour of an individual. The objective of the study is to estimate the level of fertility of the residents of Madras metropolitan area and also to study the influence of age at marriage on fertility. An in-depth analysis of the individual fertility behaviour, age at marriage and other related socio-cultural factors has been conducted. Schedules and questionnaires have been used for data collection. The criterion for the selection of the respondent has been a married woman who has a minimum of one child and who is in the reproductive age group of 15 to 49 years. In order to conduct an in-depth study, Madras metropolitan area was chosen and 100 households were selected at random. In the present study, women were the sole respondents. The sample consists of both working and non-working women as the area of study being a metropolitan area. Age at marriage has been taken as one of the important variables against fertility and analysis has made from the data collected.

Results and Discussion

Since age at marriage marks the beginning of the reproductive span of a woman's life, there seems to be a close connection between age at marriage and the fertility performance of the women. A significant relationship between age at marriage and the mean fertility of women at different age groups is viewed.

As shown in Table 7.1 the average number of pregnancies for the women who got married in the age group between 15 to 19 is 3.8 per woman, which is comparatively higher than the women who got married in the age group of 20 to 24, whose average number of pregnancies is 2.2 whereas for the women who got married between the age group of 25 to 29, the average number of pregnancies is 1.7. But the average number of pregnancies is slightly high in the age group of 30 to 34, i.e. 2.5 per woman. The overall findings of the study support the hypothesis of fertility decline with increase in the age at marriage.

Table 7.1

Age at marriage and average number of pregnancies

Age at marriage	*No. of women N*	*Average of pregnancies X*
15–19	20	3.8
20–24	46	2.2
25–29	32	1.7
30–34	2	2.5
Total	100	2.3

Many studies have shown a strong negative relationship between age at marriage and fertility, e.g. Audinarayana (1985), Bongaarts and Potter (1983) and Wyon and Gordon (1971). World Fertility Survey (1984) has reported, 'although age at marriage is a topic of interest to demographers in its own right, it has been singled out for intensive study primarily because of the impact of nuptiality on fertility'. Age at marriage has a positive correlation with the average number of live births of the women. As shown in table 7.2 the average number of live births per woman is more for those women whose age at marriage falls in the range of 15 to 19 years. Least number of live births is seen among those women who married in the age group of 25–29. There is a difference of 0.1 per cent between the average number of pregnancies and live births. There are only two women reported in this study who got married between 30 to 34 years. And their fertility rate is high at 2.5 per woman for both pregnancies and live births.

Table 7.2

Age at marriage and average number of live births

Age at marriage	*No. of women N*	*Average of live births X*
15–19	20	3.06
20–24	46	2.03
25–29	32	1.6
30–34	2	2.5
Total	100	2.13

Historically speaking, early marriage especially for females was the norm in India. The mean age at marriage in 1891–1901 for females was 12.7 years. It rose to 17.16 years in the year 1971. The mean age at marriage for women in Madras metropolis was 23.3 years. The average ideal age at marriage for girls is 23.4 years. But the average actual age at marriage for the women respondents was 22.8 years. So, it is clear from Table 7.3 that the average actual age at marriage is less than the average desired age at marriage. The actual and the ideal age at marriage is high in the age groups of 20 to 24 years, only two respondents have reported their actual age at marriage between 30 to 34 years. But none have felt that the ideal age at marriage can exceed 29 years.

Table 7.3

Actual age at marriage and ideal age at marriage

Age at marriage	*No. of women N*	*Average of live births X*
15–19	20	8
20–24	46	55
25–29	32	37
30–34	2	—
Total Mean	100 X=22.8	100 X=23.4

Conclusion

In order to ascertain the influence of age at marriage on fertility, 100 female respondents have been selected at random in Madras metropolitan area during the year 1990. It is clear from the study that the average actual age at marriage is less than the average desired age at marriage. Age at marriage is found to have a negative correlation with the fertility of the women. The findings of the study support the hypothesis of fertility decline with increase in the age of marriage.

References

Agarwala, S.N., 1966, 'Raising the Marriage Age for Women: A Mean to Lower the Birth Rate', *Economic and Political Weekly,* 1 (19): 797–798.

Audinarayana, N., 1985, *Age at Marriage and its Determinants Among the Hindus and the Muslims in Rural Andhra Pradesh,* Unpublished Ph.D. Thesis, S.V. University, Tirupati.

Bongaarts, John and R.G. Potter, 1983, *Fertility, Biology and Behaviour: An Analysis of Proximate Determinants,* New York: Academic Press.

Bongaarts, John, 1987, 'Does Family Planning Reduce Infant Mortality Rates?', *Population and Development Review,* 13 (2): 323–334.

Cassen, R.H., 1978, *India: Population, Economy, Society,* New York: Holmes and Meier Publishers.

Census of India, 1971, Series 1, India, Part II-A Special, Reports and Tables based on 5 Per Cent Sample Data, New Delhi: Government of India.

Das Gupta, M., 1974, *Factors Affecting Age at Marriage in India,* London School of Economics (Unpublished).

Das, N.C., 1969, 'A Note on the Effect of Postponement of Marriage on Total Fertility and Female Birth Rate', IUSSP, International Population Conference, London.

Goyal, R.P., 1974, 'Fertility and Family Planning in Urban Delhi', in A. Bose et al. (eds), *Population in India's Development,* New Delhi: Vikas Publishing House.

Gulati, S.C., 1969, 'Impact of Literacy, Urbanisation and Sex Ratio on Age at Marriage in India', *Arthavijnana,* 11 (4): 685–697.

Karkal, M., 1965, 'Age at Marriage', *Journal of Family Welfare,* 14 (3): 51–56.

Kurup, R.S. and K.A. George, 1965, *Population Growth in Kerala: Its Implications,* Bureau of Economics and Statistics, Trivandrum-10.

Malthus, T.R.Z., 1798, *An Essay on Population,* New York: E.P. Dutton.

Mandelbaum, David G., 1974, *Human Fertility in India: Social Components and Policy Perspective,* Berkeley: University of California Press.

Population Reports, 1985, *Minilaparotomy and Laparoscopy: Safe, Effective and Widely Used,* Baltimore: The John Hopkins University.

Raman, M.V., 1973, *Summary Statement: Calcutta Fertility Survey 1970* (Mimeo), Conference of IUSSP Subcommittee on Comparative Fertility Analysis, Brussels.

Talwar, P.P., 1967, 'A Note on Changes in Age at Marriage of Females and their Effect on the Birth Rate in India', *Eugenics Quarterly*, 14: 291–295.

UN, 1961, *The Mysore Population Study*, New York.

World Fertility Survey, 1980, World Fertility Survey Conference, Record of Proceedings, Vol. III, London.

——, 1984, Scientific Report No. 71, December.

Wyon, B. and D.E. Gordon, 1971, *The Khanna Study*, Cambridge, MA: Harvard University Press.

Zachariah, K.C., 1983, *Anomaly of the Fertility Decline in Kerala*, Report No. 1 from RPO 671–70, Washington, D.C.: World Bank.

8

Fertility Preferences and Use of Contraceptive Methods in Himachal Pradesh

Comparative Analysis of Two Surveys NFHS-I and NFHS-II

SAVITA THAKUR

The comparative results of the two surveys show that in spite of good health services, knowledge of contraceptive methods and about family size, more than 39 per cent of currently married women do not accept family planning methods. A strong son preference is evident among women who do not have any male child in their family. The time and development has no impact on the preference for ideal number and sex of child, though a little change, has been reported towards female child preference during NFHS-I and NFHS-II. So there is a need to change the values attached behind son preference by providing equal social and economic opportunities to females in the remote hilly areas of the state.

Parenthood is generally previewed by the couples as an important milestone in their lives. Decisions regarding the timing and number of children have a far reaching impact on their lives. Mostly, couples are confident of attaining parenthood hence they preconceive the idea of their family. But firm decision and the number of children is not made until the birth and the sex of the first child.

In India social economic and religious values are affected with the birth of a child. In spite of serious efforts to limit the size of population, the rate of growth of population in India has been increasing since 1951. It has been observed that at least at this stage there is a need to establish the relationship between fertility preference and acceptance of family planning methods. In India, family size is strongly affected by the social factors and since most of the families are patriarchal in nature, hence family is considered incomplete till one has at least one male living child in the family. Preference for male child has been studied by Prabhu (1965); Kapadia (1966); May and Heer (1968); Miller (1981); Amin and Mariam (1987); Jaffery (1989); Vlassaff (1990); Bhende and Kanitkar (1993); Gill (1995); Thakur (1999); Das Gupta (1987); Basu (1989); Nag (1991); Parasuraman, Roy and Surender (1994); Murthi, Guio and Dreze (1995) and Kulkarni, Kumar and Saikia (1996) and they found in their studies that a strong reference for sons has been deep rooted in India, affecting both attitude and behaviour with respect to children. The achieved family size in almost every society is below the biological maximum. Apart from the reduction due to mortality, the achievement of the size of the family below the biological maximum is accomplished through various methods of deliberate control (D'Souza 1985).

The main objective of this paper is to highlight the changes which took place for fertility preferences as well as knowledge and use of contraceptive methods among ever married respondent of NFHS-I and NFHS-II. In order to view the fertility preferences, their desire for children in future, the extent of sex preference, ideal number of children by sex and their current family planning status data on NFHS-I and NFHS-H have been analysed.

Desire for more Children

During NFHS-I, 72 per cent and during NFHS-II, 89 per cent of currently married women in Himachal Pradesh were those, not wanting any more children. As compared to 27 per cent in NFHS-I, 11 per cent in NFHS-II said they want another child. The women who want children, their desire for additional child with preferred sex of the desired child is calculated by their actual living children. A drastic change with regard to the desire for more children has been found between the two surveys. As compared to 84 per cent with one child and 22 per cent with two children during NFHS-I, only 28 per cent with one child and 33 per cent with two children during NFHS-H want more children.

Table 8.1

Percentage distribution of currently married women by desire for children preferred sex of child and mean ideal and number of children by actual number of living children

		0	*1*	2	3	4	5	6	
Desire for a Additional child	NFHS-I	92.5	84	22	8.1	3.7	3	3.5	27.1
	NFHS-II	86.2	28.3	3.3	2.5	1.3			10.9
Preferred sex of the child	NFHS-I								
	Son	33.3	46	78.1	95.3				53.9
	Daughter	0.6	6.8	10.6	4.7				5.3
	NFHS-II								
	Son	17.6	50	79.2	92.3				47.5
	Daughter	2.6	18.5	12.3	7.7				11.6
Mean ideal	NFHS-I	2	2	2.1	2.4	2.8	—	—	2.4
No. of children	NFHS-II	1.9	1.9	2	2.3	2.5			2.2
	NFHS-I								
Ideal	Son	0.9	1	1.1	1.4	1.6	—	—	1.3
composition	Daughter	0.6	0.7	0.8	0.9	1			0.8
of children	Does not Matter	0.5	0.3	0.3	0.2	0.2			0.3
	NFHS-II								
	Son								1.1
	Daughter								0.8
	Does not matter								0.3

Source of Data: NFHS-I, NFHS-H, H.P.I.I.P.S. Mumbai (India).

The data in Table 8.1 also reveals that the desire for more children declines rapidly as the number of living children increases. Among women who want another child there is strong preference for having a son as the next child. The desire for a son is particularly strong among couples having two or three children. Desire for daughter with no children and with one child has increased from 0.6 to 2.6 and 6.8 to 18.5 per cent, respectively, between two surveys. Overall the data show that preference for son has declined from 54 per cent to 47.5 per cent between two surveys. On the other hand, preference for daughter has also increased from 5.3 to 11.6 per cent, showing a positive change towards female child. Results support the study of Jejeebhoy and Kulkarni 1989 that daughters are also considered as emotional security to the women.

Ideal Number and Ideal Composition of Children

It is assumed that the family size preference will be influenced by the ideal number and ideal composition of children. On the other hand, the regulation of the size of family would be achieved through the adoption of family planning methods. The Table 8.1 clearly reveals that the ideal number of children falls within the fairly narrow range of two–three children for a large majority of women during both surveys. The mean ideal number of children ranges from 2.0 and 1.7 for women with less than two children and 2.8 and 2.5 for those who already have more than four children in NFHS-I and NFHS-II, respectively. It is evident from the Table 8.1 that family size norms are quite moderate because a proportionally large number of women say that their ideal number of children is less than the number they already have. Persistence of a strong preference for sons over daughters can be seen in this table. Overall, the ideal family consists of 1.3 sons in NFHS-I and 1.1 in NFHS-II and 0.8 daughters for both periods. There is a general tendency for women who have more daughters to exhibit a weaker preference for sons but no matter what the current composition of the family is, son preference persists. Overall, the data with regard to ideal size and sex preference shows that there is very less change between the two surveys showing that the people in Himachal Pradesh have strong preference for two children with at least one son in their family.

Knowledge and Use of Contraceptive Methods

The successful limitation of family size by the couples depends not only on their small family size but also on their psychological acceptance of family limitation, knowledge of birth control methods and availability of contraceptives. The decision to limit the family size rests with the individuals of the family, although the government strongly advocates that couples should not bear more than two children, in their own as well as for the interest of the nation and in order to achieve this objective, a well structural family planning programme has been instituted. The extent to which the couples make use of those government sponsored facilities depends on their motivation to limit family size, attitude towards government facilities and their socio-economic conditions.

Family Planning

Knowledge of family planning is nearly universal in Himachal Pradesh. About 99 per cent women during NFHS-I and 100 per cent during NFHS-II were aware about every modern method. Currently, married women are most familiar with female sterilization, followed by male sterilization, the IUD, condom and the pill.

Contraceptive Use

In comparison to the universal knowledge of family planning methods, practice of contraception is moderate in Himachal Pradesh. During NFHS-I, 58.4 per cent women were using any methods and 54.4 per cent were using any modern methods. The use of any method has increased to 68 per cent and modern methods to 61 per cent during NFHS-II, only 5 per cent increase of any modern method has been found between two surveys.

The data also shows the differentials in current use by the number and sex of living children. A positive association exists between the number of living children a woman has and current use of contraception. Contraceptive use increased from only 7 per cent and 2.8 per cent, for women who have no living children, to 76 per cent and 86 per cent for women with three living children during NFHS-I and NFHS-Il, respectively. The data on the prevalence rate by the sex composition of living children indicate the existence of son preference, at each parity, the current use of family planning is the lowest for women having no sons and highest for women having all sons. As expected, sterilization is a particularly popular method for women who do not have any sons. Among women having two or more living children, current use is highest among those who have two or more sons. The only difference between the two surveys is that the percentage of accepting any family planning method without any male child has increased from 16.5 per cent to 26.2 per cent in NFHS-II and to any modern method from 11.2 per cent to 18.1 per cent, which shows a little change in the perception of the young generation towards sex of the child.

In spite of the health services provided by 2400 health institutions, including 39 hospitals, one medical college, 39 community health centres, eight rural hospitals, 246 primary health centres, 165 civil dispensaries and 1954 health sub-centres, only 58 per cent during NFHS-I and 68 per cent during NFHS-II, showing 10 per cent increase of married women who have gone for any family planning methods between two surveys.

Reasons for Non-use of Contraception

Currently married women who were not using any contraceptive method and who said that they do not intend to use contraception at any time in the future were asked the main reasons for their intended non-use. Information on reasons for non-use is crucial for designing successful information programmes and for understanding the obstacles to further increase in contraceptive prevalence. Reasons for not intending to use any method are indicated in Table 8.3. Data in Table 8.2 shows that 42 per cent during NFHS-I and 40 per cent NFHS-II were not using any methods. Out of the target proportion of women, maximum of them revealed that they do not intend to use contraception because they want more children, particularly sons. Majority of women less than 30 years of age gave this reason.

Table 8.2

Per cent distribution of currently married women by knowledge of contraceptive methods and use with number and sex of living children

	NFHS-I			NFHS-II		
	Any method	*Any modern method*	*No using any method*	*Any method*	*Any modern method*	*No using any method*
Knowledge of F.P. methods	99.1	98.9	—	100.0	100.0	—
Current use of F.P. Methods	58.4	54.4	41.6	67.7	60.8	39.2
No. & sex of living children						
None	6.8	3.8	93.2	2.8	1.1	97.2
1 child	20.1	15.4	79.9	32.0	22.8	68.0
1 son	22.5	18.5	77.5	37.1	26.8	62.9
No sons	16.5	11.2	83.2	26.2	18.1	73.8
2 children	64.6	57.9	35.4	74.2	65.4	25.8
2 sons	77.9	73.5	22.1	84.4	79.5	15.6
1 son	63.1	55.4	36.9	74.1	63.2	25.9
No sons	31.6	21.3	68.4	43.3	31.4	56.7
3 children	76.4	73.1	23.6	86.3	80.2	13.7
2 sons	89.4	86.5	10.6	94.2	90.2	5.8
2 sons	87.0	84.5	13.0	92.8	87.8	7.2
1 son	66.2	62.1	33.8	80.9	72.7	19.1
No sons	19.4	14.1	80.6	43.2	35.0	56.8
4 + children	75.3	72.8	24.7	82.4	76.4	17.6
2 + sons	79.5	76.9	20.5	88.3	84.1	11.7
1 son	68.0	65.4	32.0	74.5	65.5	25.5

Data Source: NFHS-I NFHS-II, H.P.I.I.P.S. Mumbai, India

A minor proportion reported that contraception is either against their religion or that they or their husbands are against the use of family planning. Half of older women reported their actual or perceived sterility as the main reason for not intending to use contraception in future.

Table 8.3

Per cent distribution of women who are not using any contraceptive methods by main reason not currently using

Reasons for not using any methods	*NFHS-I*	*NFHS-II*
Wants children	33.0	43.9
Worry about side effects	2.2	0.3
Afraid of sterilization	0.3	0.2
Opposed to family planning	0.3	0.2
Husband oppose	3.2	0.2
Other people oppose	0.3	0.2
Menopausal/had hysterectomy	18.7	7.0

Data Source: NFHS-I, NFHS-II, H.P.I.I.P.S. Mumbai, India

The most important reasons for non-use of family planning are broadly the same during both the surveys, i.e. families who are yet to complete their desired family size, although the desire to have a son is more important reason for their non-use of any family planning method. It can be concluded that in spite of good health services provided by the government, knowledge of contraceptive methods, achieved family size, more than 39 per cent of currently married women do not accept family planning method. A strong son preference is evident among women who do not have any male child in their family. The time and development has no impact on the preference for the ideal number and sex of the child. A little change has been reported towards female child preference during NFHS-II. So there is a need to change the social and economic values attached behind son preferences in the family through the extensive effective implementation of family planning programmes as well as through the expansion of education by giving equal job opportunity to females in the remote hilly area of the State.

References

Amin, R. and A.C. Mariam, 1987, 'Son Preference in Bangladesh: An Emerging Barrier to Fertility Regulation', *Journal of Biosocial Science*, 19 (2): 221–228.

Bhende, A. and Tara Kanitkar, 1993, *Principles of Population Studies*, Mumbai: Himalaya Publishing House.

D'Souza, V.S., 1985, *Economic Development, Social Structure and Population Growth*, New Delhi: Sage Publications.

Jaffery, P. Andrew, 1989, *Labour Pains and Labour Power: Women and Child Bearing in India*, New Delhi, London and New Jersey: Zed Books Ltd.

Jaffery, Roger and Alka M. Basu, 1996, *Girl Schooling, Women's Autonomy and Fertility Change in South Asia*, New Delhi: Sage Publications.

Jejeebhoy, Shireen J. and Sumati B. Kulkarni, 1989, 'Reproductive Motivation: A Comparison of Wives and Husbands in Maharashtra, India', *Studies in Family Planning*, 20 (5): 264–272.

Kapadia, K.M., 1966, *Marriage and Family in India*, Bombay: Oxford University Press.

Kaur, K., 1995, *Population Growth, Family Size and Economic Development*, New Delhi: Deep and Deep Publications.

Kulkarni, S., B.S. Kumar and U.S. Saikia, 1996, 'Son Preference and Fertility Decline in India', Paper Presented at the IUSSP Seminar on Comparative Perspectives on Fertility Transition in South Asia, International Union for the Scientific Study of Population, Rawalpindi, pp. 17–20.

May, D.A. and D.M. Heer, 1968, 'Son Survivorship and Family Size in India: A Computer Simulation', *Population Studies*, 22 (3): 199–210.

Miller, B.D., 1981, *The Endangered Sex Neglect of Female Child in Rural North India*, Ithaca: Cornell University Press.

Murthi, M., A.C. Guio and J. Dreze, 1995, 'Mortality, Fertility and Gender Bias in India', *Population and Development Review*, 21 (1): 745–782.

Nag, M., 1991, 'Sex Preference in Bangladesh, India and Pakistan and Its Effect on Fertility', *Demography India*, 20 (2): 163–185.

NFHS-I, 1992-93, *Himachal Pradesh: National Family Health Survey India*, Mumbai: IIPS.

NFHS-II, 1998-99, *Himachal Pradesh: National Family Health Survey India*, Mumbai: IIPS.

Parasuraman, S., T.K. Roy and S. Surender, 1994, 'Sex Composition of Children and Fertility Behaviour in Rural Maharashtra', in K.B. Pathak, U.P. Sinha and Arvind Pandey (eds), *Dynamics of Population and Family Welfare*, Bombay: Himalaya Publishing House.

Prabhu, P., 1965, *Hindu Social Organization*, Bombay: Popular Prakashan.

Thakur, S., 1999, *Women and Development: The Changing Scenario*, New Delhi: Mittal Publications.

Vlassaff, Carol, 1990, 'The Value of Sons in an Indian Village: How Widows See It', *Population Studies*, 44 (1): 5–20.

9

Son Preference and Reproductive Behaviour in Rural Punjab

PRABHJOT MALHI AND SUKHVINDER SINGH

In recent times, the demographic implications of sex preferences for children have emerged as an important research concern. According to McClelland (1983), there are three possible direct effects of preferences for the sex of children on fertility behaviour. Sex selection may change fertility rates, change the sex ratio of population, and change the birth order of sexes within the families. The most obvious demographic consequences of parental preferences for the sex of children have been found to result in imbalanced sex ratios at birth (e.g. Yamaguchi 1989). Sex preferences have important consequences for the overall level of fertility also. Sheps (1963) reported that in a hypothetical population, if all couples desired at least two sons, families would have on an average 3.88 children, while if all couples desired a balanced sex composition of one son and one daughter, the average family size would be around three children. Sheps, thus, concluded that higher the preference for one sex over the other, higher would be the average family size.

Previous research on sex preferences for children has shown that parents, particularly in the Asian countries, demonstrate a decided preference for sons (e.g. Williamson 1976; Cleland, Verrall and Vaessen 1983), although desire for a daughter after several sons has also been recorded (Chowdhury and Bairagi 1990; Rahman and Da Vanzo 1993). Studies show that couples who have more sons among their surviving children are more likely not to desire additional children and accept contraception (e.g. Karki 1988; Malhi 1993a; Pong 1994). Having sons not only motivates parents to use contraception, but also reinforces its continuation (Gadalla, McCarthy and Campbell 1985) and is also related to the use of more effective birth control methods and acceptance of sterilization (Arnold and Liu 1986; Malhi 1993b). Couples with sons have longer birth intervals and fewer subsequent births (Bairagi and Langsten 1986; Chowdhury and Bairagi 1990). In fact, a number of authors have argued that a strong preference for sons helps to sustain high fertility and also acts as a major inhibiting factor in the implementation of the family planning programme (see e.g. Cain 1984; Nag 1991).

However, not all studies have found son preference to be related to higher fertility. For example, Cleland, Verrall and Vaessen (1983) used the World Fertility Survey data and found that sex composition of surviving children did not influence either fertility intentions or contraceptive behaviour despite a strong desire for sons. Some of the earlier studies conducted in India also failed to find any relationship between number of living sons and contraception. For instance, Repetto (1972) analysed data from Bangladesh, Jordan, and India and found that the fertility decisions were unrelated to desire for male children. He argued that couples base their fertility decisions on the economic benefits and costs of children and not on their sex. Repetto suggested that couples who already have boys may desire more children because of the perceived financial benefits associated with having sons, while couples with more girls in their families may restrict child bearing because of the perceived economic burden associated with having several daughters.

It is important to note, however, that sex preferences for children may not influence fertility and family planning acceptance under all conditions. According to Williamson (1976), several conditions need to be present before stated preferences can influence fertility behaviour. First, parents must typically desire a small or moderate number of children since large families are likely to include children of both sexes. Second, couples who have had the desired number of children must control their fertility. Lastly, parents must have some assurance that children will survive till adulthood. Apparently, these conditions were not present in the early 1979s in India; hence the earlier studies show only small effects of sex preferences on fertility. It has also been argued that son preference may not be an important determinant of fertility given the experience of several Asian countries like South Korea, Taiwan, and Singapore which have experienced substantial declines in their overall fertility levels despite the prevalence of a very strong preference for male children. Moreover, Arnold (1985, 1987, 1992) has argued that son preference does not exert a strong impact on fertility mainly because couples tend to have a son early in their reproductive life by sheer biological chance.

Although the social and economic determinants of sex preferences are to some extent documented (e.g. Jejeebhoy and Kulkarni 1989; Basu 1991), less is known about the impact sex and birth order of children have on the reproductive behaviour of the married couples (see Das 1987; Rajaretnam and Deshpande 1994). A number of earlier studies have indicated that the order in which couples have boys and girls is important in determining subsequent fertility behaviour (see e.g. Mason and Bennett 1977; Park 1978; Dixon and Levy 1985). However, birth order effects have typically not been examined in India. In the present article, the effect of sex composition, birth order, and number of living children is examined on the fertility behaviour of women in the rural areas of Punjab. The specific objectives are to study the pattern of gender preferences and to estimate the extent to which sex preferences have constrained the success of family planning programme and related fertility decline in the state.

The Setting, Data and Methodology

The state of Punjab is one of the most economically prosperous states in the country. Over the years, both fertility and mortality rates have been steadily declining. The crude birth rate in the last one decade declined from 31.2 per thousand (1981) to 27.1 per thousand (1992). The total fertility rate has also declined from 4 children in 1981 to 3.1 children in 1991 (Registrar General of India 1981; Ministry of Health and Family Welfare 1992). The recent census results reveal that the decennial population growth rate of the state has fallen substantially from 23.89 per cent (1971–81) to 20.26 per cent (1981–91). The contraceptive prevalence rate (CPR) has been rapidly increasing and it has increased from 17.2 per cent in 1970 to 69.6 per cent in 1989, the highest rate recorded in the country (Ministry of Health and Family Welfare 1992).

Gender inequality in the state is particularly striking on indicators such as sex differentials in child mortality and access to paid employment. Despite overall levels of relatively low infant and child mortality, girls in the state experience wide spread discrimination in the access to food, clothing, and medical care which is reflected in some of the most marked sex differentials in child mortality observed in the country (Dyson and Moore 1983; Das Gupta 1987). The sex ratios in the state remain historically low and in 1991, there were only 882 females per 1000 males. Women's participation in income generating activities is abysmally low and only 4.4 per cent of women were recorded as economically active in 1991 (Census of India 1992).

The data used in the present study comes from a sample survey conducted by the Centre for Research in Rural and Industrial Development (CRRID) in 1989–90 in the rural areas of seven districts of Punjab and the study was sponsored by Ministry of Health and Family Welfare. The sample comprised the 450 currently married women in the reproductive ages of 15–44. The questionnaire used in the survey elicited information from the women on the socio-economic background of their households, fertility history, family size desires, and current use of contraception.

Sex preferences were analysed by examining the (i) mean desired family size, (ii) per cent not desiring additional children, (iii) per cent desiring additional sons and daughters, and (iv) current use of contraception by the sex, birth order, and number of living children. Arnold's (1985) method was also applied to this cross-sectional data to estimate the extent to which contraceptive use rate would increase, and desired family size would decline in the absence of sex preferences. This technique assumes that in the complete absence of sex preferences, at any parity, all the couples would behave in a similar fashion as those who are most satisfied with their existing sex composition of children. The observed rates are compared with the expected rates (for details see Arnold 1985, 1987).

Results and Discussion

Table 9.1 presents the mean desired children, per cent not desiring additional children, per cent desiring additional sons and daughters, and per cent using modern contraceptives by number, sex and birth order off living children for women in rural Punjab. On all the measures shown, there is strong evidence to reveal that a very marked preference for male children exists among married women in the state.

The preference for sons is most obvious if one compares women whose all children are of one sex. In general, at every parity, women with all sons desire fewer children, are less likely to want more children, and are more likely to be practicing contraception as compared to respondents who have all daughters. For example, among women with two children, the average desired family size was 2.07 children, whereas it was 3.05 children for those with two daughters, a difference of one living child. Further, the percentage of women not desiring additional children increased from 25 per cent for those with two girls to 93 per cent for those with two boys.

Table 9.1

Mean desired children, per cent not desiring additional children, per cent desiring additional sons and daughters and per cent practising contraception by number, sex and order of living children

Number, sex and birth order	*Mean desired children*	*% Not desiring additional children*	*% desiring additional*		*% practising contraception*			*Number*
			Son	*Daughter*	*Spacing*	*Permanent*	*Total*	
No Child	2.23	4.5	95.7	79.5	2.3	0.0	2.3	44
One Child	2.22	16.6	80.0	16.7	20.0	1.7	21.7	60
Girl (B)	2.41	6.9	33.1	10.3	13.7	0.0	13.7	29
Boy (B)	2.04	25.8	67.7	22.6	25.8	3.2	29.0	31
Two Children	2.4	66.1	33.1	1.6	42.5	15.0	57.5	127
2 G	3.05	25	75.0	0.0	20.0	0.0	20	20
1 G, 1 B	2.39	64.5	35.5	0.0	51.6	3.2	54.8	31
1 B, 1 G	2.44	58.8	41.2	2.9	41.2	11.8	53	34
2 B	2.07	92.8	4.8	2.4	47.7	33. 3	81	42
Three Children	3.16	89.5	10.5	0.0	25.4	52.6	78	114
3 G	3.67	33.3	66.7	0.0	0.0	0.0	0	3
2 G, 1 B	3.31	69.2	30.8	0.0	30.8	30.8	61.6	13
1 G, 1 B, 1 G	3.21	78.6	21.4	0.0	35.7	35.7	71.4	14

Cont'd...

...Cont'd

1 B, 2 G	3.38	75	25.0	0.0	50.0	37.5	87.5	8
1 G, 2 B	3	100	0.0	0.0	14.3	71.4	85.7	-21
1 B, 1 G, 1 B	3,16	100	0.0	0.0	21.1	57.9	79	19
2 B, 1 G	3.13	93	6.7	0.0	33.3	60.0	93.3	15
3 B	3.05	100	0.0	0.0	19.0	61.9	80.9	21
Four or more Children	4.54	89.5	8.6	0.1	20.9	58.1	79.9	105
More Girls than Boys, B last	5.07	85.2	14.8	0.0	37.0	40.7	77.7	27
More Girls than Boys, G last	4.65	73.9	26.1	0.0	17.4	47.8	65.2	23
Same Number of Girls and Boys, B last	4	100	0.0	0.0	18.2	68.2	86.4	22
Same Number of Girls and Boys, G last	4	100	0.0	0.0	18.2	72.7	90.9	1 1
More Boys than Girls, G last	4.65	94.1	0.0	5.9	11.8	70.5	82.3	17
More Boys than Girls, B last	4.4	100	0.0	0.0	0.0	80.0	80	5
Total	3.05	64.9	34.2	9.8	26.2	31.3	57.5	450

In order to detect whether couples desire some balance in the sex composition of their desired family, women who wanted more children were asked the sex of the additional children desired. Surprisingly, there was no evidence to indicate that women with all boys consider it important to haven balanced sex composition of children. At each parity, the percentage women desiring daughters among those who do not have a living daughter was very small, and this desire becomes negligible as the number of living sons increase in the family. In sharp contrast, the percentage of women wanting sons among those who do not have a son is very substantial, even at parity three and above. Moreover, a large majority of the rural couples desire a second son while a desire for a second daughter is virtually non-existent. These results are in contrast to some of the earlier studies conducted in India where a desire for a daughter after several sons has been observed (see e.g. Khan and Prasad 1985; Rajaretnam and Deshpande 1994).

Preference for sons is also evident from the contraceptive use pattern of the couples. At each parity, the use of family planning methods increased monotonically as the number of living sons in the family increased. It is noteworthy that the highest contraceptive use rate was prevalent among those couples with at least two living sons, highlighting the model preference of the rural couples in Punjab. At parity two, the use of birth control methods increased from 20 per cent for couples who had no son to a little above 50 per cent for those with one living son, to 81 per cent for those with two surviving sons. The results are even more striking if one examines the data by type of contraceptive method used. At every parity, all the couples with no living son were found to be using temporary methods of family planning. It seems that couples are unlikely to adopt an irreversible method of contraception until they have achieved their desired number of sons. Moreover, it was found that the sterilization acceptors had on an average 2.07 living sons, while acceptors of spacing methods had only 1.36 living sons. These findings reinforce the conclusion that the success of the family planning programme in the rural areas of the state, to a large extent, depends on the couples having achieved a desired family composition with at least two surviving sons.

In order to detect whether the order in which couples have boys and girls is important for influencing subsequent fertility decisions, comparison of couples with different birth order of sons and daughters was made (controlling for the number as well as sex composition of children). Although previous research indicates that couples whose last child is a boy have on an average higher contraceptive acceptance rate (e.g. Arnold 1987), no consistent trend is apparent in the present data. The results indicate that there is a tendency, albeit small, for women to desire a male as their first child as those who have boys as their first born have higher acceptance of family planning and are also less likely to desire additional children. These results are, however, not always consistent thereby indicating that birth order effects are not so marked.

The strength of son preference can also be examined comparing the distribution of women, according to the number and sex of their children (see Arnold and Liu 1986). Since more male than female children are born, it would be expected that in the complete absence of sex preferences, at each parity there would be marginally higher number of couples with all boys than couples with all girls among their children. The present results reveal that at parity two, there are twice as many couples with all boys than couples with all girls, and at parity three, there are seven times more all boys families than all girls families. This is primarily because couples who have all daughters are less likely to terminate child bearing and continue having more children till such time that they have a son. In contrast, couples with all boys among their children are less likely to want more children, since a desire for a daughter, particularly after two sons, is fairly muted.

The strong impact of son preference on fertility intentions and contraceptive acceptance has significant demographic implications. To access the extent to which desired family size would fall and contraceptive use rate would increase in the absence of sex preference, the quantitative method of Arnold (1985) was applied to the data shown in Table 9.1. It was estimated that if sex preferences were completely eliminated in rural Punjab, the desired family size would fall from the present 3.05 children to 2.77 children, a decline of 9 per cent. It is further estimated that the proportion of women who do not want any more children would increase approximately by 14 percentage points in the absence of gender preferences. Contraceptive use rate would also show a marked improvement and would increase from the present 58 per cent to 72 per cent. An increase of 14 percentage points in the family planning acceptance rate in the absence of sex preferences highlights the extent to which son preference has constrained the family planning programme in the state. These findings are in sharp contrast to Arnold's (1992) contention that the demographic impact of sex preferences, even in countries which depict a fairly strong preference for male children, is at best marginal.

To understand why a preference for male children is so strong in Punjab, it is important to bear in mind the cultural and economic factors which operate in the state. Das Gupta (1987) has argued that the culture of the dominant caste group in Punjab, namely the *Jats*, places a premium on successfully bearing and rearing sons because the prevailing patriarchal norms accord the Punjabi women a very low social status. The Punjabi practice of marrying women into an extended household of strangers, physically as well as psychologically, isolates them from their natal home. The flow of resources is inevitably from the women's parental home to the husband's home and this coupled with high marriage costs makes the girls an economic liability. Women in Punjab are excluded from owning property, particularly land, and have some of the lowest levels of participation in income generating activities. Without an independent economic base, women gain power mainly through their ability to produce children, particularly sons (also see Dyson and Moore 1983).

In sum, the results clearly indicate that preference for male children is exerting a substantial impact on the fertility desires and family planning behaviour of the rural couples. It is important to bear in mind as the overall demand for children declines, the impact of son preference on fertility behaviour will become stronger and future declines in fertility may be more difficult to attain in the state.

References

Arnold, F., 1985, 'Measuring the Effect of Sex Preferences in Fertility: The Case of Korea', *Demography*, 22: 280–288.

——, 1987, 'Effect of Sex Preferences on Fertility and Family Planning: Empirical Evidence', *Population Bulletin of the United Nations*, 23/24: 44–45.

——, 1992, 'Sex Preferences and its Demographic and Health Implications', *International Family Planning Perspectives*, 18: 93–101.

Arnold, F. and Z. Liu, 1986, 'Sex Preferences, Fertility, and Family Planning in China', *Population and Development Review*, 12: 221–246.

Bairagi, R. and R.L. Langsten, 1986, 'Sex Preferences for Children and its Implications for Fertility in Rural Bangladesh', *Studies in Family Planning*, 17: 302–307.

Basu, A.M., 1991, 'Demand and its Socio-Cultural Context', in J.K. Satia and S.J. Jejeebhoy (eds), *The Demographic Challenge*, Bombay: Oxford University Press.

Cain, I., 1984, *Women's Status and Fertility in Developing Countries: Son Preference and Economic Security*, Working Paper No. 110, Centre for Policy Studies, New York: The Population Council.

Census of India, 1992, *Final Population Totals: Brief Analyses of Primary Census Abstracts*, Paper 2, New Delhi: Government of India.

Chowdhury, M.K. and R. Bairagi, 1990, 'Son Preference and Fertility in Bangladesh', *Population and Development Review*, 16: 749–757.

Cleland, I., I. Verrall and M. Vaessen, 1983, 'Preference for Sex of Children and their Influence on Reproductive Behaviour', *Comparative Studies*, No. 27, Voorburg: World Fertility Survey.

Das, N., 1987, 'Sex Preference and Fertility Behaviour: A Study of Recent Indian Data', *Demography*, 24: 517–530.

Das Gupta, M., 1987, 'Selective Discrimination Against Female Children in Rural Punjab, India', *Population and Development Review*, 13: 77–100.

Dixon, R.D. and D.E. Levy, 1985, 'Sex of Children: A Community Analysis of Preferences and Pre-determination Attitudes', *The Sociological Quarterly*, 26: 251–271.

Dyson, T. and M. Moore, 1983, 'On Kinship Structure, Female Autonomy, and Demographic Behaviour in India', *Population and Development Review*, 9: 35–60.

Gadalla, S., J. McCarthy and O. Campbell, 1985, 'How the Number of Living Sons Influences Contraceptive Use in Menoufia Governorate, Egypt', *Studies in Family Planning*, 16: 164–169.

Jejeebhoy, S.J. and S. Kulkarni, 1989, 'Reproductive Motivation: A Comparison of Wives and Husbands in Maharashtra, India', *Studies in Family Planning*, 20: 264–272.

Karki, Y.B., 1988, 'Sex Preference and the Value of Sons and Daughters in Nepal', *Studies in Family Planning*, 19: 169–178.

Khan, M.E. and C.V.S. Prasad, 1985, 'A Comparison of 1970 and 1980 Survey Findings on Family Planning in India', *Studies in Family Planning*, 16: 312–320.

Malhi, P., 1993a, 'Sex Preferences for Children: Implications for Fertility and Contraceptive Use in People's Perceptions and Reproductive Behaviour in North West India', Report Submitted to Ministry of Health and Family Welfare, Centre for Research in Rural and Industrial Development, Chandigarh.

——, 1993b, 'Impact of Women's Education on Sex Preferences, Value and Aspirations for Children: Evidence from Haryana', *Man and Development*, 15 (4): 46–62.

Mason, A. and N.G. Bennett, 1977, 'Sex Selection with Biased Technologies and its Effect on the Population Sex Ratio', *Demography*, 14: 377–388.

McClelland, G.H., 1983, 'Measuring Sex Preferences and their Effects', in N.G. Bennett (ed.), *Sex Selection of Children*, New York: Academic Press.

Ministry of Health and Family Welfare, 1992, *Family Welfare Programme in India, Year Book 1990–91*, New Delhi: Government of India.

Nag, M., 1991, 'Sex Preference in Bangladesh, India, and Pakistan and its Effect on Fertility', *Demography India*, 20: 163–185.

Park, C.B., 1978, 'The Fourth Korean Child: The Effect of Son Preference on Subsequent Fertility', *Journal of Biosocial Sciences*, 10: 95–106.

Pong, S.L., 1994, 'Sex Preference and Fertility in Peninsular Malaysia', *Studies in Family Planning*, 25: 315–332.

Rahman, M. and J. Da Vanzo, 1993, 'Gender Preference and Birth Spacing in Matlab, Bangladesh', *Demography*, 30: 315–332.

Rahman, M., J. Akbar, J.F. Phillips and S. Becker, 1992, 'Contraceptive Use in Matlab, Bangladesh: The Role of Gender Preferences', *Studies in Family Planning*, 23: 229–242.

Rajaretnam, T. and R.V. Deshpande, 1994, 'The Effect of Sex Preference on Contraceptive Use and Fertility in Rural South India', *International Family Planning Perspectives*, 20: 88–95.

Registrar General of India, 1981, *Survey on Infant and Child Mortality*, New Delhi: Government of India.

Repetto, R., 1972, 'Son Preference and Fertility Behaviour in Developing Countries', *Studies in Family Planning*, 3: 70–76.

Sheps, M.C.I., 1963, 'Effects on Family Size and Sex Ratio of Preferences Regarding the Sex of Children', *Population Studies*, 17: 66–72.

Williamson, N.E., 1976, *Sons or Daughters: A Cross-Cultural Survey of Parental Preferences*, Beverly Hills: Sage Publications.

Yamaguchi, K., 1989, 'A Formal Theory for Male-Preferring Stopping Rules of Child Bearing: Sex Differences in Birth Order and in the Number of Siblings', *Demography*, 26: 451–465.

10

Poverty and Population

A Study of Reproductive Ideals and Attitude Towards Family Planning Among the Rural Poor in Uttar Pradesh

ARUN KUMAR SHARMA

At the time of Independence, India did not have a good data base in demography. Even the national level estimates of vital rates were of doubtful quality. Census, as the main, source of population data had provided data on size, distribution and growth of a population at national and sub-national administrative levels. Therefore, in the beginning, demographers concentrated on developing appropriate analytical techniques to estimate vital rates for the country as a whole and then for different regions in the country separately. Some attempts were made to relate demographic patterns to socio-economic characteristics of regional/state populations.

Soon in 1951, the Government of India adopted family planning programme as an instrument of development planning. Simultaneously, the Government of India, a small number in international organizations, and research centres and voluntary organizations in India started collecting data on aspects of fertility and mortality through large-scale and small scale surveys. In addition, action research and simulation exercises were undertaken to help demographers in exploring mechanisms of fertility decline. Studies done in Uttar Pradesh showed that there were significant regional variations in infertility and family planning in the state. They also showed that while a number of factors of social change were causing reduction in fertility in rural areas, some factors were causing a temporary rise. Other endings were: (a) high castes had responded to family planning programme more favourably than the intermediate and low castes; (b) Muslims had higher fertility than Hindus even in educated communities; (c) hilly areas had lower fertility and higher age at marriage than the plains; (d) occupation, literacy and social status determined fertility and family planning status in both urban and rural areas; and (e) in some cases, social habits of groups and marriage customs were more important determinants of fertility than occupation, literacy and social status (Rao 1974). These studies produced an Indian version of the theory of demographic transition which explained reduction in fertility in terms of improvement in mortality and socio-economic conditions, and yet laid stress on family planning information, education and communication (IEC) to re-establish balance between fertility and mortality. Few efforts were made to unearth the rationality of persistence of high fertility in a transitional and dual society that contemporary India is.

A large number of researches have been conducted in Uttar Pradesh after mid-1970s by Population Centre Lucknow, Population Research Centre of Lucknow University, Operations Research Group, National Institute of Health and Family Welfare, and an increasing number of scholars from the BHU, IIT-Kanpur, and other institutions. These studies have shifted their attention from study of trends and differentials to management aspects of the programme and specific issues such as fertility behaviour among minorities, slum dwellers, rural poor and tribals, area-wise change in nuptiality patterns, non-acceptance of family planning programme even in absence of desire for additional children, and breast-feeding practices. These studies and 1981 census data have shown that there are tremendous variations in fertility according to religion, urban-rural residence, caste, duration of marriage, occupation, birth order and educational levels (Khan 1999; Saksena and Srivastava 1980; Gupta 1986; Census of India 1981).

Among all the religious groups, Muslims have the highest fertility level and Christians have the lowest level. The Muslim religious leaders operating at the grassroots level feel that family planning is against the socio-religious beliefs of Muslims (Sawhney, Kumar and Saseendran 1990). Uttar Pradesh has five Muslim organizations: Muslim Majlis, Jamia-ul-ulema, Amarath Shariah, Jamayethe Islami and Muslim Education Society. First four of them are openly propagating the view that family planning is against Islam (Mahadevan 1989). However, there are significant variations within the community (Sawhney, Kumar and Saseendran 1990) and attitudes of the young elite are encouraging. Sharma (1989b) has argued that Muslims are highly stratified and demographers needed to look at their behaviour at the strata level.

Saseendran and Kumar (1989) have explored regional differences in family planning in Uttar Pradesh, and their causes. They made use of 1981 census data to run multivariate regression analysis at the district and the regional levels. Their findings show that per capita income, and literacy and work participation among females explain the variations in the couple protection rate (CPR) significantly at the district level. At the national level CPR is explained by proportion of Muslims male literacy, work participation among females, total literacy, per capita income, female literacy and urbanization.

Some studies have examined aspects of the programme development and interface between the family planning organization and target population (Misra et al. 1981; Sawhney, Kumar and Saseendran 1989; NIHFW 1989; ORG 1988). Their focus is on managerial aspects of the programme and not so much on contextual logic of fertility behaviour. The authors have noted that motivators and extension workers often lack empathy. When the clients do not pay heed to workers' advice, the only thing they are known to be saying is that what they are telling and working for (i.e. for promoting the idea of birth control) is true, but it is certainly up to the people to accept it or not to accept it. In the absence of proper understanding of clients' circumstances and alternatives probably they have no better answer to offer. Also, it has been reported that fertility among slum dwellers, the poor, and the tribals is particularly high and the incidence of infant and child mortality affects fertility and family planning behaviour (Kumar 1983; Sharma 1989b; Sharma, 1990).

Meta-analysis of studies in Uttar Pradesh shows that population research in India is either descriptive or managerial. There are few theoretical attempts to explain data or develop a theory of fertility in Uttar Pradesh. The dominant thinking among demographers seems to be that as Uttar Pradesh and other BIMARU states develop socially and economically, as some other states have done, their fertility will start declining. The old theoretical dependence on the theory of demographic transition has been strengthened by the politically sweet slogan that development is the best contraceptive. Thus, the main explanatory variables are developmental variables, e.g. education, income, infant mortality, etc. or ethnic, e.g. caste and community. They can easily be weld into a single conceptual framework of 'ethclasses' which was proposed by Gordon (1964) in the Western context.

It needs to be accepted that population in India had natural fertility in the past for a very long period of time and high fertility, therefore, has acquired its own traditional and ethnic rationality. The interesting question is not why is fertility in Uttar Pradesh high that many researchers have posed, but under what conditions does fertility decline. Sharma (1989a) has built a discursive model of fertility among the poor in Uttar Pradesh and related it to life goals, structure of objectives, consciousness of objectives, and locus of control. Looking at the situation in high and low fertility regions we may hypothesize that conditions which make people take new initiative in life, and internal locus of control, will cause reduction in fertility.

Several analysts have indicated that economic development in the post-Independence India has aggravated inequalities. Both industrialization and green revolution have helped the already better off sections of urban and rural areas and put the underprivileged sections to disadvantages and, thus, widened the gap between the elite and the masses. Bang (1984) maintains that colonial politics and industrialization have marginalized the poor and reduced their faith in their own resources, and themselves. Can alienated people who lack initiative in general be enthusiastic and rational in terms of their reproductive behaviour is a question to ponder.

But the poor are not a homogeneous group. There are many cultural, ecological, historical, psychological and occupational differences among the poor. So far population sociologists have compared the poor with the non-poor. There is now a need to examine differences within the category of the poor and establish their causes. In this context, the present paper attempts to relate reproductive ideals to locus of control among the poor in rural Uttar Pradesh.

This study is based on data obtained from rural poor of Kanpur and Varanasi districts. These data were collected as a part of a general study of poverty from four developed and four under developed villages[1]; in all 506 poor could be studied. They are all poor on both objective grounds and subjectively in their own eyes. In objective terms, they had an earning less than ₹ 550 per month (per adult male earner); those who had any agricultural land had only 2 acres or less. In subjective terms, only those objectively poor were included in the study who thought that they were poor. It was decided that only one working male per

Table 10.1

Percentage distribution of the respondents by their answer to the question, 'who may be held responsible for poverty'

Responsibility	Poverty in general						Respondents own poverty					
	Developed villages		Less developed villages		Total		Developed villages		Less developed villages		Total	
	No.	%	No.	%	No.	%	No.	%	No.	%	No.	%
1. Self	39	14.55	46	19.32	85	16.8	45	16.79	50	21.01	95	18.77
2. Others												
(a) Parents	13	4.85	17	7.14	30	5.93	16	5.97	7	2.94	23	4.55
(b) Society	13	4.85	16	6.72	29	5.73	10	3.73	7	2.94	17	3.36
(c) Fate	189	70.52	153	64.29	342	67.59	187	69.78	166	69.75	353	69.76
(d) Government	9	3.36	6	2.52	15	2.96	7	2.61	8	3.36	15	2.96
Sub-Total	224	83.58	192	80.67	416	82.21	220	82.09	188	78.99	108	80.63
3. No One	2	0.75	—	—	2	0.4	1	0.37	—	—	1	0.2
4. No Response	3	1.12	—	—	3	0.59	2	0.75	—	—	2	0.4
Total	268	100	238	100	506	100	268	100	238	100	506	100

household in the age group 10–50 years should be interviewed. This is the age group of males whose wives are expected to be in the reproductive ages. The field work was conducted by two investigators, specially selected for this purpose, during September, 1986 – May, 1987. Data was collected by both quantitative and ethnographic methods.

Attribution of Poverty

On the issue of the locus of control two close-ended questions were asked. The first question was related to poverty in general and the second to the respondents' own case. An attempt was made to know who may be held responsible for poverty in general and one's own poverty in particular – self, government, parents, society, fate, etc. Table 10.1 gives the percentage distribution of respondents according to their answer to this question. The table shows that an overwhelming majority of the poor (more than 80%) attribute poverty to some external factors. Among these factors, fate is the most frequent category. Only 18.77 per cent poor say that they themselves are responsible for their own poverty, and only 16.80 per cent attribute general poverty to some personal factor, in this respect the differences between the developed and the less developed villages are marginal. Though a little greater proportion of respondents in the less developed villages attribute general as well as their own poverty to 'self'.

Thus, in this study, the poor are divided into two groups: respondents attributing poverty to self and respondents attributing poverty to other factors. For this classification only general poverty and not own poverty has been considered.

Characteristics of Respondents

Table 10.2 summarizes data on the socio-economic characteristics of the poor. It gives a sociological profile of respondents. It is evident from the table that characteristics of those respondents who attribute poverty to self differ significantly from those who attribute poverty to other factors. The former are younger, more from high castes, more literate, more in non-agricultural activities (e.g. service, business or self employed), have more work and better income than the latter. More of them are married and live in semi-*pacca* or *pacca* house.

Table 10.2

Characteristics of the respondents

Characteristic	*Respondents attributing poverty to self*	*Respondents attributing poverty to other factors*	*Total*
Average age	33.9	35.1	34.9
Brahmins and other high castes (%)	38.8	34.0	34.8
Married (%)	88.2	83.6	84.4
Literate (%)	82.4	65.3	68.2
Cultivators (%)	31.8	41.1	39.5
Landless (%)	25.9	36.8	35.0
Workers with work for less than 6 months in the last year	28.2	39.5	37.6
Proportion living in Kachcha houses (%)	69.4	81.7	79. 6
Medium income (in ₹) during the months of work	375	300	305

Living Conditions

In the survey, respondents were asked to rate their relative position in their society. We asked: 'How are your living conditions as compared to others in your village?' Their responses are shown in Table 10.3. As expected majority of them rate their condition to be bad or average; 12.5 per cent say that it is very good. Only 0.8 per cent says that it is very good. Chi-square for difference (Kritzer 1986) reveals that the difference between respondents who attribute poverty to self and those who attribute poverty to other factors is not significant.[2]

Table 10.3

Relative condition of the poor

Condition	*Respondents attributing poverty to self*		*Respondents attributing poverty to other factors*		*Total*	
	No.	*%*	*No.*	*%*	*No.*	*%*
Very Good	3	3.5	1	0.2	4	0.8
Good	9	10.6	54	12.8	63	12.5
Average-neither good nor bad	37	43.5	154	36.6	191	37.7
Bad	26	30.6	173	41.1	199	39.3
Very Bad	6	7.1	36	8.6	42	8.4
Non-Response	4	4.7	3	0.7	7	1.3
Total	85	100.0	421	100.0	506	100.0

X^2 (Very good or good) = .07, X^2 (Average) = 1.4

Ideal Family Size

Population sociologists have conventionally used ideal family size[3] as an important instrument of measuring family size preferences. It has been maintained that it predicts future course of fertility quite well – some evidence from researches in India and abroad that IFS has not been found to be correlated with actual fertility in longitudinal researches has still not lessened its importance as an important academic and policy index of fertility (Westoff, Dishler and Kell 1957). Unlike fertility whose examination requires large sample, ideal family size can be meaningfully studied even in small surveys. This study has collected data on ideal family size and also on ideal family composition. Table 10.4 exhibits the pattern of these data. It shows that mode of the distribution is three (two sons and a daughter) followed by two and four. As much, it is a good sign. Conforming to the norm of three will imply a rather slow growth of population. But the aspects of family composition and presence of son-preference makes it an absurd entity. Statistical theory of stopping rules shows that when mortality is high ideal family of two sons and one daughter causes an average family to be of size five and not three (Sharma 1985). It may be noted that even among the rural poor there are at least 22 per cent respondents who will be satisfied with only two children (one son and one daughter).

Chi-square for difference shows that the difference in proportion of respondents reporting three or less children as ideal between respondents who attribute poverty to self and those who attribute poverty to other factors is statistically not significant, i.e. it may emanate simply from sampling fluctuation. As shown elsewhere (Sharma 1989), caste and education are correlated significantly with ideal family size in this study, having no interaction effect. Thus, we may conclude that the variations in ideal family size among the poor are largely due to caste and educational differences and not due to locus of control. This also shows that spread of education effects all castes uniformly.

Table 10.4

Distribution of respondents ideal family size and composition

Ideal family size (children)			*Respondents attributing poverty to self*		*Respondents attributing poverty to other factors*		*Total*	
Total	*Sons*	*Daughter*	*No.*	*%*	*No.*	*%*	*No.*	*%*
0	0	0	—	—	4	1.0	4	0.8
1	1	0	1	1.2	6	1.4	7	1.4
1 irrespective of sex			—	—	1	0.2	1	0.2
0	0	0	22	25.9	90	21.4	112	22.1
1	1	0	1	1.2	9	2.1	10	2.0
2 Sex composition not mentioned			—	—	1	0.2	1	0.2
4	2	2	43	50.5	210	49.9	253	50.0
4	3	1	—	—	3	0.7	3	0.6
4	4	0	3	3.5	1	0.2	4	0.8
Five or more children With no sex preference			1	1.2	1	0.2	2	0.4
Five or more children With son-preference			2	2.4	8	1.9	10	2.0
Non-response			5	5.9	22	5.2	27	5.3
Total			85	100.0	421	100.0	506	100.0

x^2 (IFS>3) = 127

Attitude Towards Family Planning

Mere reduction in IFS is not enough. To be able to exercise their free decision to limit family size to two–four children, people must have favourable attitude towards family planning and also have knowledge of effective family planning methods. It is, therefore, quite disappointing to observe that in this study many respondents (6.3%) are still against family planning and many more hold an ambivalent position (indicated by high incidence of indifference or non-response) (Table 10.5). It is again shown that respondents who attribute poverty to self and those who attribute poverty to other factors do not differ significantly with respect to attitude towards family planning. Contrary to expectations more respondents who attribute poverty to self are clearly against family planning than the respondents who attribute poverty to other factors.

Table 10.5

Percentage distribution of respondents by attitude to family planning

Attribute	*Respondents attributing poverty to self*		*Respondents attributing poverty to other factors*		*Total*	
	No.	*%*	*No.*	*%*	*No.*	*%*
Favourable	65	76.5	323	76.7	388	76.7
Against F.P.	11	12.9	21	5.0	32	6.3
Indifferent/Others	—	—	55	13.1	55	10.9
Non-response	9	10.6	22	5.2	31	6.1
Total	85	100.0	421	100.0	506	100.0

X^2 (Favourable) = .002

Knowledge of Family Planning Methods

Many national surveys have created a myth that knowledge of family planning methods is widespread. The present study showed that only about 70 per cent have knowledge of at least one method[4] (Table 10.6). Almost all of them know about sterilization. A little less than half of the respondents know about condoms. Other methods are reported by less than 18 per cent. Also, there is no significant difference between respondents who attribute poverty to self and those who attribute it to other factors with respect to knowledge. However, relatively more number of respondents among respondents who attribute poverty to self have known about condoms and IUCDs.

Table 10.6

Percentage distribution of respondents by knowledge of family planning method

Method	*Respondents attributing poverty to self*		*Respondents attributing poverty to other factors*		*Total*	
	No.	*%*	*No.*	*%*	*No.*	*%*
Sterilization	59	69.4	288	68.4	347	68.6
Condoms	45	52.9	191	45.4	236	46.6
IUCD	18	21.2	70	16.6	88	17.4
Oral Pills	5	5.9	31	7.4	36	7.1
Self Control/Others	3	3.5	35	8.3	38	7.5
At least one	60	90.6	298	70.8	358	70.7
Non-Response	12	14.1	117	27.8	129	25.5
No knowledge	13	15.3	6	1.4	19	3.8

X^2 (At least one method) = .001

Causes of High Fertility

In response to a question on whether the poor derive any benefit from large family almost all the respondents answered in negative – that is, no benefits accrue to the poor from high fertility. Then, why do the poor have larger family than the non-poor? Table 10.7 presents respondents answers to this question.

Researchers working in the less developed countries have often explained high fertility in villages in terms of contribution of large family to household economics. Theoretical economists have also envisaged a positive correlation between income and fertility as children may be treated as consumers durables. Even when empirical correlations are found to be negative, they are not considered to be inconsistent with the basic theory; negative correlations simply indicate that the high income families may desire children of higher quality. Our data reveal that positive contribution of large family among the poor may be a myth. Answers to the indirect question on causes of large family affirm that not advantage but carelessness, lack of planning, religiosity, illiteracy, ignorance, lack of knowledge of family planning methods may be the real reasons behind high fertility. On this question also differences between respondents attributing poverty to self and to other factors are marginal.

Table 10.7

Causes of high fertility among the poor

Attribute	*Respondents attributing poverty to self*		*Respondents attributing poverty to other factors*		*Total*	
	No.	*%*	*No.*	*%*	*No.*	*%*
Illiteracy/Ignorance	15	17.7	72	17.1	87	17.1
Lack of entertainment	7	8.2	43	10.2	50	9.9
Belief in God/God sends them	15	17.7	70	16.6	85	16.8
Economic contribution/ Contribution to labour power	8	9.4	32	7.6	40	7.9
Carelessness or lack of planning	12	14.1	88	20.9	100	19.8
Lack of knowledge about F.P. methods	9	10.6	76	18.0	85	16.8
Power	1	1.2	—	—	1	0.2
Others	6	7.0	36	8.6	42	8.3
Non-response	12	14.1	4	1.0	16	3.2
Total	85	100.0	421	100.0	506	100.0

This study does not examine acceptance of family planning. There are some reasons for this: (a) family planning acceptance in the field was low; (b) the responses did not appear to be reliable and emphasis or probing on this matter could cause errors even in responses on other items; and (c) people were generally reluctant to discuss it with young investigators. It was noticed that family planning programme has not become peoples movement. Respondents consider it to be a government's programme in which government's and not their own interest is involved. Some family planning workers of that area confided that when they approach the people they are told that people will do it (i.e. accept sterilization) only if houses or other tangible benefits are granted to them after that. Government departments must partly be blamed for this state of affairs. To fill up their quotas workers in some departments have not only delivered age proved incentives but also added to that something from their own pocket.

Conclusion

As such, reproductive goals among the rural poor in Uttar Pradesh are undergoing transition from natural to volitional and limited fertility. Yet preference for sons and specific desires for sons and daughters make it difficult to implement the ideals. Our data shows that with respect to IFS, the poor are differentiated. The factors behind this differentiation are caste and education and not psychological. By and large people are in favour of birth control but their knowledge of effective methods leaves much to be done. People have heard about sterilization and nirodh but their knowledge of working of contraceptives and human physiology is rather poor. It may be said that above empirical ending that respondents attributing poverty to self and to other factors do not differ significantly must be interpreted with caution. The concept of fate in the Indian tradition is not same as the Western world has. In India, a typical theory of life makes people attribute outcome of their past efforts to fate or chance and yet they prepare themselves seriously for the future. Thus, with respect to future the gap between respondents attributing poverty to self and those who attribute poverty to other factors may be inconsequential.

Our observations show that in village life today crude physical power is more vital than economic power. It may be said that *lathi* (stick) is central to survival. One may not get labour even by paying double the market wage rate. One's power in society depends on *lathis* one has under his command. *Lathis* add to political power also which has permeated all areas of life. We have seen above that the respondents have not mentioned it. Rather they explained high fertility among the poor in terms of ignorance and carelessness. But in the rural context these facts are not inconsistent. Insecurity breeds alienation (helplessness) and that kills efficacy, planning, and initiative producing this syndrome. In this context family planning work requires some fresh thinking both on the part of academicians and social workers. Following are some theoretical lessons:

(a) The poor in rural Uttar Pradesh have been marginalized. Their locus of control is external and this explains their lack of enthusiasm for family planning. The degree of marginalization depends on caste and education.

(b) Malthusian pressure rather than social mobility aspirations may motivate people to control fertility in the future.

(c) Lack of social security is a major factor behind poor acceptance of family planning.

Notes

1. Development status of villages was fixed by the author himself on the basis of socio-economic conditions and infrastructural facilities (Sharma 1989a/b/c?).
2. The Chi-square for difference has only 1 degree of freedom. Thus, at 5 per cent level of significance, Chi-square higher than 3.84 is significant.
3. In social demography family size refers to number of own children and not to total number of family members.
4. If the percentage is calculated only for target couples the figure will be somewhat higher than shown here as the sample includes some who are not currently married couples whose wives are in reproductive ages.

References

Bang, T., 1984, *Kisan Mazdoor ki Loot,* Varanasi: Sarva Seva Sangh Prakashan.

Bose, A., 1988, *From Population to People,* Vol. 2, Delhi: B.R. Publishing Company.

Census of India, 1981, *Fertility and Child Mortality Estimates of Uttar Pradesh,* Occasional Paper No. 7 of 1987, New Delhi: Office of the Registrar General of India, Demography Division.

Gordon, M., 1964, *Assimilation in American Life,* New York: Oxford University Press.

Gupta, R., 1986, *Fertility Tables: Uttar Pradesh,* Series 2i, Part VI A & B, New Delhi: Office of the Registrar General of India.

Khan, M.E., 1999, *Management Information Systems in Health and Family Welfare Programme,* Baroda: Operations Research Group.

Kritzer, H.M., 1986, 'Using Categorical Regression to Analyze Multivariate Contingency Table', in B.D. Berry and M.S. Lewis-Back (eds), *New Tools for Social Scientists* (157–165), New Delhi: Sage Publications.

Kumar, A., 1983, *Slums: A Socio-Demographic Study,* Lucknow: Jaithosh Parkashan.

Mahadevan, K., 1989, *Population Dynamics in Indian States,* New Delhi: Mittal Publications.

Misra, B.D. and A.K. Sharma, 1978, 'Family Size Norms in India', *The Economic Times,* Bombay, June 8.

Misra, B.D., Ali Ashraf, Ruth Simmons and George Simmons, 1981, *Organizations for Change: A Systems Analysis of Family Planning in Rural India,* New Delhi: Radiant Publishers.

NIHFW, 1989, Report of a Study of Health Service Delivery System in a District (2 Parts), New Delhi: National Institute of Health and Family Welfare.

ORG, 1988, *Indian Population Project-II in Uttar Pradesh, Vol. 3: Findings from Endline Survey,* Baroda: Operations Research Group.

Rao, K.C., 1974, *Studies in Family Planning,* New Delhi: Abhinav Publications.

Saksena, D.N. and J.N. Srivastava, 1980, *Child Mortality and Family Formations Patterns in Lucknow City,* Lucknow: Population Research Centre.

Saseendran, P.P. and Mithilesh Kumar, 1989, *Determinants of Family Welfare Programme in U.P.: An Analytical Study of CPR and Socio-Economic Variables*, Lucknow: Population Centre.

Sawhney, Nirmala and N.C. Roy, 1990, *An Assessment Study of Coverage and KAP of Immunization Programme in Uttar Pradesh*, Lucknow: Population Centre.

Sawhney, Nirmala, Mithilesh Kumar and P.P. Saseendran, 1990, *Socio-Religions Dimensions of Family Welfare Programme: A Case Study of Muslim Elite*, Lucknow: Population Centre.

Sharma, A.K., 1990, 'Reproduction Among the Rural Poor in Uttar Pradesh', *The Journal of Family Welfare*, 34 (3): 51–60.

——, 1985, *Social Inequality and Demographic Processes*, New Delhi: Mittal Publications.

——, 1989a, *Developing the Underdeveloped: A Socio-Psychological Study*, New Delhi: Northern Book Centre.

——, 1989b, *Issues in Social Demography*, New Delhi: Mittal Publications.

——, 1989c, 'What the Poor Think About Their Poverty', *The Indian Journal of Social Work*, 50 (1): 171–182.

Sharma, Lallan, 1990, *Socio-Demographic Characteristics of Slums in Eastern Uttar Pradesh: A Fact Finding Study*, Lucknow: Population Centre.

United Nations, 1985, *Levels and Trends of Fertility in India*, Asian Population Studies Series, 62–B, New York.

Westoff, C.F., E.C.M. Dishler and E.L. Kell, 1957, 'Preference in Size of Family and Eventual Fertility Twenty Years After', *American Journal of Sociology*, 62 (5): 491–497.

11

Technology for Human Reproduction and Construction of Gender

A Case Study in Amritsar City

JASMEET SANDHU AND ANURADHA

Human reproduction is a social process. It is the social character of human life and of human reproduction that differentiates human societies from those of animals (Michaelson 1981: 18). Human reproduction is social in the sense that it takes place mostly within a social institution, i.e. marriage, and leads to family formation. It is also attended to and assisted by others. Whenever a couple enters into a marital union in India, there are social pressures on them to reproduce. If there is delay, intentional or unintentional, it is a matter of concern for others. The kin, the neighbours and the friends express concern, ask questions and give suggestions. Different folk techniques as well as the modern techniques are suggested to the couple.

Human reproduction is social for yet another reason, i.e. that there is human intervention in the case of human reproduction. Ever since times immemorial, different folk techniques and social practices are used to restrict family size and to strike a balance between population and resources. With the availability of the modern methods of contraception there is greater human intervention in human reproduction.

A reproduction revolution began some 200 or more years ago when medical men took over the management of child births (Stacy 1992). In the last few decades, the amount of human intervention has increased to such an extent that it is now possible to bring about conception outside the human womb, i.e. in a petridish or a test tube, to determine the health status of the foetus in the womb and even to operate upon the foetus in the womb itself. Very soon the genetic counselling and genetic engineering would become a routine medical process.

With increasing human and medical intervention, family formation is no longer a simple natural process. It has become a highly complicated process, involving more than just two individuals and, thus, has acquired greater implications.

In this article, the focus is on the use of one such reproductive technology, i.e. antenatal tests, for the purposes of family formation and its implications for social construction and maintenance of gender. In India the use of such tests has become popular in the last two decades. These tests are not only used to detect the abnormalities of the unborn foetus but also to determine the sex of the unborn child. As a matter of fact these are mainly used for the second purpose rather than the first one. The diagnosis of sex of the foetus then helps the couple to decide whether to retain the unborn child or to get it aborted. This has resulted in the ugly practice of female foeticide. In fact, these antenatal tests have come to be known as 'Sex Determination Tests' because of the popular use these tests are put to. Many scholars, social philosophers, feminists and thinkers have expressed their opinion on the use or abuse of this technique and its resultant consequences. Here, an effort is made to empirically know the perspective of the women who undergo these tests and then to understand the use of this technology for gender construction, and its maintenance. Some of the questions to be answered are: who are the women who go in for such tests and why? How do they make decisions to make use of this technology and how do they subjectively feel about the use of such tests in reproduction? And, finally the implications of its use for gender relations.

Sex Determination Tests

In the medical terminology, there is nothing like sex determination tests. However, there are numerous antenatal tests such as chorion villus sampling, Amniocentesis, ultra sonography, etc. These tests were introduced to detect genetic disorders and abnormalities in an unborn child. With the help of these tests, it is also possible to determine the sex of the unborn child. In India, these antenatal tests were popularized as sex determination tests because of the strong preference for sons. Singh and Jain (1985) conducted a study to understand the knowledge of the people about Amniocentesis technique. The study revealed that the test was more popular in North India than in South India because of strong son preference in the North and most of the people knew about this test as a sex determination test rather than the one to detect genetic abnormalities in the unborn child. This popularity of the tests led to the mushrooming of the clinics offering this test.

The use of such tests led to the rise of another phenomenon of female foeticide or 'extermination of female foetuses' (Arora 1996). This phenomenon generated a controversy in India in terms of its moral, religious, social and demographic implications and this led to the enactment of certain laws against their use in some Indian states like Punjab and Maharashtra.

Scholars are divided in their opinion regarding the consequences of these tests. Some scholars look at the utilitarian aspect and consider these tests as a useful technique for limiting the family size. For instance, Balasubrahmanyan (1982) considers sex selection as an example of science responding to natural human preferences and according to her, sex determination technologies and their use reflect the philosophy of the world population control establishment. Similarly, Kumar (1983a) also feels that as a consequence of use of such tests ratio of the females would decline and that will improve their status in the society. She further adds that long term effects of sex selection tests are frequently exaggerated and no research has been conducted on the pattern of Indian preferences for children.

On the other hand, Dube (1983 and 1997) points out that some social problems and certain kinship systems are associated with the imbalances in sex ratio resulting from the use of sex determination tests. Pimpley (*The Indian Express* 1989) considers these tests as discriminatory against women who already are under-privileged sections of the country. Similarly, Arora (1996) is also highly critical of these tests. According to her, their use is victimizing for women. She is of the view that these technologies have adverse side effects for women, have disturbing implications for social relations and their proneness to be misused is quite high, but, still these have acquired people's approval because vested interests ensure the production and reproduction of patriarchy which 'supports the use of such a technology and help in the construction' and maintenance of gender inequalities. In India, women are eulogized for their reproductive role. In the absence of a dominant role in production, their reproductive role becomes the most important role. Reproduction technologies help the women in performing this role as per the role expectations of the society, community and family and in the process maintain the existing gender realities.

Although, the existing literature has tried to bring out the manifest and latent consequences of use of antenatal tests, yet there is a lack of empirical studies in this area. The questions which need to be answered empirically are: who are the women who undergo these tests? How do they decide about the use of these tests? How do they perceive these tests and what are the implications of these tests for the existing gender relations? These questions are being delved into in the next section.

Method and Discussion

The study was exploratory in nature and was conducted with a view to ascertain he perspective of those urban women that undergo sex determination tests and use technology for their family formation. Fifteen profiles of women in an industrial suburb of Amritsar city in Punjab, who had undergone sex determination tests to beget sons, were collected. Snowball technique was used to gather information.

Socio-Economic Profile

Socio-economic and demographic profile of the respondents is presented in Table 11.1. It reveals that the respondents belonged to both the Sikh and the Hindu religions and were between 22–36 years of age. Except for one, all were literate and most of them had education up to Matric level. They were from castes like Brahmin, Khatri, Jat, Mehra and Majhbi. They were married between the age of 14–25 yrs. Their husbands were engaged in petty trade, shop keeping, fanning and in petty jobs. Their monthly household income ranged between ₹ 700 and ₹ 4,000. They had two–four living children. Together they had 26 daughters and 14 sons. Most of them had one son, one daughter or one son and two daughters.

A look at the profile reveals that the women who adopted this reproduction technique were in the prime years of their reproductive span. They were literate and belonged to lower middle and middle classes. They were from high, middle and low castes. They had two or more living children but had more living daughters than sons.

Table 11.1

Socio economic and demographic profile of the respondents

Characteristics	*Response category*	*Number*
Religion	Hindu	11
	Sikh	4
Age (in years)	21–25	5
	26–30	4
	31 or more	6
Caste	High	13
	Low	2
Educational back ground	Illiterate	1
	upto Primary level	2
	upto Matric	12
Age at marriage (in years)	upto 18	5
	18–20	5
	More than 20	5
Monthly household income (in ₹)	700–1,500	3
	1,500–2,300	9
	2,301 or more	3
Type of household	Joint or Extended	9
	Nuclear	6
No. of living children	2–3	12
	More than 3	3
Sex composition of the children	1 Son 1 Daughter	7
	1 Son 2 Daughters	3
	1 Son 3 Daughters	1
	2 Son 2 Daughters	2
	2 Daughters	1
	3 Daughters	1

Preference for Sons

An effort was made to know whether these women preferred children of a particular sex or not with a view to understand the use of sex determination tests in the context of their value system. Eleven out of the fifteen women considered sons as more important than daughters. The remaining four did not state any such preference but remarked that children of both the sexes would complete a family. Those who expressed preference for sons stated the reasons like continuation of the family name and support during old age. All of them stated that it was absence of sons which motivated them to make use of the latest available technology to beget them. No woman underwent this test during her first pregnancy. It was only after these women had produced daughters that they made use of this reproductive technology to have sons in their families. None of them had a living son when they considered the use of this technology. In fact, eight of them had two or more living daughters and seven of them had one living daughter. This shows that although the women had imbibed the traditional values concerning sons and, therefore, attached great importance to sons yet, none of them got the sex of her first child tested. It is only after having one or more living daughters that they wanted to have a son because they felt or were made to feel that their family was incomplete. So, they went in for this modem reproduction technique only to complete their families.

Knowledge and Use of Sex Determination Tests

Although except for one all the respondents were literate and there were many clinics offering such tests, yet respondents' primordial ties were the main source of information about them. Six of the respondents came to know about these tests from their neighbours, three from their relatives, two from friends and two from their husbands. Only two respondents read about these tests in the newspapers. So, social networks played an important role in imparting information to the respondents and in motivating them to 'take another chance' to beget sons and to complete their families. These networks also reflect the larger community's perspective and, thus, reinforce the desired behaviour.

After being aware of these tests, the decision to actually accept this technology was not entirely that of the respondents. Rather, they were impelled and forced to undergo these tests by their husbands and in-laws. In as many as 10 cases, the women went through these tests because of the fear of divorce or remarriage by their husbands. They were made to realize that if they were to lead a happy married life then they were expected to bear the sons for the perpetuation of the family name. Some of the respondents stated that they were beaten and/or ill treated by their husbands and were threatened of divorce and remarriage by their husbands as well as in-laws. It was under such familial and societal pressures that they decided to undergo these tests. Only in five cases the husband and wife jointly decided to undergo these tests, i.e. without any threats or pressure but as a conjugal unit.

Views About Family Planning and Foeticide

All the women were aware of the modern methods of contraception and 13 of them had also used various methods at different stages of their married life. Only two women stated that they did not use any such method as they wanted to bear children at close intervals so as to complete the task of child bearing early in their lives.

When asked to express their views concerning female foeticide as a consequence of use of sex determination tests, 13 of them favoured and tried to justify sex selective foeticide. Some of them also mentioned that female foeticide involves health hazards and is also burdensome physically as well as psychologically and yet they were against producing 'unwanted' daughters to be ill treated later on. Some of them also considered female foeticide as a method of family limitation and, thus, tried to justify and legitimize their action. They were of the view that this way they can limit their family size and can also have the children of both the sexes in their family.

Views Concerning Ban on these Tests

Respondents were asked to express their views on whether the sex determination tests should be banned or not. Twelve of the fifteen respondents clearly stated that these should not be banned, two women wanted these tests banned and one respondent did not take a clear stand. Those who were in favour of these tests argued that with the help of these tests women can produce sons as is expected from them in the family and society and can escape being the victims of their husband's and in-laws' wrath and cruelty. They opined that a son is a must in a family and with the help of the tests they can have sons and can also limit their family to two as is being popularized by the government. In the absence of sons people will go on having daughters till they get a son as has been happening earlier, when this technique was not available. In the process of justifying they were trying to legitimize the existing gender roles and realities.

Some of the respondents even expressed the view that rather than banning the tests, the government should keep check on their misuse or should lay down some conditions for their use. They were of the opinion that such reproduction techniques would free the women from the drudgery of producing unwanted children. Some even commented that these tests would improve the status of women because their number will decline and they will be more valued and preferred.

Those who wanted the tests to be banned expressed the opinion that this practice leads to a 'sinful' practice of female foeticide and more and more women are being pressurized rather victimized by their family members to adopt this technique to beget sons.

Conclusion

The above discussion clearly confirms that women have a low status in the patriarchal Punjabi society. Begetting sons is the chief expectation attached to the role of a married woman. She gets status in the in-laws family only after she produces a son for the family. If she fails to perform her expected role then she is ridiculed, ill treated, beaten and threatened of divorce and remarriage by her husband and in-laws. Although it is a well-known fact that not a woman but a man is responsible for the sex of the child, yet the woman always gets the blame and is victimized. The urban women studied, thus, had no sons, and therefore some of them were made to feel guilty for not performing the expected role. According to them, they found some respite with the availability of these tests. These women used this technique only to complete their families and a family is considered incomplete without a son. These tests were not used to produce more than one son or only sons. The urban Punjabi women by and large have imbibed the two children, i.e. one male and one female, family norm. Strong son preference and low status of women prevailing in the society is the main cause of popularity of these tests. The decision to accept this technology is not always that of the couple but 'others' especially the relatives of the husband and neighbours and friends also play a significant role in this regard. The onus of producing a son is on the women, whether with or without the help of this latest reproduction technology. Here is one more evidence to the view that people accept a particular technology only if it blends well with the existing social structure. This particular technology of sex determination blends well with the existing social structure and its acceptance testifies to the prevailing son preference and low status of women and it also helps furthering the prevailing social reality. Although the whole procedure is highly burdensome for the women both physically as well as psychologically, yet, the women have by and large welcomed this technology and want to make use of it in order to perform the roles expected of them and, thus, escape victimization. In its absence they feel they would be burdened with unwanted pregnancies and births and that according to them is neither going to solve their personal problem or familial problem nor the national problem?

The women feel that this particular technology helps them build 'small and ideal' families and frees them from the drudgery of carrying unwanted and numerous pregnancies leading to numerous childbirths. The women are living and are enacting their roles, in a particular social structure and it is here that they make sense of their lives. In that context their perspective is an extension of the prevailing social perspective. In a patriarchal set-up there is little scope for individual agency for women and they acquire a gendered perspective. Thus, women identify the needs of the patriarchy as their own needs. Others, mostly women, in that regard, socially condition them. They feel guilty for having not produced a son because of their gendered role socialization and low self-esteem. They are pressurized to use technology to beget sons. In this way, they become victims of these technologies and, thus, unconsciously construct and reproduce gender inequality and help in its perpetuation.

Thus, the use of technology for reproduction becomes discriminatory and victimizing for the women and helps in the construction and maintenance of gender inequality. The technology itself may be gender neutral but its acceptance, the way it is being put to use and its popularity reflect a strong gender bias and perpetuate the same.

References

Arora, Dolly, 1996, 'The Victimizing Discourse: Sex Determination Technologies and Policy', *Economic and Political Weekly*, XXXI (7): 420–424.

Balasubrahmanyan, V., 1982, 'Medicine and the Male Utopia', *Economic and Political Weekly*, XVII (43): 17–25.

Dube, L., 1983a, 'Misadvantages in Amniocentesis', *Economic and Political Weekly*, XVII (8): 279–280.

——, 1983b, 'Amniocentesis Debate Continued', *Economic and Political Weekly*, XVII (38): 1633–1635.

——, 1997, *Women and Kinship: Comparative Perspective on Gender in South and Southeast Asia*, Tokyo: United Nations University Press.

Kumar, D., 1983a, 'Male Utopias or Nightmares', *Economic and Political Weekly*, XVII (3): 61–64.

——, 1983b, 'Amniocentesis Again', *Economic and Political Weekly*, XVII (24): 1075–1076.

The Indian Express, 1989, 'Ban on Sex Tests Not Favoured', May 10: 3.

Michaelson, K. (ed.), 1981, *And the Poor Get Children*, New York: Monthly Review Press.

Sandhu, J. and Anuradha, 1991, 'Sex Determination Tests and Women', *The Tribune*, Sunday Reading, April 14.

Singh, G. and S.V. Jain, 1985, 'Opinion of Men and Women Regarding Amniocentesis', *The Journal of Family Welfare*, 3: 13–15.

Stacy, Meg (ed.), 1992, *Changing Human Reproduction*, London: Sage Publications.

Section III

Emerging Challenges

12

Changing Demographic Structure and its Implications for Old Age Support

A Situational Analysis in the Developing Countries

P.K.B. NAYAR

In 1959, it was estimated that there were 200 million people aged 60 years and over in the world (eight % of the population). This is expected to increase six-fold to 1.2 billion (i.e. 14%) in 2025. The size of world's elderly has been growing for centuries; what is new is the rapid pace of ageing. The increase in the 60+ population in the industrialized countries of Europe and North America and of late Japan (for convenience they may be termed 'more developed countries' or MDCs) and the rest as less developed countries (LDCs) generally has outpaced the total growth of their elderly population in recent decades. In the LDCs, the growth rate of the elderly accelerated sharply after 1960 and is subsequently higher than that of the world's population of all ages. LDCs as a whole are ageing much faster than the MDCs. In 1995, the world's 60+ population increased by more than 12 million persons and nearly 80 per cent of this increase occurred in the LDCs (US Census Bureau 1986a); 37.5

per cent of the elderly population lives in LDCs of Asia (China 17.9%, India 8.2% and Japan 9.6%). The global age structure would change its strictly triangular shape to that of a dome by 2025 if projected decline in fertility and mortality in the LDCs proceeds as expected. There are several important features in this shift in age structure that have important bearings on old age security.

Change in Sex Ratio

The steady increase in the gap between male and female life expectancy, first experienced in the MDCs, has now become a global phenomenon in recent years. Table 12.1 shows this picture. In the MDCs, this has reached almost its peak. Many LDCs are close on the heels.

The pace is rather slow in India and Bangladesh but the experience of the state of Kerala in India where male and female life expectancy at birth is 69 and 74, respectively, would indicate the direction of the wind in this matter.

As women in most countries live longer and marry men older than themselves, they are much more likely to be living alone without a spouse in old age (UN 1991a). In Morocco 76 per cent, India 70.3 per cent, Indonesia 64.3 per cent and Malaysia 60.0 per cent old, 60 plus women are widows (UN 1991b). Widowhood and loneliness make women particularly vulnerable in old age (feminization of ageing). Men by comparison are more likely to have wives to care for them in old age and have greater possibilities of marrying younger women if widowed (UN 1991b). Women not only age without a spouse but with much reduced socio-economic support as well.

Intra-Group Differentials in Ageing

Within countries, different age groups within old grow at different rates. Over time, the elderly population itself may grow older on an average (increase in median age of the old and in

Table 12.1

Male and female life expectancies in selected MDCs and LDCs

Countries	*Life expectancy*			
	At birth		*At age 60*	
	Male	*Female*	*Male*	*Female*
More Developed Countries				
France	74.2	82.2	19.7	25
United Kingdom	74.7	79.6	18.8	22.5
Russian Federation	58.3	71.7	13.1	18.6
USA	73.6	99.2	19.3	22.9
Canada	74.6	80.9	19.4	24
Japan	77.2	84	21	26.4
South Korea	70.6	78.1	17	21.5
Less Developed Countries				
China	66.8	70.5	15 .5	18.4
India	60.1	61.4	15.3	17.5
Bangladesh	58.6	58.26	15.1	15
Malaysia	69.6	74.6	16.5	18.8
Thailand	65.8	72	—	—
Sri Lanka	70.9	75.4	—	—
Philippines	63.1	66.7	15.5	17.3
Brazil	64.7	70.9	16.6	19
Mexico	69.5	75.5	16.7	21.3
Argentina	68.4	75.6	18.7	22.4
Chile	72.4	78.4	—	—
Egypt	65.1	69	15.5	1 7.3
Tunisia	69.6	73.1	17.7	19.1
Zimbabwe	58	62	14.9	16.7

Source: UN, Demographic Yearbook 1999, Table 22.

index of ageing) as a larger proportion survives to age 75 and beyond. In many countries of the world, the oldest old (75+) are the fastest growing segment among elderly. They constituted 23 per cent of the world's 60+ in 1996; 30 per cent of them were in MDCs and 19 per cent in the LDCs. In that year, 43.6 per cent of the world's oldest old lived in just four countries: China 17.9 per cent, India 8.2 per cent, USA 11.8 per cent and Japan 5.7 per cent (absolute numbers). In terms of the percentage of the population, Sweden has the highest proportion, 8.5, Norway has 7.6 and United Kingdom and Denmark 7.2 each while Bangladesh, Myanmar, Indonesia and Jordan have less than 1 per cent oldest old in their population. The numerical growth and increasing heterogeneity of the oldest old challenge social planners to seek further information about this growing group since the oldest old consume disproportionate amounts of health and long-term care-services.

Age Composition

Another characteristic of the change in age structure is the shift in the proportion of working and non-working age groups. Here, the tendency is for the working age group (15–64) to hold a more or less stable position, and for the two non-working groups (child 0–14, old 65 and above) to change positions. Actually the shift has been from child to the old.

Table 12.2 gives the global scenario in this regard. The effect of this process is that more and more health and social welfare inputs will have to be transferred from the care of children whose number is falling to the care of the aged whose number is rising. The health and welfare needs of the two categories are different. The need for paediatric hospitals will decrease and the need for geriatric hospitals and age-care programmes including old age homes will increase. Governments in these countries will have to redistribute their financial outlays to meet these changed needs appropriately.

Table 12.2

Population composition 1990 and 1999

		Below 15	*15–64*	*65 and above*
World	1990	32.0	61.0	6.0
	1999	29.7	63.4	6.9
North America	1990	21.0	66.0	12.0
	1999	21.3	66.1	12.6
Europe	1990	19.0	66.0	13.0
	1999	17.4	67.8	14.7
Africa	1990	45.0	51.0	3.0
	1999	42.5	54.3	3.2
Asia	1990	32.0	62.0	4.0
	1999	29.9	64.2	5.9
Oceania	1990	26.0	64.0	9.0
	1999	25.3	64.8	9.9
Latin America	1990	35.0	59.0	4.0
	1999	31.6	63.0	5.4

Source: UN, Demographic Yearbook 1999.

Change in Dependency Ratio

A related concept in this regard is the dependency ratio which expresses the level of burden of children and old people on the working age group. Table 12.3 gives information on this item. It clearly indicates the magnitude of burden. One feature revealed in this table is that while there is increase in the child dependency ratio, there has been an increase in the old dependency ratio over time. Here, the LDCs are pursuing the path followed by the MDCs earlier.

The table shows that in the MDCs there will be 57.5 per cent dependents (children 28.8, old 28.8) in 2025 as against 54.8 per cent in 1950 (children 43.0, old 11.8). In contrast, there will be smaller number of dependents (52.2%) in the LDCs. In fact, there is a steep fall in the LDC ratio of dependents, from 71.5 in

1950 to 52.2 in 2025. The changes in the child and old population ratios are even more spectacular. In the case of child dependency, there will be a fall from 65 in 1950 to 39.9 in 2025. In the case of old, the figures for the two periods are 6.6 and 12.2. Clearly, the increase in the old dependency ratio is significant to warrant serious attention of the policy makers.

Table 12.3

Change in dependency ratios 1950, 1990 and 2025

	1950	*1990*	*2025*
Developed regions			
Total	54.8	50.4	57.5
0–14	43.0	50.4	28.7
65+	11.8	18.1	28.8
Developing regions			
Total	71.5	66.7	52.2
0–14	65.0	59.3	39.9
65+	6.6	7.4	12.2
Asia			
Total	68.7	61.0	48.5
0–14	61.8	52.9	34.3
65+	6.8	8.9	14.3
Africa			
Total	84.3	92.5	67.4
0–14	78.5	86.7	60.7
65+	5.8	5.9	6.7
Latin America			
Total	78.2	72.7	49.3
0–14	72.0	64.9	35.6
65+	6.2	7.8	13.8

Source: Peter Lloyd-Sherlock, *Old Age and Urban Poverty in the Developing World*, 1997.

The needed transfer of resources and inputs from child care to old care has additional qualitative and hidden dimensions than are indicated by mere changes in numbers. Old people require proportionately more health care and social service inputs than children as the per head cost of maintaining an old person compared to that of a child is higher. The period of childhood is fixed and known while the period of old age is moving and unknown (though predictable on the basis of existing parameters).

The Economic Factor

Another point that needs consideration in the context of rapid ageing in the LDCs is the mounting welfare needs of the old in countries where existing provisions are grossly inadequate. The social security needs of a population can be accessed from two indices, among others labour force participation and population living in poverty. In the LDCs not all persons in the working age group are actually employed. A sizable number of women are outside the work participation stream though they work as housewives. Another significant number of persons, both women and men, are not employed due to several structural and market factors. A small work participation rate coupled with low level of technology as in the case of the LDCs would result in low GNP and low per capita income. Similarly a high proportion of the population living in poverty also would indicate the need for major welfare intervention by the government. Table 12.4 gives details regarding work participation rate and poverty level for selected LDCs.

It is fairly well established that among the poor, the old constitute a disproportionately larger number and among the old, women outnumber the men (feminization of ageing).

Table 12.4 shows that women are fewer in work participation than men with the exception of Tanzania (where they are equal to men). In seven states, participation of women is only 50 per cent of men. Since in many of these countries patriarchic forms of inheritance prevail, women will have neither any property nor any savings to provide for the rainy day. Cain (1991) found that by and large all existing property laws and customs protect male assets. Given the low level of work participation and high level of poverty, even the capacity of the young to take care of their old is severely circumscribed. All these point to the need for massive public assistance programme for the elderly in the LDCs.

Table 12.4

Labour force participation and people living in poverty

Country	*Labour force*		*Participation (1996)*	*People in poverty*
	M	*F*	*Total*	*(1990)*
Egypt	51.2	21.7	33.7	21
Sudan	46.8	25.8	36.6	67
Kenya	54.1	463.	51.6	46
Tanzania	52.6	50.1	51.4	19
Argentina	54.8	24.2	38.0	20
Brazil	59.9	32.0	39.2	63
Chile	54.6	25.4	34.3	34
Mexico	54.3	25.1	32.6	55
Venezuela	52.0	26.6	34.2	53
Bangladesh	56.6	43.5	47.1	53
China	63.7	55.6	54.9	12
Bhutan	58.4	38.9	51.5	90
India	57.4	28.6	43.6	48
Indonesia	56.2	37.2	39.5	14
Malaysia	50.2	30.1	38.5	19
Philippines	51.4	31.1	39.	52
Sri Lanka	54.6	30.1	36.8	32
Thailand	63.8	55.2	52.2	34

Source: ILO: *World Labour Report 1997–98*, Tables 6 and 7.

Health Aspects

In many of the LDCs the basic health needs of the population have not been met in spite of the 'Health for All by 2000' programme. Nor is there indication that this will be achieved in many countries within a minimum time frame. One aspect in the health situation in the world is the epidemiological transition in the MDCs. In these countries, there is a shift in the morbidity pattern, a movement from communicable and debilitating diseases like fever, diarrhoea and infectious diseases to non-communicable and degenerative diseases like cardio- and cerebro-vascular diseases, malignant neoplasm, diabetes, hypertension and the likes. However, the more developed among the LDCs are also experiencing the latter syndrome and are faced with the double burden of coping with both disease patterns simultaneously. Old age morbidity falls in the second category even though in the LDCs debilitating diseases also take a high toll from the old. Old age diseases are mostly chronic, treatment is prolonged and costly and cure is elusive. Incidence of illness is higher among the poor than the rich and this, coupled with the high cost of treatment, compels many of the victims to forego proper treatment. Government provisions for the health in most LDCs are inadequate and private hospitals are beyond the reach of the poor. There is no health insurance for all in these countries.

Problem in a Nutshell

The findings in the preceding section may now be summarized.

1. Elderly population in the LDCs is growing at a faster rate than the general population. Within the elderly, the oldest old are growing at an even more rapid rate than the total population and even the young old.
2. Sex ratio among the old is strongly skewed towards women and most old women are widows.
3. Dependency ratio is also rising in the direction of old age dependency. Its qualitative dimension is even more significant than its numerical dimension.

4. Work participation in the LDCs is generally low and women's work participation is even lower; in majority of countries this accounts for only one-half of that of men.
5. Since the laws of inheritance in many LDCs are generally tilted against women and since a sizable proportion of women are unemployed, the majority of women spend their old age in poverty and misery.
6. Since women live longer and since women's illnesses are non-fatal, they undergo longer period of morbidity in old age than men.
7. In many LDCs there are sizable segments of the population who are living in poverty and so in old age, both men and women, more women than men, spend old age in destitution.

Implications for Old Age Support

Income Security

The implications of changes in the demographic structure on old age security are serious and unique and have to be examined in the above context. Until recently, both the absolute number and proportion of the old in the population of LDCs were quite small and there were traditional modes of management of old age care and problems of old age. The traditional society in general and the traditional family in particular provided near-adequate social security to the old. Problem arose because the size of the older population increased rapidly, the period of old age expanded and the pattern of old age morbidity also changed. At the same time, changes unfavourable to the old happened in the family and society. The nuclear family emerged as with its individualistic orientation of members, general poverty increased and old age care and security became beyond the capacity of the family alone to manage. In this state of affairs, intergenerational relationships moved from primary group orientation to secondary group orientation and from affectivity to neutrality. Studies conducted in different parts of the world (Nayar 1990) indicate that even where the old are taken care of by kins there is in most cases a *quid pro quo* involved. Where the old contributes to the family pool or performs services that are desired by the kins, the care given is always warm and satisfying; where old do not have anything to contribute in money or services, the attitude and care from the young become lukewarm or even cold. This happens in case of poor, sick and disabled old, with women having to bear the double burden of neglect, and abandonment. It is here that the need for public support in terms of social support or security arises. Even the affluent sections among the old have problems which they or their family cannot solve and the state will have to step in. In the MDCs, almost the entire population is covered by social insurance programmes of one sort or another. In many other parts of the world, especially in the more developed among the LDCs, old age pension schemes have become social institutions though their nature and coverage have differed from country to country. The goal in most public old age pension schemes is to provide all qualifying individuals with an income stream during their retirement years which is (1) continuous, (2) adequate, (3) constant in terms of purchasing power, and (4) capable of maintaining the socio-economic position of the retired in relation to that of the active population. Since World War II, public pension plans have played an increasingly important role in providing retirement income to older people in most countries. The number of countries with an old age/disability/survivor's programme has increased from 33 in 1940 to 170 in 1999 (US Department of Health and Human Services 2000). The World Bank estimates that the existing formal public programmes provide coverage for approximately 30 per cent of the world's 60+ population with some 40 per cent of the working age population making contribution towards that support (World Bank 1992). A caveat is necessary about these pensions when we deal with the LDCs. In the LDCs, formal pension programmes cover only around 10 per cent of the population, mainly government servants and those retiring from organized sector industries. In the unorganized sectors, only very few countries have any form of formal old age support of which the most important is the destitute old age pension programmes. However, they do not cover the entire needy population and the amount does not qualify under any of the objectives mentioned earlier about the existing pension programmes. In India, the model pension amount under this scheme comes only a little more than US$2.00. Even when meagre, there is need to extend the scheme to all the qualifying persons in the LDCs and to peg the amount of pension to basic needs.

Health Needs

Next to economic security, health needs assume priority. Indeed, for the old, health is as much a concern as income support. This is because old age is a period when all latent diseases manifest themselves; most old age diseases are chronic, the treatment is prolonged and costly and there is no complete cure and most people cannot afford the high cost of geriatric health care. All these are serious concerns for the old man looking with anxiety towards his last days. This is irrespective of economic status but for the poor there is an additional amount of frustration and indifference coming out of anxiety and helplessness. Here again, the formally protected categories (retirees from government and organized sector) have some medical insurance but the other groups have to spend from their limited income and the income less and marginalized groups are left high and dry. Government health care programmes aided by UN and other international agencies exist in most countries but they are unable to give even partial health insurance to their people even though they provide medical assistance to the poor free or at subsidized rates. The problem in health care in the LDCs is that a sizable segment of the old are marginalized in the manner of health; government services are inadequate, the aged cannot afford private health care because it is highly expensive. Further, governments in most LDCs are not in a position to invest massive inputs in the health care sector.

Globalization and Ageing

The problem is going to be accentuated with the globalization of the pharmaceutical industry and the tendency for privatization of health care. The unprecedented spread of civil society organization in many LDCs and the insistence of international agencies and donor countries on sharing government programmes with them will tend towards further privatization of health care system. Emerging trends in the LDCs indicate that the phenomenon of medicalization of ageing and commoditization of the aged already thriving in the MDCs are finding fertile soils in many LDCs. If this spreads, the non-affluent sections of the society stand to lose.

The medicalization of morbidity will result in yet another outcome. The supreme emphasis on clinical solutions to all morbidity problems will de-emphasise much of the social and behavioural causes of many of the modern degenerative diseases including HIV/AIDS which is coming up as a major killer disease today. Also, many old age problems like visual and sensory impairment and joint pains require primary care and preventive measures as long run strategies of cure.

The effort of the non-clinical experts and social scientists is on compression of morbidity which means postponement of diseases to the very last stage of life. It is argued that illness and many other health-related problems of the elderly are influenced by potentially modifiable social factors such as (a) income, (b) safe environment, (c) social support system and (d) public financing for health. These will reduce the period of morbidity and when death finally occurs, this will be mainly due to degenerative causes. The supreme role of the government in providing basic infrastructural amenities and minimum health needs and in acting as a cushion against economic hardship preventing health care among the poor has to be underscored in both promotive and preventive health care. Some sort of community shared health insurance, like the one existing in China, will be an affordable answer to the problem of health care and health insurance of the poor.

Building Social Network

There are two more areas where strengthening of the existing social institutions could give added support and security to the aged, viz., strengthening the social network and support system on the one hand and involving them in public decision-making bodies. Building social network should begin from the family which should facilitate the maintenance of the social support and network system to rehabilitate the old in their former social surroundings. Social network has been found to go a long way in removing loneliness caused by several factors and in increasing the personal worth of the old (Nayar 1990). Government could facilitate the mobility of the old by proper transport concessions.

Voice in Decision-Making Bodies

Societies are moving from more authoritarian structures to a more democratic way of life. In the traditional society, the authority of the old was an established factor. In the modern society and even in the family, the word of the old does not have smooth sail. In some families the old are not even informed, let alone consulted, about the matters that vitally affect them. It may not be possible to re-establish the old climate of authority of the family head, but it will not be difficult to provide representation for the old in elective bodies at the different levels, especially at the local village community level where the old will not only feel recognized but their voice is also being heard. This is an insurance against loneliness and neglect and it will act as a strong integrating factor.

Note

This is a paper presented at Session I, Round Table 'Demography, Ageing and Social Support' of Research Committee 11 Sociology of Ageing at the XV World Congress of Sociology, Brisbane, 7–13 July 2002.

References

Adeokun, L.A., 1984, *The Elderly All Over the World*, Paris: International Centre of Social Gerontology.

Cain, Mead, 1991, 'Welfare Institutions in Comparative Perspective: The Fate of the Elderly in Contemporary South Asia and Pre-industrial Western Europe', in K. Pelling and R. Smith (eds), *Life, Death and the Elderly: Historical Perspectives*, London: Routledge.

Estes, C.L. and Associates, 2001, *Social Policy and Ageing: A Critical Perspective*, London: Sage Publications.

Goldstein, M.C., S. Schules and J.N. Ross, 1983, 'Social and Economic Sources Affecting Intergenerational Relations in a Third World Country: A Cautionary Tale from South Asia', *Journal of Gerontology*, 38 (6).

ILO, 1997, *World Labor Report 1997–98: Industrial Relations, Democracy and Social Stability*, Geneva: ILO.

Kending, H.L., A. Hashimoto and L. Coppard (eds), 1992, *Family Support for the Elderly: The International Experience*, New York: Oxford University Press.

Kinsella, Kevin, 1988, *Ageing in the Third World*, International Population Report Services No. 79, Bureau of Census, Washington, D.C.: Center for International Research.

Lloyd-Sherlock, Peter, 1997, *Old Age and Urban Poverty in the Developing World*, Suffolk, UK: The Ipswitch Book Co.

Nayar, P.K.B., 1990, *The Old Old and Oldest Old: A Study of Their Problems and Needs*, Trivandrum: Centre for Gerontological Studies.

Schultz, J., 1993, 'Generations: International Challenges of an Aging World', *Generational Review*, XVII (4).

Selby, P. and M. Schechter (eds), 1982, *Aging 2000: A Challenge for Society*, Hingans: Sandoz Institute for Health and Socio-Economic Studies and UNDIESA.

Sen, Kasthuri, 1994, *Ageing Debate on Demographic Transition and Social Policy*, London: Zed Books Ltd.

Tout, Ken, 1986, *Ageing in Developing Countries*, London: Oxford University Press.

Tracy, Martin B., 1991, *Social Policies for the Elderly in the Third World*, Westport: Greenwood Press.

United Nations, 1991a, *The World Ageing Situation*, New York: UN.

——, 199b, *The World of Women 1970–1990: Trends and Statistics*, New York: UN.

——, 1992, *Demographic Yearbook 1991*, New York: UN.

——, 2000, *Demographic Yearbook 1999*, New York: UN.

US Department of Commerce, 2001, *An Ageing World 2001: International Population Reports*, Washington: US Department of Commerce.

——, 1986a, *Global Aging into the 21st Century*, Washington: US Department of Commerce.

——, 1986b, *Population and Health Transitions*, International Population Reports, Washington: US Department of Commerce.

US Department of Health and Human Services, 2000, *Social Security Programs Throughout the World*, Washington: US Department of Health and Human Services.

Wenger, C., 1989, 'Support Networks in Old Age: Constructing a Typology', in M. Jeffries (ed.), *Growing Old in the 20th Century*, London: Routledge.

Williamson, J.B. and F.C. Pampel, 1993, *Old Age Security in Comparative Perspective*, New York: Oxford University Press.

World Bank, 1992, *World Development Report: Development and Environment*, Washington, D.C.: World Bank.

13

Problems of the Aged in Unorganized Sector

A Case Study of Old Age Pensioners in Haryana State

AMARJIT MAHAJAN

Does the term 'old age' conjure up images of frustration and pity; sickness and poverty; despair and senility or maturity and serenity; warmth and responsibility? Age effects are developmental, that is, they are ontogenetic or systematically related to time (Goulet and Baltes 1970). Aging is a process. If the term 'aging' is used descriptively, it refers to a sequence of changes across a life span (Eisdorfer and Cohen 1980). Though aging is a multidimensional process and it is not easy to determine when it starts, yet for the purpose of understanding it can be discussed at four levels: biological, psychological, sociological or situational and socio-psychological or behavioural.

Biological aging refers to anatomical and physiological changes that occur with age. For example, the capability to reproduce offspring is a phenomenon associated with biological aging. Changes in sensory-motor performance, muscle strength, brittleness of the skeletal structure, visual acuity, reaction time and balance are other examples of biological aging which may influence attitudes and behaviour (Deering et al. 1983). The biologists are of the opinion that aging begins when growth and development stop (Harris 1980). The critics, however, opine that biological aging would differ from individual to individual because they have different medical history, live and work in different situations, have different levels of income and nutrition and have varied psychological and social problems.

Psychological aging is being studied in terms of changes in the central nervous system, in sensory and perpetual capacities and inability to organize and utilize information. Psychologists are also concerned with changes in personality and with external behaviour of the aging person. In short, psychological aging consists of a general decline in the mental abilities that accompany old age. Harris (1980) is, however, of the view that older people who continue to exercise their brain and grow mentally actually delay or reverse their psychological aging.

Sociological aging refers to changes in social roles. The most frequently cited crises that are related to social aging include: loss of spouse, vulnerability to disease, compulsory or voluntary retirement, loss of income, reduction or loss of status, loss of authority, birth of a grandchild, reduction in social contacts and assumption of 'terminal sick role'. Social aging, as distinct from biological and psychological aging, refers to that stage in the life span of an individual that is designated as old age by the group (Bhatia 1983). Every society, however, has its own conception of aging. It is the society which defines age related roles, privileges and expectations.

Psychosocial aging refers to systematic changes in personality, needs, expectations and behaviour as well as changes in status and roles and changes in relation to others (Deering et al. 1983). The behavioural aspect of aging refers to meanings an individual associates to the above noted changes and the efforts he makes to bring about internal and external adjustments to the perceived changes. Disengagement from active, social and economic life may result into a feeling of meaninglessness and loneliness.

Attempts have also been made to combine different conceptions of aging. Some people use their chronological age as a criterion for their own aging, whereas others use such physical symptoms as failing eyesight or hearing, increased tendency to fatigue, decline in sexual potency. Still others assess their aging in terms of their capacity for work, their output in relation to the standards set in earlier years, their lack of interest in competing with others, lack of motivation to do things, or a tendency to reminiscence and turn their thoughts to the past rather than dwell on the present or the future (Grienleigh 1955).

It is difficult to define old age precisely because the term 'old' is used to describe persons of different ages depending on the circumstances and on the area of operation. In spite of these difficulties, a person is treated as having become old on the basis of certain criteria. The villagers have certain criteria that they apply in describing a person as old. The loss of teeth, gradual weakening of eyesight, pain in knee joints, shrinking of skin, the appearance of grey hair, unsteadiness in walking and talking the arrival of a grandchild, particularly the offspring of the son, are very important criteria (Marula Siddaiah 1966). For the present study the criterion of chronological age has been used to identify the aged persons. Men of 60 years and plus and women of 55 years and over were treated as old persons.

The literature on aging suggests that the problems associated with the aged are the outcome of physical, psychological, social, religious, environmental and cultural factors (Pyrek and Snyder 1978). In short, it is being emphasized that for the purpose of dealing with the problems of the aged, one should adopt 'whole-person-system' models. Further, the problem of the aged has to be understood in their social and cultural contexts.

In the traditional Indian society, the old persons occupied position of prestige, privilege and power. It was believed that, with age, man acquired knowledge and experienced and his variegated life experiences would help the younger generation in a number of ways. The *varna-ashrama-dharma* scheme of life also associated honour and respect to the old persons. The *Grihya Sutras* ordained filial piety. Such religious dictates gave the old persons in the Indian society authority, security and honour and enjoined upon the son to look after his old parents. Failure on the part of sons was considered a serious demerit and earned social opprobrium (D'Souza 1982). Such a system provided economic, social and emotional security to the aged.

The institutions of joint family, caste and village community, which formed the building blocks of traditional social structure in India, ensured economic security and high social status to the aged. The demographic factors and the processes of industrialization and democratization have brought about radical changes in the basic institutions affecting adversely both economic security and social status of the aged.

The Indian population which was 361.1 millions in 1951 rose to 683.8 million in 1981, an increase of 89.36 per cent in three decades. The increase is attributed to a better control over famines, epidemics, etc. and better health services. Decline in death rate results into increase in life expectancy. The last three decades (1951–1981) indicated a much sharper increase in the growth rate of the total population and the 60+ years age group is most remarkable during the period 1961–71. The rate of growth of the aged population in this decade was 31.46 per cent as compared to 24.75 per cent for the total population. The similar pattern of differential growth rate is expected during 1971–81. The increase of life expectancy and population growth rate has important implications for understanding the position of the aged in India (Ranade 1977).

From the life cycle perspective there are two significant stages in which the culture more often accepts dependency needs – at the beginning and at the end (Cantor 1980). It is, therefore, expected that the present working generation must support the preceding working generation. However, increase in the proportion of the aged persons in the total population implies an overwhelming expansion of the non-productive segment (Monk 1980). Taking into account the rise in the longevity of the population and fall in infant and child mortality, the dependency ratio of the population (dependency ratio being the ratio of those in the age groups of 0–15 years and 60+ years, to those who are in the non-dependent age group of 15 to 60 years) is bound to increase. An important implication of this kind of development is that the position of the aged is expected to worsen because the natural tendency would be to divert the limited resources of the family towards the upbringing and development of the younger generation and this will be more in the case of lower segments of society (Ranade 1984).

Such a situation would demand from the aged either to learn to live with deficit or make good losses which they are bound to suffer. Pfeiffer (1977) is of the view that successful adoption during old age involves replacing some of the losses, remaining active and making do with less. What are some of the losses to which old persons should adjust? The most frequently cited crises that are related to loss include: widowhood, increased vulnerability to disease, pain and hospitalization, loss of income, reduction or loss of status, reduction or loss of physical, sensory and cognitive functioning and preparation and pre-occupation with death and dying (Butler and Lewis 1973; Palmore 1973).

The concept of deficit has little meaning independent of an accompanying idea of what it is to be adapted. A deficit may be redefined as the result of what society chooses to use or not to use, believe or not believe. Indeed, in some primitive cultures, older women become very powerful witches and older men lovable story tellers (Eisdorfer and Cohen 1980). If we measure the assets of the elderly rather than their deficits, would the pattern of research assume a different shape?

The demographic changes do not necessarily imply that the old persons assume a status of dependency and play no role or contribute nothing to the family. There is substantial reciprocity between generations – the flow of assistance is not one-way. The elderly, in turn, help children when there is an illness in the family, provide child care and give advice about child rearing and major family decisions.

In addition to the demographic variable, D'Souza holds changing Indian structure responsible for old age problem. He opines: 'In the emerging industrial social order the economic, political and value system are undergoing a fundamental change, altering basically the social structure. The new industrial economy, political democracy and rationally oriented value system support one another and together tend to alter the social structure in a radical manner' (D'Souza 1971).

The increasing tendency for the family to break up into smaller units even when the parents are alive has increased the vulnerability of the old. The traditional roles and personal security provided to the elderly under the extended family structure is seriously threatened by increased mobility and urbanization (Maldonado 1975). Similarly, the forces of modernization have adversely affected the status of the aged. It is being contended that the status of the aged declines with technological and economic development because the status in the industrial set-up is achieved based on individual's acquired formal skills and education. As the industrial society is oriented towards the individual rather than the group, the aged are bound to be rendered useless generating a feeling of meaninglessness in them.

A few studies, however, indicate that family and kin still play an important role in providing economic and social security to the aged (Desai and Naik 1971; Vatuk 1980). Most of these studies refer to the middle and higher classes where the aged owned the means of production or had sufficient economic resources. In the lower segments of society, the working generation is not able to extend social and economic support to the aged (Chowdhry 1968), not because they do not want to but because they cannot afford. It is this segment which becomes most vulnerable with increasing age. Positive association has been found between aging and disability among those engaged in occupations of lower prestige (Haber 1970). The aged cannot be treated as forming a homogeneous category. The problem of affluent old would be completely different from that of the poor old persons. As the present study is confined to the poor aged, we shall highlight some of the major problems they are likely to face.

Economic needs are the most crucial problems of the poor aged. In discussing the economic aspect of aging, the subjects of economic roles, economic status and policy issues can be separated for convenience. The economic roles of the elderly are important in a variety of ways. They determine possible income flows. They establish the individual in the society and they involve meaningful use of time. The poor old persons, due to their poor health and lack of economic resources, have to withdraw consequences thereof. In discussing economic status, we have to keep in mind the health status because chronic ailment along with malnutrition are important threats to economic status of the individual. The interaction of health status and economic status is especially noteworthy in old age and particularly among those whose livelihood depends upon their physical labour.

The problem of the old persons engaged in the unorganized sector, particularly those with low and irregular wage/income is more acute because they were not able to allocate finances for old age. When they were physically fit and were working they lived hand-to-mouth. As such the question of saving did not arise.

In spite of adverse economic and health conditions, they continue to work till their physical strength allows them. When they fail to earn their livelihood the old persons perceive the informal network of kin (particularly children) as the most appropriate source of social support. It is to this network that older persons turn first. Only when assistance from the informal system is unavailable or kin can no longer absorb the burden of support (because they themselves are almost below the poverty line), do older persons turn to the formal organizations, like government old age pension scheme, for support.

The aged in the Indian society have always constituted problems at some levels but it is only recently that they have begun to represent a major social problem. What makes aging and the aged a social problem is its recognition by society as an important aspect of behaviour that needs attention. The recognition is the direct outcome of changed age pyramid, value system and withdrawal of support system from the family and community. The Constitution of India recognises the duty of the state towards the elderly persons. Article 41 provides: 'The State shall within the limit of economic capacity and development, make effective provision for securing the right to work, to education and to public assistance in cases of unemployment, old age, sickness and disablement'. Keeping in view the Constitutional provisions the state of Haryana has shown concern for the care of the old persons, particularly those who have no means of support and no kin to look after them, in the shape of working out an old age pension scheme.

As stated earlier, aging is a multi-dimensional problem. Therefore, it becomes essential to have an overview of the basic facts about the aging population, the aged and the society. To satisfy such an objective, several studies are needed. Unfortunately we are still at a point where much knowledge is anecdotal and most of the research studies had very limited empirical base. The present study does not claim to advance a theoretical framework on aging. The scope of the present study is limited to identifying the problems of the aged poor who were working in the unorganized sector and are now dependent upon the state's old age pension.

The present study was limited to the recipients of old age pension scheme in the state of Haryana. The only information we have about the beneficiaries is that they are poor, destitute, old and residents of the state of Haryana (formal requirements for entitlement to old age pension), but have no information regarding their socio-demographic background, needs and problems so that priorities could be established. Keeping in view the knowledge available on aging in India, particularly on the poor segments of society and the scope of study, an exploratory design of research was adopted. With the help of such a design we would not only be able to know their background which has forced them to assume the status of destitute but also highlight the needs and the problems of the aged poor.

Universe and Sampling

On 31 January 1980, there were 10,146 recipients of old age pension in the state of Haryana who were treated as the universe of the study. From the records of the Department of Social Welfare of Haryana state, a comprehensive list of all the recipients district-wise was prepared (based on the alphabetical order of the name of the district). It was decided to take 8 per cent sample of the recipients based on simple random sampling technique. In this way every twelfth case was included in the sample which came to 812 cases. The complete addresses of such cases were recorded for the collection of core data with the help of an interview schedule. However, when these cases were contacted at their respective places, it was found that there were 15 cases that could not properly listen and respond to the questions, 27 cases were not available at the official addresses as they had gone somewhere. We were left with 770 cases who were interviewed but on scrutiny it was found that 21 interview schedules were filled partially because the recipients did not cooperate. In this way, we were left with 749 cases, on which the study is based. Out of the total sample, there were 369 males and 380 female recipients and with regard to their rural-urban background, 499 cases were from the rural areas and 250 cases were from the urban centres.

Findings

The present study is limited to old age pensioners in Haryana. It is, thus, obvious that the respondents under study come from lower economic strata. Under these circumstances one may argue that the description of the background is meaningless because the study is confined to a particular group. It is admitted that only those persons are entitled to old age pension whose income from all sources does not exceed a particular limit. It does not, however, explain their social background, caste affiliation, previous economic status. Further, such an information also helps us to know the family composition and the extent to which such a basic institution provides safeguards to the economically inactive, poor and aged persons.

Education, occupation and income are the variables which are generally taken to determine the economic status of an individual. Let us first look at these attributes of the respondents. Almost all the pensioners, irrespective of their sex and rural urban background, were illiterate which would have direct bearing on the type of occupations in which they were engaged in when they were in the labour force.

No doubt, the pensioners were professing various types of occupation but to put them in a tabular form, different occupations have been grouped into certain prestige categories. Grade I includes occupations like priesthood and owner cultivator; grade V includes petty shopkeeper, goldsmith, *halwai* and blacksmith; Grade VI includes labourer, carpenter, barber, hawker, domestic servant, weaver, potter, tailor, *chhaj* maker etc.; and grade VII includes occupations like sweeping and shoe making [D'Souza's (1969) occupational prestige categories have been used].

Majority (72.36%) of the pensioners were engaged in occupations of Grade VI followed by Grade VII, Grade I and Grade V occupations. The fact that most of the pensioners were engaged in occupations of Grade VI, which includes occupations like labourer, hawker, carpenter, etc. and hence were leading a life from hand to mouth. Such type of occupations is physically strenuous. In other words, the individual can do this type of work only when he/she is physically strong and stout. The pensioners are quite old to do such type of work. Most of the respondents were engaged in this type of occupations which had no provision for retirement benefits and had also lost physical strength to carry on these occupational activities. Under these circumstances, there was no alternative with them except to depend upon government assistance. An interesting feature of the data is that a large percentage of the women were also in the labour force when they were physically fit. Such a situation further supports the contention that people of only lower economic status seek and depend upon governmental assistance. In short, prior to their inability to earn their livelihood most of the pensioners were engaged in occupations of lower prestige and with low economic returns. This would become clearer if we look at their past earnings.

Majority (81.17%) of the pensioners were having an income not more than ₹ 200 per month. When we look at the high income side, we notice a progressive decrease of the percentage of people earning higher income.

The low income of the majority of the pensioners irrespective of their sex can be attributed to the nature of their occupational activities. As stated earlier most of the pensioners were engaged in occupations like agricultural labourer, hawker, vegetable vendor, etc. which implied that their earnings were very meagre and had no permanent source of income even when they were physically fit to work. We found no marked difference in the rural and urban areas with regard to past income which is attributed to the nature of their occupations. Out of those who had no income, women were overrepresented, because of the fact that a few women who were engaged in family occupation had no independent income as such. The description of education, occupation and income of the pensioners indicates that they belonged to the lower strata of the society. Let us now look at the social attributes.

Indian society is hierarchically divided based on caste system. In most of the studies conducted in India, the caste status was found to be congruent with the economic status. As the present study is confined to the pensioners who belong to lowest economic status, one may expect that they would also belong to those castes which have lowest social prestige.

The caste composition of the pensioners has been classified into four categories: (1) Higher castes comprising *Brahmin, Khatri, Jat* and *Rajput* (2) Middle ranging/trading castes comprising *Arora, Aggarwal, Kamboj, Saini, Mahajan,* etc. (3) Backward/Artisan castes comprising *Teli, Lohar, Maniyar, Jhimar, Kumbhar, Nai, Sonar,* Carpenter, etc. and (4) Scheduled castes comprising *Balmiki, Ramdasia, Majhbi Sikh, Dhanak, Chamar, Harijan,* etc.

The tabulation of data helps us to conclude that old age pension benefits are not being availed by the members of lower castes only but upper caste members also get such benefits due to their lower economic status. Our results, therefore, do not support the contention that caste status and economic status are co-terminus. We notice that scheduled castes were overrepresented in comparison with the higher castes. Nevertheless, there were 25.23 per cent pensioners of the higher castes among the total sample of the pensioners. If we combine the columns 5 and 6 (Backward and Scheduled Castes) and term them as 'lower castes', we would notice that majority (57 54%) of the pensioners belonged to the lower castes. If we arrange the pensioners according to their caste background, we would find that middle ranging and trading castes occupy the bottom position, that is, they had least number among the pensioners. Their least representation can be attributed to their strong familial links as well as their efforts to continue earning on their own instead of depending upon the welfare policies of the government or other voluntary organizations. It can, thus, be concluded that poverty is not confined to the lower castes but transgresses the boundaries of caste. In short, caste status and economic status were not found to be congruent.

Tabulation of data on marital status indicates that in comparison with the widowers, the percentage of the widows was quite high (50.14% male and 78.94% female). This type of difference is mainly due to the age differences at marriage. According to the Indian traditions, the bride is always younger to the bridegroom. So it is natural that the older dies first.

Another important feature of the marital status found from tabulation was the significant percentage (21.14%) of the single male respondents. In case of the female pensioners, there was only one spinster. Such a difference indicated adherence of the women folk to the social norms which prescribed that each adult person must get married. The deviation on the part of male pensioners may be due to their poverty or something else. We need not pay more importance to this aspect because it is not within the purview of our study. However, the unmarried have certain specific problems. As they do not have wives/children to bank upon at their old age, their problem is more acute than others which demand a separate study.

The problem of the aged can well be appreciated if we look at their family composition. Such information would help us to know the role being played by the family institution in the present day Indian society. In case we find a large number of the pensioners living alone it would imply that they have been discarded by their kinsmen at a time when the old persons need the help of their kinsmen most.

Approximately, 53 per cent of the pensioners were found to be living alone which implies that they were left to their own fate by their kinsmen. They were either abandoned or their spouses and children were no more to look after them. More than 10 per cent of the pensioners were living with their spouses and another 7 per cent had dependent children also with them.

Out of those who were dependent upon their married sons and other relatives, more male pensioners (25.20%) were living with them than the female pensioners (17.36%). On the other hand, more female pensioners (6.63%) than the male pensioners (2.72%) were living with their married daughters or sisters and other affinal kinsmen. Though their number was quite small, a few pensioners were found to have been accommodated in the joint family system.

One of the important features of the data is contrary to the general belief that old persons are taken care of by their children or kinsmen that only 219 (28.17%) old people were looked after by their kinsmen. If we look at the different reasons given for such a situation, we notice that economic factors in the shape of dependency and inability to work were the main forces of strained relationships. It was not only because of the inability of the aged to earn but also because of the low earning capacity of other members. Additionally. a few respondents had health problems demanding constant care which other members could hardly provide because of their being involved in a struggle for survival. Under such situations how could the family members assume additional burden? The results do not support the general contention that the aged persons unnecessarily interfere in the family affairs. In short, it was the lack of economic power in the hands of the pensioners in particular and their families in general that was responsible for their being abandoned by their kinsmen. In short, family system in the present day Indian society and particularly among the lower segments of the society has failed to come up to its role obligation in providing protection and congenial atmosphere to the aged, forcing them to assume the status of a destitute.

The respondents were asked to arrange their different problems in rank order. The most acute problem was given rank number one and the least important was placed at the bottom. Most of the respondents (65.55%) perceived health problem as more serious than the psycho-social problem. Economic needs and problems were placed at the bottom of the rank order. The respondents felt that it was their bad health which was the root cause of their economic dependency and helplessness. As most of them were engaged in those occupational activities which demanded greater physical strength, they could not continue such activities due to their poor health. It was, thus, natural for them to assign greatest importance to health problems.

Further, inability to have full and balanced diet due to poor economic conditions, coupled with biological aging process, has adversely affected their health. The common ailments were diabetes, asthma, tuberculosis, cataracts, pain in joints and abdomen, etc. Out of the 95 physically handicapped pensioners,

65 were orthopaedically handicapped, 15 cases were blind and 11 were deaf and dumb. There were four cases who were suffering from multiple disabilities. It was encouraging to rind that approximately 44 per cent of the pensioners were free from any serious health problem but most of them were the victims of malnutrition, adversely affecting their mobility and physical strength.

We would be interested to know as to what they did throughout the day. In other words, what is their routine?

Tabulation of data draws our attention to a large number of pensioners (approximately 54%) who were not engaged in any constructive activity, they would sit idle, gossip and play cards. Such a situation can be attributed to the lack of any programme for utilizing their time, their poor health and lack of zeal on their part. In the absence of any alternative, they somehow kill time and face boredom.

It is encouraging to note that more than one-third of the pensioners (more women than men) were still engaged in some type of odd jobs and were free from boredom. To understand their work activity the following points would be in order:

1. The percentage of the pensioners spending their time on work activity should not be construed as their active engagement in economic activity for the purpose of earning. They were mostly engaged in family work or domestic functions. As such their time was being fruitfully utilized.
2. The difference in percentage of the male and female engaged in work could be attributed to the nature of work. Activities like utensil cleaning, sweeping and mopping the residence, helping the ladies in domestic functions are exclusively done by the females. We have seen earlier that the number of widows was more than the number of widowers. Apathy on the part of kinsmen, lack of support from the relatives and poverty might have forced these widows to take up odd jobs in the households of others. By such activities they could supplement their meagre pension amount. Approximately 5 per cent of the pensioners were found to be taking care of the younger children of the

households. The above analysis helps us to conclude that barring the handicapped, most of the pensioners were physically active but were not doing anything because of lack of alternative activities suiting their health.

Concluding Remarks

The problem of the poor aged can be dealt with at two levels. First, in checking the circumstances which force them to become destitute and secondly, in evolving suitable alternative work activities. The study highlights the fact that family in the lower segments of society no more acts as a support system to the aged persons. This demands that alternative support systems have to be evolved. Most of the respondents were engaged in occupations of low prestige in the unorganized sector and had no retirement benefits. It is, therefore, suggested that some provisions in the shape of Provident Funds or other retirement benefits should be worked out even for those who are engaged as self-employed and in the unorganized sector. The study also reveals that most of the pensioners were free from serious ailments but due to lack of alternative work activities suiting their health, they were forced to become destitute. It is, therefore, suggested that with the help of voluntary associations some programmes should be worked out so that their time is fruitfully utilized and the old persons also get a sense of belongingness relieving them from economic hardship, boredom and idleness. In short, unless serious thought is given to the problem of those working in the unorganized sector, the problem would remain perennial and a stage would come when the state government would not be able to meet the growing demands.

References

Bhatia, H.S., 1983, *Aging and Society*, Udaipur: Arya Book Centre.

Butler, R.N. and M.I. Lewis, 1973, *Aging and Mental Health*, St. Louis: Mosby.

Cantor, M.H., 1980, 'The Informal Support System: Its Relevance in the Lives of the Elderly', in E.F. Borgatta and N.G. McCluskey (eds), *Aging and Society,* London: Sage Publications.

Chowdhry, D. Paul, 1968, 'The Aged and the Infirm', in *Encyclopedia of Social Work in India,* Vol. I, New Delhi: Government of India.

Deering, M. et al., 1983, *The Aging Worker,* New Delhi: Sage Publications.

Desai, K.G. and R.D. Naik, 1971, *Problems of Retired People in Greater Bombay* (Mimeo), Bombay: Tata Institute of Social Sciences.

D'Souza, V.S., 1969, *Social Structure of a Planned City,* New Delhi: Longman.

——, 1971, 'Changes in Social Structure and Changing Roles of Older People in India', *Sociology and Social Research,* 55 (3): 1.

——, 1982, 'The Aged in India', Paper Presented at the World Assembly on Aging, Vienna, 26 July–6 August.

Eisdorfer, C. and D. Cohen, 1980, 'The Issue of Biological and Psychological Defects', in E.F. Borgatta and N.G. McCluskey (eds), *Aging and Society,* London: Sage Publications.

Goulet, L.R. and P.B. Baltes (eds), 1970, *Life Span Developmental Psychology Research and Theory,* New York: Academic Press.

Grienleigh, L.I., 1955, 'Some Psychological Aspects of Aging', *Social Case Work,* 36: 99–106.

Haber, L.D., 1970, 'Age and Capacity Devaluation', *Journal of Health and Social Behaviour,* II (3): 167–182.

Harris, R., 1980, 'Biological and Psychological Factors in Aging', in E.F. Borgatta and N.G. McCluskey (eds), *Aging and Society,* London: Sage Publications.

Maldonado, D. Jr., 1975, 'The Chicago Aged', *Social Work,* 20 (3): 213–216.

Marula Siddaiah, H.M., 1966, 'The Declining Authority of Old People', *Indian Journal of Social Work,* 27.

Monk, A., 1980, 'More on the Economies of Aging', in E.F. Borgatta and N.G. McCluskey (eds), *Aging and Society,* London: Sage Publications.

Palmore, I.E.B., 1973, 'Social Factors in Mental Illness of the Age 51', in E.W. Buss and E. Pfeiffer (eds), *Mental Illness in Later Life,* Washington, D.C.: American Psychiatric Association.

Pfeiffer, E.Z., 1977, 'Psychopathology and Social Pathology', in J.E. Birren and K.N. Schaie (eds), *Handbook of Psychology of Aging,* New York: Litton.

Pyrek, J. and L.H. Snyder, 1978, 'The Human Development Inventory, a Measuring Instrument with Programmatic Implications', in J. Pyrek et al. (eds), *Human Development Assessment and Care Planning*, Minneapolis: Centre for Aging and Human Development.

Ranade, S.N., 1977, *A Study of the Aged in Delhi 1970–74*, Delhi: Delhi School of Social Work.

——, 1984, 'Special Aspects of Aging in India', Background Paper Submitted at the International Federation on Aging: Problems, Priorities and Programmes of Service and Research, New Delhi, November 16–17.

Vatuk, S., 1980, 'Withdrawing and Disengagement as a Cultural Response to Aging in India', in L.F. Christine (ed.), *Aging in Culture and Society*, New York: Bergin.

14

Problems and Needs of Aged Widows

Some Neglected Dimensions

SOBHA B. NAYAR

Widows constitute around 75 per cent of the elderly women (60+) in India. In the 70 + age group, they account for 84 per cent. The proportion is the highest in the state of Kerala in India, where 92 per cent of 70+ women are widows against only 23 per cent above are widowers in that age group. The uniqueness of the problem of aged widows is not only that they are the largest segment of aged women but also that they form the bulk of the elderly population. The traditional role of the widow in India is quite depressing. She is forbidden from wearing ornaments and colourful dresses and also appearing before visitors in the family and participating in auspicious functions. In patriarchal families, when the husband dies, she loses her major source of support-material and morale. The widow is marginalized on every front by both the family and the society. When she becomes old, these problems are added to the problems of aging, i.e. severe fall in income, failing health and inadequate home-care facilities. As life span increases, which is more in the case with women, all these problems get accentuated and the old widow will be faced with an agonizing and prolonged end.

Against this background, a study was conducted in Kerala, India, to find out the present status of widows. Traditionally, women in Kerala had enjoyed a higher status than women in the rest of India. Kerala is leading India in the matter of female literacy, birth rate, death rate, infant and maternal mortality rate and expectation of life at birth. After India's Independence, the state has witnessed a number of progressive reforms aimed at empowering women. Naturally, the effect of these will be reflected in the position of widows, including old widows. Data for the present study was obtained by a re-analysis of the data collected for an earlier study on the problems and needs of the old (Nayar 1998). We took a sub-sample of 240 old widows from among the 320 old women in the study sample. The length of widowhood was as given below:

More than 20 years	26%
10 to 20 years	36%
5 to 10 years	28%
Less than 5 years but more than 2 years	10%

(We did not take widows whose husbands died less than 2 years ago as such respondents would not have an opportunity to experience the full gamut of the problems).

In the matter of age, 58 per cent of the respondents were in the age group 60–69, 29 per cent in the category of 70–79 years and the rest 13 per cent in the age group of 80+. While 15 per cent had no education, 42 per cent had education up to 7th standard, 31 per cent had high school education and 12 per cent had college education. Enquiry into the number of surviving children for the respondents showed that 8 per cent had no surviving child, 17 per cent had only one child, 24 per cent had two to three children, 29 per cent had four to five children and rest 22 per cent had six or more children.

Previous and Present Employment

While 51 per cent did not have any employment during their life time, 22 per cent worked on the farm, 12 per cent held white collar jobs and the rest (15%) had other types of jobs before touching age 60. Currently, only 7 per cent were working. It may be pointed out that the work participation rate for old women (60+) in Kerala, as per the latest census, is 12 per cent. The low rate of work participation of our respondents is indicative of the lack of freedom for widows to work.

Income

The present annual income of our respondents is given below:

No income	38%
Up to ₹ 2000	23%
₹ 2000 to ₹ 4999	21%
₹ 5000 to ₹ 10,000	12%
Above ₹ 10,000	6%

(Note: US$ = ₹ 42)

The source of this income was as follows:

No income	38%
From pension	
(Statutory, destitute and widow's pension)	19%
From land, building and other sources	27%
From own savings, contribution from kin	16%

It will be seen that more than one-third of the widows have no income and another nearly one-fourth had only less than ₹ 200 per month. Altogether, the financial position of 61 per cent of the old widows in our sample has been precarious and they are left to the mercy of their kin for maintenance. It may be pointed out that for an old widow, management of land and collection of rent is a difficult operation and she is dependent on her kin for these services. When kinship bond is not so thick, she could expect some pilferage from this source. Both her old age and widowed status are handicaps in getting a fair deal in this regard. This is more so in the case of failing and sickly widows.

Living Arrangements

The pattern of living of our respondents is given in Table 14.1. The most preferred pattern of residence is with daughter (39%), closely followed by living with son (30%). The daughter's preference is partly due to the hangover of matriliny which prevailed in the state until recently.

Table 14.1

Living arrangement of elderly widows

Staying	*Number*	*Per cent*
Alone	26	11
With daughter	94	39
With son	72	30
With grandson	12	5
With grand daughter	14	7
With other relatives	19	8
Total	240	100

One point which was brought to our attention by the respondents in the matter of residence was that when there is more than one son or daughter (which was the case with 75% respondents), the choice of residence was not always that of the widowed mother but that of the children who used a judicious combination of need for the mother's service in their family and affordability. Out of 12 per cent respondents living with grand children (male or female) 8 per cent have their sons/daughters abroad and the mother is taking care of the grand children and managing the family property. It may be noted that 11 per cent are staying alone. But this includes only 3 per cent of those who have no surviving child. The others do have children but are brought to this situation (living alone) by a variety of circumstances: children are away and the mother does not want to leave the native village and home; problems of adjustability especially with in-laws, love for independence, children do not want to keep the mother with them; quarrel between mother and children, etc. However, all those staying alone have minimum source of maintenance and those who are poor are healthy and could earn a living or manage matters without others' help.

As already stated, our respondents had only limited options in their decision on where and with whom to stay. The widow had to follow the son/daughter who was willing to accept her. In a few cases, at least, children took care of their old mother for reasons other than pure filial obligations. In some cases, it was the mother's wealth/income; in other cases, it was the mother's usefulness to the family – assistance in kitchen work, home management, child care and other household chores. We were told that in such cases when the children grew older, there was a reduction in the amount of consideration shown to the mother. Our study also revealed that attitude and behaviour were also partly related to age and degree of health of the widow. Older widows and those with chronic diseases were treated with less warmth. The widow is generally marginalized in the allotment of space in the house for rest and sleep. In at least 20 per cent of the cases, the respondent was not happy with the arrangement. This was the case even with those who had sufficient personal income for their maintenance. On the one hand, there were social norms regarding with whom a widow should stay in old age; on the other, the widow was unable or unwilling to break the norms because of her limitations as a widow and being old. The amount of dissatisfaction with the living arrangement is reflected in part by the responses given in Table 14.2 on amount of home care and services received by our subjects.

This table shows that among those who were staying with others (children/grand children/relatives), 11 per cent were not satisfied with the quality of food, 7 per cent were dissatisfied with the quantity of food, 19 per cent were not satisfied with the medicines and health care received during illness and 24 per cent were not happy with the care and services received from the members of the household. At least 3 per cent reported domestic abuse in the form of wounding remarks and behaviour especially by grandchildren, denial of urgently needed services, and enforced loneliness. They felt that if their husband was alive, these situations would not have arisen or at least they would have got a sympathizer to share their woes.

Table 14.2

Level of satisfaction of needs of widows living with kin (%)

Item	*Adequate*	*Inadequate*	*Total*
Quality of food	89	11	100
Quantity of food	93	7	100
Medicines and health care	81	19	100
Home care and services	76	24	100

Health Scenario

Since health is a very important concern of an old person, especially when this period in life is marked by multiple disease syndromes, we enquired into the health condition of our subjects who were asked to rate their health status on a five-point scale. Table 14.3 gives the information by age-group. Only 19 per cent reported above-average health and, of these, 12 per cent were in the age group 60–69 and 6 per cent in the age group 70–79. Only 39 per cent of the subjects assessed their health as average. Those who reported below-average health were 42 per cent, of whom 16 per cent considered themselves as in a very bad health. To be sure, 4 per cent of them were in the age group of 70–79 and 6 per cent in the age group of 80+. The incidence of illness among widows found in our larger study (of which the paper is a re-analysis of widow respondents only) was more than that among old women in general. (The figures for all the old women and for widows respectively are: very good 9 and 6; good 16 and 13; average 40 and 39; bad 24 and 26 and very bad 11 and 16). Depression was also more among widows than non-widows in the study (37% and 31% respectively). The major illnesses reported are disorders of the reproductive system, rheumatism, chest diseases, diabetes, blood pressure and visual and hearing impairments. We have reported earlier (see Table 14.2) that the subjects mentioned inadequacy of medical attention received by them. In many cases, regular treatment for diabetes and blood pressure was not taken. Some of them were suffering from cataract. Even though treatment is simple and inexpensive no remedial action was taken and both the victim and the kin considered it as an illness of old age to be borne with. Since the widow had no choice or bargaining power, she suffered all this without complaint. We found that this has created an attitude of pessimism among many widows and much of the cause of their depression could be attributed to this situation of helplessness.

Table 14.3

Subjective assessment of health by respondents (%)

Health status	*Age group*			*Total*
	60–69	*70–79*	*80 Plus*	
Very Good	4	2	0	6
Good	8	4	1	13
Average	26	11	2	39
Bad	14	8	4	26
Very Bad	6	4	6	16
Total	58	29	13	100

Conclusion

In this paper, some of the problems of old widows that are generally assumed away by society have been examined. The problems are rooted in the social values that give women subordinate position in society and to widowed women an even more subordinate position. When a widow becomes old, the pangs of old age with its inseparable companions – poverty or reduced income and ill-health – join her to make the already miserable life even more miserable. A widow's movements, both within the family and outside, are restricted. She is kept out of the main production stream and, thus, denied access to an independent source of income. Other restrictions inhibit her free use of any property that she may have inherited or acquired. All these happen when she needs more of these to compensate for her husband's loss. In physical and social distance, she is outside the inner circle of the family and stands a little away from other members. She is treated as an appendant in family dynamics. A widow is expected to be more modest than a non-widow and this normatively imposed role prevents her from expressing her legitimate needs and aspirations. In our study, we have seen that even in a progressive state like Kerala, she faces discrimination at every point and this has affected her health and well-being. Only specific widow-oriented programmes will be able to break the vicious circle.

References

Audinarayana, N. et al., 1996, 'Living Arrangements of the Elderly Women in Rural Tamil Nadu', Paper Presented at the International Congress on Aging, Trivandrum.

Chen, Marti and Jean Dreze, 1995, 'Recent Research on Widows in India', *Economic and Political Weekly*, September 30: 2435–2449.

Dantavate, P. et al. (eds), 1989, *Widows, Abandoned and Destitute Women in India*, New Delhi: Radiant Publishers.

Desai, N. (ed.), 1988, *A Decade of Women's Movement in India*, Bombay: Himalaya Publishing Co.

Ghosh, S.K., 1989, *Indian Women Through the Ages*, New Delhi: Ashish Publishing Co.

Gulati, Leela, 1994, 'Widowhood and Aging', Paper Presented at the Widows in India Conference, Bangalore, March.

Irudaya, Rajan, U.S. Mishra and P.S. Sharma, 1995, 'Living Arrangements Among the Indian Elderly', *Hong Kong Journal of Gerontology*, 9 (2): 20–28.

Kitchlu, T.N., 1979, 'Profile of Widows in Delhi', *Social Work*, 25 (10): 33–35.

Lal, S., 1972, 'Some Characteristics of the Widows in Rural Society', *Rural India*, 35 (9): 205–208.

Nayar, P.K.B., 1998, *Problems and Needs of the Elderly* (Mimeo), New Delhi: ICSSR.

Sahayam, M.D., 1988, 'Aged Females: The Most Deprived Among the Deprived', *Indian Journal of Social Work*, 49 (3): 269–270.

Singh, G. and S. Gill, 1986, 'Problems of Widowhood', *Indian Journal of Social Work*, 47 (1): 67–72.

Vatuk, S., 1975, 'The Aging Women in India: Self-perception and Changing Roles', in D'Souza (ed.), *Women in Contemporary India*, New Delhi: Indian Social Institute.

15

Changing Parental Exchange System

Among Elderly and their Married Children

ANUPAM BAHRI

Being a parent involves interaction with children throughout the life cycle. This lineage interaction can vary in frequency, quality and type depending on the age, interest and needs of two generations. During early childhood the relationship between parent and the child is constant and largely unidirectional, in that the children are highly dependent on the parents for multidimensional support. During adolescence, the interaction declines in frequency and becomes more reciprocal as both generations influence each other. The relationship at this time may be characterized by conflict over values, beliefs and behaviours. As children grow up and eventually establish their own families they begin to experience interaction from the parental perspective. The relationship with their own parents may decrease further in quantity and quality as new demands are placed on them. Finally, as new demands enter midlife, more dependent on adult child, in this situation the relationship once again becomes primarily unidirectional, but in the opposite direction from that of adult children.

More help is given to parents, especially with respect to health care. However, there may be a continuing socio-culture and economic exchanges in both directions, although whether the direction is parent to child or child to parent may depend on the socio-economic status of the two generations.

Within the family there are physical, emotional, economic and social resources that can be exchanged in a serial or reciprocal manner, depending on the need and stage of life. Serial exchanges tend to be prevalent and generally represent a downward flow of assistance from the older generation to the younger generation because of a sense of responsibility and affection. Reciprocal exchange or two way flow, is most common among the middle old and oldest old generations, especially among the middle class. Johnson (1961) found that 93 per cent of the elderly in the study who had adult children engaged in the reciprocal pattern of exchanges.

This process of exchange usually involves services such as babysitting, nursing, counselling, shopping, household maintenance, gifts such as money, clothes, appliances, and air or train tickets for visit or interaction in the form of face-to-face visits, telephone calls or letters. The form and frequency of exchange varies greatly among families and is influenced by a number of social factors. These include residential propinquity, social class, children's sex, race and ethnicity, age of the middle and oldest generations and the degree of filial maturity. The greater the extents, to which elderly parents live in close proximity to children, the greater the likelihood of visiting and exchanging goods or services as a token of emotional attachment and mutual affection.

Class difference in frequency and types of exchange has been found in many studies (Troll and Bengtson 1979; Neugartan 1979; Lacy and Hendricks 1980). Shanas (1979), in a study of family help patterns among approximately 25,000 people over 65 in Britain, Denmark and the United States, found that members of every class were engaged in reciprocal assistance. However, since the size of the family, living arrangements family values and economic positions vary by social class, the amount, form and frequency of mutual aid also varies. Studies have shown that working class parents are more likely to exchange services; that the middle class is more likely to exhibit patterns of serial exchange from oldest to youngest generation, while reciprocity is more common among the working class and there is more face to face interaction amongst the working class; and more telephonic and letter writing among the middle class because of greater social and geographical mobility.

There is also sex difference in familial exchange relationships. Son often perceived assisting older parents as an instrumental act resulting from an obligation to repay a past debt. In contrast, daughters because of long standing, expressive lineal mother daughter ties perceived assistance as an expressive act which they want to or need to perform. As a result, sons generally provided more financial assistance and frequently took decision about the care of the parents. Daughters were seemed to be the primary care giver. This may occur because women are more likely to play the traditional nurturing role, because the mother daughter relationship is strengthened during the adult years, especially after the daughter has become a mother. Daughters worry more about parental health than sons do and that the health of the father generates more concern and worry than that of mother.

From the perspective of elderly parents, it's appearing they primarily offer financial assistance to sons and services to daughters. However, there are great inter-family variations, depending on class and on the individual interest of the parents. If they are still employed, younger grandparents may have neither the time for, nor the interest in performing baby sitting or other service roles. As a result, they may replace this personal assistance in the form of gifts, monetary assistance or loan.

Another factor influencing the type and frequency of exchange and assistance is filial responsibility or filial maturity. This represents the extent to which the adult children feel obligated to meet the basic needs of their aging parents. While the family is an important source of aid and support for the elderly, the expectation of the parents and children as to what should be done may or may not coincide. The chronological age of the children may determine their desirability to assist and interact with their parents. Adult children with very old parents may also be retired and have their own economic and health concerns. Therefore, they may be less able or willing to assist their ageing parents and may abdicate some of their filial responsibility to public or private social service agencies.

From the perspective of the aging parents, the expectations for filial responsibility seem to be higher with increasing age among females and among the widowed or divorced, if they have few economic resources, health fails and if their general level of morale and life satisfaction is low. In short, perception of the filial responsibility may influence interaction pattern in later years, where expectation differs, family solidarity is weakened, overt conflict is visible and public and private social agencies may be required to fill the void for visiting, health and household services.

In summary, exchange between parents and adult children vary in frequency, type and quality across the life cycle. The form and frequency of communication and assistance between adult children and ageing parents is influenced by such factors as residential propinquity, social class, sex of the child, ethnicity, age and health of the two generations, and the degree of filial responsibility felt by the children.

Most research has focused on the type and frequency of exchange between aging parents and adult children. Quantity rather than quality has been the central concern. Johnson and Bursk (1977) and Johnson (1978) found that quality of the relationship is influenced by the health, economic and housing situation of the elderly and by attitudes to their personnel ageing experience. The level of the effect was higher when the parents were in good health and held positive feelings about their personal ageing process. They also noticed that there was more quality interaction in relationship when parents were socially active outside the extended family. The studies on old age in India are still in their infancy as most of the studies were conducted in the 1960s, or efforts were made to explore the problems of old people. Later in 1970s and 1980s social scientists paid attention to issues like the status and role of the old people in rural and urban community and their adjustment in old age. As per Indian studies, Mishra (1987) in his study conducted in retired male government employees in Chandigarh found a direct link and positive correlation between their health conditions and their subsequent adjustment. Poor health often leads to the redefinition of the scope of their parental role. Poor health leads to more assistance from adult offspring and it also contributes significantly negative self feeling.

In other studies conducted by Jamuna (1984, 1987, 1988, 1989, 1990, 1991), Jamuna and Ramanmurti (1984, 1989) and Asha and Subramaniam (1990), the problem of aging like adjustment patterns, role activities and acceptance decides husband-wife communication has been examined in detail. They found that as the ageing process goes on it brings in several changes for the individual in terms of role playing and adjustments to be made at various stages. It requires adjustment to changing relations of authority and difference, to changing health situation, intergenerational problems, following 'exit' situations like dead and bereavement. All these call for adjustment between the aging individual and other members of the family as well as the community. Taking a clue from the research studies conducted in the area and in order to fill the gap in the existing studies, the researcher in the present study has stressed upon quantitative methods, keeping in view the nature of problem and the magnitude of population.

Objectives

The main objectives of this study are:

1. To find out the influence of social factors upon interpersonal exchange among elderly and their married children.
2. To find out how far interpersonal exchange influence the well-being of the elderly.

Research Methodology

The location of the study was Chandigarh; as according to the 2001 census, amongst the states and union territories of India, Chandigarh had the highest growth rate of the aged.

Chandigarh was planned as an administrative capital city for the state of Punjab in 1951, and overtime has emerged as one of the largest and most significant of the new cities in India. First master plan was prepared in 1949 by the American firm of Mayer, Wintlessly and Glass in association with brilliant young architect Mathew Nowicki. However, Nowicki died in an air crash in 1950 while returning to the United States and the new city had its first setback. Albert Mayer was heartbroken and refused to continue the initial plan, which was later on improved by Le-Corbusier.

Le-Corbusier considered the city plan as a biological phenomenon and according to him it has a brain, heart, lung and feet like a human being: it is on this analogy that the city of Chandigarh has been planned. To the north lies the capital complex comprising the Secretariat, High Court, Legislative Assembly which constitute the head, the city centre represents the heart which is located at the junction of two important arteries, Madhya Marg (V2-station) and Janpath (V2-captial). The network of roads for vehicular traffic and footpaths for pedestrians constitute the circulation system. The spacious parks and green belts which run through the city act as lungs. The industrial Area to the east and Panjab University to the west represent the limbs, the former fulfilling the materialistic and the later the spiritual needs of the city.

The universe of the study was the aged who were residing together with their married children in Chandigarh. To identify this universe, the Election Commissioner's office, located in Sector 17, was approached. With the help of the Chairman, Election Commission, the researcher was able to prepare a sector-wise list of elderly voters who were residing with their married children. In all, there were 11,826 such cases. Since the population of 60 plus elderly residing together with married children in Chandigarh was very high and they were not equally distributed in different sectors, therefore it was decided to follow a multistage sampling procedure.

To begin with, depending upon the strength of this population in all the 56 sectors (excluding the Colonies and Industrial Area Phase I and Phase II), the sectors were arranged in descending order. To know about the cutting off point which split the sectors into two equal halves, each having 50 per cent of the population, cumulative frequency was calculated, which came out to be 4, 24, 413 and then divided by two, to know about the midpoint was 2, 12, 206. The dividing point lies between Sectors 35 and 41 (see Annexure I). Twelve sectors were above the cutting off point and 35 were below it. Two sectors were randomly chosen with the help of random number table from the first half (sector 20 and 22) and three sectors from the second half (sector 42, 19 and 7). The list of households, thus, obtained and was considered the sampling frame from which a random sample of households was proportionately selected; information was gathered from elderly parents and their married children with whom they were staying together in the selected households. In this way the researcher was able to select 198 households in five different sectors for which a sample of 343 elderly and 198 children were interviewed. Sector-wise distribution of elderly and their married children is given in Table 15.1. The elderly were interviewed at the place of residence and married children were interviewed at work place.

Table 15.1

Sector-wise distribution of the elderly and their married children

Sectors	*Total number of households*	*Elderly staying with their married*	*Elderly selected children*	*Married children selected*	*Households selected*
7	165	270	54	33	33
19	160	265	53	32	32
20	255	470	94	51	51
22	240	435	87	48	48
42	170	275	55	34	34
Total	990	1715	343	198	198

The parental exchange was studied by taking into consideration the type and extent of change which took place among them and was articulated into three parts – receiving, giving and both receiving and giving. Each part was studied from three dimensions called financial, personal and advisory. Financial receiving includes payment of bills, essential needs, luxury items and received cash, etc. Personal help includes the help in light and heavy house-keeping, laundry, grocery shopping, cooking, running errands, fixing things around the house, aiding in transportation, and help in illness, and help in renovating house. In advisory help, they receive the help in life problems, running the house, money or business matters.

The socio-economic characteristics were measured with the help of these factors: age, sex, marital status, education, occupation, monthly income, and the health status is also considered in order to judge whether these factors affect on their exchange relationship.

Well-being was measured along with two components – cognitive and affective.

1. In the cognitive dimension the researcher asked questions like, were things getting better with growing age, the dearest time of their lives, happier when they were younger, best year of their lives, etc.

2. In affective measures questions like why most of the things you do are boring, 'feeling of monotonous', 'you feel old and tired', 'plan things for future', etc.

Results

To investigate exchange the researcher reviewed it at the three levels – financial, personal and advisory. Overall analysis of financial, personal and advisory help was carried out. For this, three categories were made – dependent, independent and inter-dependent. The following table will enlighten the extent to which these socio-economic factors affect on these exchanges (financial, personal and advisory) among elderly and their married children.

Financial Help

A separate table was made to measure the financial help among the elderly and their married children with the help of questions as mentioned earlier. Table 15.2 will enlighten the financial exchange between elderly and their married children.

Table 15.2

Financial exchange among elderly and their married children

Financial help	*Elderly*	*Married children*
Giving Help	104 (30.3)	56 (28.3)
Receiving Help	87 (25.4)	59 (29.8)
Both Giving and Receiving	152 (44.3)	83 (41.9)
Total	343 (100)	198 (100)

It is clear from Table 15.2 that 30.3 per cent elderly as compared to 28.3 per cent of married children were giving help. Against this 29.8 per cent of married children as compared to 25.4 per cent of elderly were receiving financial help. It was found that 41.9 per cent of elderly and 44.3 per cent of married children were both giving and receiving financial help from each other, which showed their interdependency.

Personal Help

Elderly usually prefer to receive help or personal care, everyday chores and other ongoing needs from close family members. For example, aged parents who believe that their children would give assistance if the need arises have better understanding than those who are less certain about what their offspring's response would be. Table 15.3 will appraise the personal help given or received by both elderly parents and their married children.

Table 15.3

Personal exchange among elderly and their married children

Personal help	*Elderly*	*Married children*
Giving Help	27 (7.9)	70 (35.4)
Receiving Help	126 (36.7)	15 (7.6)
Both Giving and Receiving	190 (55.4)	113 (57)
Total	343 (100)	198 (100)

On the basis of the analysis of the Table 15.3 it was found that 7.9 per cent of the elderly as compared to 35.4 per cent of the married children were giving personal help. As against this, 36.6 per cent of elderly and only 7.6 per cent of married children were receiving help. In case of, however, both giving and receiving, 55.4 per cent of elderly and 57 per cent of married children showed their personal interdependence on each other.

Advisory Help

Interaction with the children buffer the effect of stressful events and situations, offer emotional sustenance and affirmation of one's identity, yield needed assistance, help time structure and meaningful ways, and provide continuity in important roles. Even those ways are very dependent on each other for personal care and assistance can reciprocate with affection, companionship and advice. Table 15.4 will fathom the advisory help given by elderly and their married children.

Table 15.4

Advisory exchange among elderly and their married children

Advisory help	*Elderly*	*Married children*
Giving Help	100 (29.2)	56 (28.3)
Receiving Help	98 (28.6)	59 (29.8)
Both Giving and Receiving	145 (42.3)	83 (41.9)
Total	343 (100)	198 (100)

From Table 15.4, it can be summarized that 29.2 per cent of elderly and 28.3 per cent of married children were giving advisory help to each other. On the other hand, 28.6 per cent of elderly and 29.8 per cent of married children were receiving help. It was, however, noticed that 42.3 per cent as well as 41.9 per cent of married children were both giving and receiving advisory help from each other. It again proved their interdependence.

Overall Interdependency Level

To ascertain if the elderly are considered as an asset or burden by their married children an overall analysis of financial, personal and advisory help was carried out. For this three categories were made – dependent, independent and interdependent. Table 15.5 will enlighten the extent to which the elderly were considered as asset or burden by married children as well as their dependency level on each other.

This table exhibited that 30.3 per cent of elderly and 22.7 per cent of married children were dependent on each other. However, 22.5 per cent elderly and 28.8 per cent of married children were independent as against these, 47.2 per cent of elderly and 48.5 per cent of married children showed their interdependency on each other. So it is very clear that majority of the elderly as well as married children are interdependent on each other.

Table 15.5

Overall interdependency level

Overall interdependency	*Elderly*	*Married children*
Dependent	104 (30.3)	45 (22.7)
Independent	77 (22.5)	37 (28.8)
Interdependent	162 (47.2)	96 (48.5)
Total	343 (100)	198 (100)

From the overall picture that emerges it can be concluded that majority of the elderly parents as well as their married children were both giving and receiving financial, personal and advisory help from each other. However, the giving and receiving help is not on equal footing in each category. Whosoever is strong is giving and the other is receiving help. This shows cordial relations of the family. Table 15.6 will show the effect of socio-economic factors on this overall dependency level.

Table 15.6

Overall exchange with regard to age amongst elderly and their married children

Overall interdependency	*Elderly*			*Married children*		
	Young old	*Middle old*	*Oldest old*	*Young adulthood*	*Middle adulthood*	*Late adulthood*
Dependent	27 (1 0.9)	36 (50)	24 (100)	52 (66.6)	3 (4.1)	4 (8.5)
Independent	100 (40.5)	4 (5.6)	—	1 (1.3)	49 (67. 1)	2 (4.3)
Interdependent	120 (48.6)	32 (44.4)	—	25 (32. 1)	21 (28.8)	41 (87.2)
Total	247 (100)	72 (100)	24 (100)	78 (1 00)	73 (1 00)	47 (1 00)

An examination of the table reveals that all the elderly belonging to the oldest old category and exactly half of the middle aged category were dependent on their married children.

In contrast somewhat less than half of the elderly belonging to young old category was interdependent, that is were engaged in reciprocal relations (both giving and receiving). If you glance at the children's table, it reveals that more than three-fourth of the children in their late adulthood were mutually exchanging help with their elderly parents. Against this, more than half the children who were in their middle adulthood and young adulthood were independent or dependent on their elderly parents, respectively.

Table 15.7

Overall exchange with regard to sex amongst elderly and their married children

Overall interdependency	*Elderly*			*Married children*		
	Male	*Female*	*Total*	*Male*	*Female*	*Total*
Dependent	116 (66.3)	10 (5.9)	126	15 (7.9)	—	15
Independent	19 (10.9)	8 (4.8)	27	62 (32.8)	8 (38.9)	70
Interdependent	40 (22.8)	150 (89.3)	190	112 (59.3)	1 (11.9)	113
Total	175 (100)	168 (100)	343	189 (100)	9 (100)	198

Table 15.7 shows that majority of elderly female (three-fourth) and little less than one-fourth of the elderly males were engaged in reciprocal exchange with their married children. A little more than half of the elderly males were engaged in one way of exchange from their married children. More than three-fourth of female children were independent and on the other hand more than half of the male children were interdependent on their parents.

A perusal of Table 15.7 reveals that majority of widow/widowers were interdependent with their married children. However, half of the married parents were independent and maintaining a reciprocity in relationship. In the same way, more than half of the married children were interdependent with their parents. More than one-fourth married children were dependent on their parents.

Table 15.8

Overall exchange with regard to marital status

Overall interdependency	Elderly			Married children	
	Married	Widowed	Total	Married	Total
Dependent	85 (29.3)	2 (3.8)	87	75 (37.87)	75
Independent	101 (34.8)	3 (5.7)	104	23 (11.61)	23
Interdependent	104 (35.9)	48 (90.5)	152	100 (51)	100
Total	290 (100)	53 (100)	343	198 (100)	198

Table 15.9

Overall exchange with regard to educational level overall elderly married children

Overall interdependency	Elderly			Married children		
	Low	Medium	High	Low	Medium	High
Dependent	50 (94.3)	20 (18.2)	17 (9.4)	53 (77.9)	5 (7.0)	1 (1.7)
Independent	1 (1.9)	75 (68.2)	28 (l 5.6)	—	50 (69.4)	2 (3.5)
Interdependent	2 (3.8)	15 (13.6)	135 (75)	15 (22.1)	17 (23.6)	55 (94.8)
Total	53 (100)	110 (100)	180 (100)	68 (100)	72 (100)	58 (100)

It is apparent from Table 15.8 and 15.9 that more than three-fourth of the elderly with low educational level were dependent on their children. Three-fourth of the elderly who had the high educational level were having reciprocity in their exchanges. On the other hand, vast majority of the married children with high educational level were interdependent with their elderly parents. A little more than three-fourth and a little less than three-fourth of the married children who had low and medium-level of education were dependent and independent, respectively.

From Table 15.7 and 15.8 it has been noted that a majority of elderly with medium and high economic status were interdependent to their children. Almost half of the elderly who have low economic status were engaged in reciprocal exchange with their children. On the other hand, majority of the married children with high economic status were involved in reciprocal exchange with their elderly parents. Against this, more than half of the children with medium and low economic status were engaged in one way of exchange.

Table 15.10

Overall exchange with regard to economic status overall elderly married children

Overall interdependency	Elderly			Married children		
	Low	Medium	High	Low	Medium	High
Dependent	85 (30.8)	1 (1.8)	1 (10.0)	53 (65.4)	6 (7.9)	—
Independent	42 (15.2)	55 (96.4)	7 (70.0)	1 (1.2)	50 (68.8)	1 (2.4)
Interdependent	149 (54.0)	1 (1.8)	2 (20.0)	27 (33.3)	20 (26.3)	40 (97.6)
Total	276 (100)	57 (100)	10 (100)	81 (100)	76 (l00)	41 (100)

Table 15.11

Overall exchange with regard to health status

Overall interdependency	Elderly			Married children	
	Bad	Good	Average	Average	Good
Dependent	35 (94.6)	50 (52.02)	41 (19.5)	15 (68.2)	—
Independent	—	26 (27.08)	1 (0.5)	5 (22.7)	65 (36.9)
Interdependent	2 (5.4)	20 (20.90)	168 (80.0)	2 (9. l)	111 (63.1)
Total	37 (100)	96 (l00)	210 (100)	22 (100)	176 (l00)

Table 15.11 reveals that a majority of elderly with good health status were interdependent. While elderly people with bad health status were dependent in comparison to those elderly with average health who were independent. On the other hand, two-third of the married children who had average health status were dependent on the parents and almost equal number of children who were in their pink of their health status were exchanging interdependent relationship with their parents and only one-third with good health were independent.

Cognitive Well Being

To know the effect of overall interdependence level on the well-being of the aged Table 15.12 the following table envisaged the result.

Table 15.12

Cognitive well-being and overall interdependence among elderly and their married children

iverall interdependency	*Elderly*			*Married children*		
	Low	*Medium*	*High*	*Low*	*Medium*	*High*
Dependent	40	30	34	29	20	10
Independent	9	55	30	2	38	12
Interdependent	2	5	155	3	25	59
Total	51 (100)	90 (100)	202 (100)	34 (100)	83 (100)	81 (100)

It is crystal clear from the table that majority of the elderly who were interdependent were (95.7%) high on their cognitive well-being level in comparison to those who were dependent (38.5%). Those who were independent (71.4%) have medium well-being level. This showed that those who are low on their cognitive well-being level were dependent on their children (78.5%) and more than half were high on their cognitive well-being level were interdependent on their married children. If we glance at the children side it depicted that a vast majority of children with low psychological well-being were dependent on their parents. Most of the children who were having high psychological well-being were found to be in the interdependency stage.

This table denoted that the vast majority of the elderly (94.2%) who were high on their effective well-being were interdependent. Three-fourth of the elderly who were low on their effective well-being were dependent. In case of married children, as the table exhibited, more than three-fourth of the children having high psychological well-being were maintaining a mutual exchange relationship with the parents. On the other hand, little more than the half of the children with medium psychological well-being were independent and less than half of the children having low psychological well-being were dependent on their parents.

Table 15.13 and 15.14 envisages that a thumping majority of the elderly (96.5%) with high overall well-being was interdependent and three-fourth of the elderly with low well-being level was dependent on their married children. More than half (61.4%) with medium well-being were independent. While nearly three-fourth of the married children with low psychological well-being were dependent upon their parents. A little less than three-fourth of the children with high psychological well-being were interdependent. However, about half of the children with medium psychological well-being were independent. Thus, it can be summerized that overall well-being does have an impact on interdependence level of both of them.

Table 15.13

Affective well-being and overall interdependence among elderly and their married children

Overall interdependency	*Elderly*			*Married children*		
	Low	*Medium*	*High*	*Low*	*Medium*	*High*
Dependent	99	4	1	14	16	—
Independent	13	57	67	8	48	14
Interdependent	9	27	129	12	34	67
Total	121 (100)	85 (100)	137 (100)	34 (100)	83 (100)	81 (100)

Table 15.14

Overall well-being and overall interdependence among elderly and their married children

Overall interdependency	*Elderly*			*Married children*		
	Low	*Medium*	*High*	*Low*	*Medium*	*High*
Dependent	70	29	5	25	14	20
Independent	7	70	0	1	48	7
Interdependent	9	15	138	8	21	54
Total	86 (100)	114 (100)	143 (100)	34 (100)	83 (100)	81 (100)

Discussion of Results

Basis of exchange between elderly parents and their married children changes throughout the life cycle, depending on each side's circumstances. As far as the present context is concerned, this pattern of exchange focus on the principle of reciprocity which operates among them and its effect on their relationship. Majority of the elderly and their married children were interdependent on financial, personal and advisory help which means both giving as well as receiving help from each other.

A small number of elderly were independent and they were only helping the children and getting nothing in return. Similarly, a small number of elderly were totally dependent on their children and they were only receiving help but giving nothing in return. The majority of the elderly who gave financial help to the children were receiving personal help from them and those who received financial help were giving personal help to their children, if their health permitted. The advisory help to each other was based on who was more intelligent and had better state of mind to offer help. It was concluded that a majority of young old elderly, with high education and economic status and good health, were engaged in reciprocal exchange with their married children. As opposite to it, the oldest with low education level, economic status and bad health were receiving help from the children. The elderly who were financially well off were, however, found to be enjoying better well-being.

Lastly, the association between socio-economic and children exchange on financial, personal and advisory help summarised that majority of the late adult married children with high education, medium economic status and good health were engaged in reciprocal relations with their parents. On the other hand, the young adult with low education, economic status and average health were receiving help from the parents. Finally, it was found that elderly who had reciprocity of relationship with their married children were enjoying high level of well-being than those who were independent or dependent.

References

Allan, G., 2005, 'Family, Domestic Roles and Social Organization', *Journal of Marriage and Family*, 67 (2): 191–206.

Allen, Katherine R., Rosemary Blieszner and Karen A. Roberto, 2000, 'Families in Middle and Later Years: A Reviewed Critique of the Literature', *Journal of Marriage and Family*, 62: 911–926.

Asha, C.B. and K.A. Subramanian, 1990, 'Problems of Elderly Women', *Indian Journal of Community Guidance*, 7 (3): 61–67.

Benerjee, Tapan, 2002, *Senior Citizen of India: Issues and Challenges*, New Delhi: Rajat Publications.

Binstock, Robert H. and Linda K. George, 2001, *Handbook of Aging and the Social Sciences*, New York: Academic Press.

Borgatta, E.F. and R.J.V. Montgomery, 2000, *Encyclopedia of Sociology*, Vol. 3, USA: Macmillan Reference.

Browing, G., A. Halgail and F. Webster, 2000, *Understanding Contemporary Society: Theories of the Present*, London: Sage Publications.

Elder, G.H. Jr. and M.K. Johnson, 2003, 'The LW Course and Aging: Challenges, Lessons and New Directions', in R.A. Settersten Jr. (ed.), *Invitation to the Life Course: Toward New Understandings of Later Life* (48–81), Amityville, New York: Baywood Publishing Company.

Hendrick, Clyde A. and Susan S. Hendrick, 2000, *Close Relationships: A Source Book*, New Delhi: Sage Publications.

Jamuna, D., 1984, 'A Study of Some Factors Related to Adjustment Among Middle Aged and Elder Women, Doctoral Dissertation, S.V. University Tirupati (unpublished).

——, and P.V. Ramamurti, 1984, Psychological Research on the Aged in India, *Journal of Anthropological Society of India*, 19(3): 269–286.

——, 1988, Age Adjustment and Husband Wife Communication of Middle Aged and Older Women', *Journal of Psychological Research*, 28: 145–147.

Jamuna, D., 1989a, 'Self-acceptance Among Aged Women Belonging to Forward Class and Backward Class Groups', *Journal of Personality and Group Behaviour*, 9(1): 13–18.

——, and P.V. Ramamurti, 1989b, 'Adjustment Patterns among Middle Aged and Older Widows and Non-widows', *Indian Journal of Applied Psychology*, 25(2): 48–50.

——, 1990, 'Caring for Elderly Women: Perspectives on the Turn of the Century', *Journal of the Indian Academy of Applied Psychology*, 16(2): 17–22.

——, 1991, 'Perception of the Problems of the Elderly in Three Generational Households', *Journal of Psychological Researches*, 35: 99–103.

Jamuna, D., 1992, *Status, Needs, Determinants of Problems of Older Women of Forward and Scheduled Caste Group*, Project Report submitted to UGC, New Delhi.

Johnson, Elizabeth S. and B.J. Bursk, 1977, 'Relationship between the Elderly and their Adult Children'. *The Gerontologist*, 17(1): 90–96.

Johnson, Elizabeth S., 1978, 'Good Relationships between Mothers and their Daughters: A Causal Model', *The Gerontologist*, 18(3): 301–306.

Johnson, H.M., 1961, *Sociology: A Systematic Introduction*, London: Routledge and Kegan Paul Ltd.

Lacy, W.B. and J.L. Hendricks, 1980, 'Development Models of Adult Life', *International Journal of Aging and Human Development*, 11: 89–110.

Mishra, S., 1987, *Social Adjustment in Old Age*, Delhi: B.R. Publishing Corporation.

Neil, J.S. and B.B. Paul, 2001, *Intergenerational Encyclopedia of Social and Behavioral Sciences*, Vol. 12, USA: Macmillan.

Neugarten, Bernice L., 1979, 'Time, Age and the Life Cycle', *American Journal of Psychiatry*, 136: 1887–1894.

Rajan, S. Irudaya, S. Mishra and P.S. Sharma, 1999, 'Indian Elderly: Some Views of Populace', *The Indian Journal of Social Work*, 60 (4): 487–507.

Ramamurti, P.V. and D. Jamuna, 1986, *Self-perception of Issues and Problems of Aged Women in India*, New Delhi: Congress of International Sociological Association.

Shanas, E., 1979, 'Social Myth as Hypothesis: The Case of the Family Relation of Old People', *Gerontologist*, 19: 169–174.

Troll, L. and V.L. Bengtson, 1979, 'Generations in the Family' in Wesley R, F.I. Nye, R. Hill and I.L. Reiss (ed.), *Contemporary Theories About the Family*, New York: The Free Press.

Troll, L., S. Miller and R. Atchley, 1979, *Families in Later Life*, Belmont: Wadsworth Publishing Co. Inc.

16

Single-Parent Families and Public Policy

RANJAY VARDHAN

Family has been conceived as the cornerstone of the society. It forms the smallest but basic unit of social organization. It is difficult to imagine how human society could function without it. As a carrier and mediator of culture, its role in socialization and personality development is well recognized. Murdock (1949) in a study entitled 'Social Structure' found that some form of family existed in every society and concluded on the evidence of his sample that family is universal. The family in Parsons' (1959) view provides a context in which husband and wife can express their childish whims, give and receive emotional support, recharge their batteries and so stabilize their personalities. However, Parsons like Murdock has been accused of idealizing the family with his picture of well-adjusted children and sympathetic spouses caring for each other's every need. He fails to explore functional alternative to the family.

The family has always been subject to changes, so as to compete with the needs of time and changing demands of society. Goode (1963) has held that most parts of the world are undergoing a family revolution. Almost everywhere in future, he predicted that the predominant type of family will be nuclear in structure, made up of parents and their unmarried children. If we analyse the present families, it can be said that nuclear families are prevalent in the West as well as in urban India. Moreover, due to the process of industrialization, urbanization, westernization, modernization, spread of education, women liberation movements, impact of mass media, etc. it can be stated that even this type of family is under change. Thorne (1982) stated that in the last decades, the family has emerged as a political issue, especially in USA. Some who claim that the family is in crisis cite as evidence the high divorce rate; the increase in single parent families; people living alone; and the employment rates of married women, especially mothers of young children. There have been calls for new federal policies to strengthen the family. Further analysis of structure of modern families indicates that the significant numbers of families are being run by single parents (male or female). Yet, social development in traditional sense has not prepared either males or females to be single parent. Single mothers and fathers need to establish strong support networks, personal friendships and new networks and work on improving their self-esteem. Many single parents learn to live on reduced incomes, find acceptable ways to deal with a non-custodian parent and redefine their relationships with their children.

Single Parents

Single parents and their children constitute a rapidly increasing population. Much of the initial research on single parent family focused on single mothers due to father's absence. More recently, single fathers, unwed teenage mothers, other single parents and adjustment process of single parents and their children received attention. Although the common assumption from early research was that single parent households are a pathological family forms, these units today provide viable alternative to nuclear family.

But rearing families as single parents is tough task and is full of challenges. Poverty is persistently linked with single parent households, especially those headed by women. Such families are poorest of all major demographic groups in the United States (Garfinkle and Mclanahan 1986). Wage differences between men and women arising from lack of labour and market preparation or experience or from discrimination, reinforces low status. Poverty may be the most stressful challenge which single parent families are facing. Thirty two per cent of single mother headed households and 16 per cent of single father households live below the poverty level (Fields and Casper 2001). Higher rate of poverty among mothers can be attributed to the higher earning power of men compared with women (Mclanahan and Booth 1989), lack of child support, payments made in full and on time, lack of affordable child care (Hilton, Desrochers and Devall 2001) and poor public assistance programmes (Sugarman 2003).

For most children, two parents are better than one, for more than just economic reasons. Fathers bring a dimension to child rearing that complements and under the best of circumstances supports mother's role. For example, research indicates that the manner in which fathers interact with their children differs from that of mothers, one which has an important role in children's social and emotional development. Krein (1986) found children in single parent families are twice as likely to drop out of high school as children living full time in two parent families. She further said that children in single parent homes are also more likely to have their own marriages end in separation or divorce and are at higher risk for unmarried parenthood. With more mothers in the workforce than ever before, many fathers are assuming a share of routine child care responsibilities. This sharing of responsibility comparatively eases the pressure on the other parent. But such help is not available to the single parent. Single parent family differs from two parent family in their resources, motivations and opportunities to function as viable units. Parents who have experienced a separation, divorce or death may also have a hard time attending to their children's needs (Amato and Booth 1996), making it difficult to nurture and discipline their children effectively.

Research reveals that the single parenthood has different effects on different family members. Children in two parent families are more likely to have at least one parent who works full time all year round. In 1997, 88 per cent of children living with a single father and only 41 per cent of children in families headed by a single mother had a parent who worked full time all year (Federal Interagency Forum on Child and Family Statistics, 1999).

Studies have found that teenagers from single parent homes were more likely to engage in delinquent behaviour and consume illicit drugs or alcohol as compared to those from intact home and have more behavioural problems and lower mathematical and reading ability than children raised in two parent families. Single parents tend to be poorly trained. Because their financial situation is marginal, they cannot hold out and tend to take the first job offered. It is a true irony that, because single parent cannot afford to refuse any work, they may not be unemployed very long and therefore, fails to qualify for special government training and assistance. They may express satisfaction with part time work because they are glad to have any work, one says that they have 'low expectations'. Nevertheless single parents are more likely to work full time and they work much longer hours. Single parents can not give adequate attention to their children. It also has an adverse impact on the children's performance in school and peer relations. Such a family also faces disruption in extended family relationships. Thus, it can be seen that single parent face tremendous socio-economic and children related problems.

Single Mothers

Women are the primary custodians for children in our society. This is particularly true in poor areas and in minority groups, where single parenting is the norm and where abuse and neglect rates are the highest. 'Left behind' women, *defacto*, in charge of farm households have been a presence in rural Africa for some time. Yousseff and Hetler (1984) estimate that one-third to as many as half of all rural households have been headed by women in countries such as Botswana and Kenya. Estimates are that 55–60 per cent of all children in the US will spend some of their childhood in single parent households; that parent is usually the mother. At any given time, about 22 per cent of all children under the age of 18 are living with one parent. The number of children living in single parent households with their mothers is more than living with their fathers. This is true for most of the societies and problem for single mother is more because in single father family, there may be another woman to help but such help is generally absent in single mother family. This problem takes serious proportions in patriarchal society as she is not accorded equal status in the society. With lesser education and work experience, she has to face different kind of challenges as compared to their male counterparts. Various studies have tried to highlight the problems of single mothers.

It has been argued that women are a deprived and discriminated lot with limited access to resources. Studies have shown that, both in developing and developed countries, female headed household have different socio-economic and demographic characteristics as compared to male headed households (Barros, Fox and Mendonca 1997; Buvinic and Gupta 1997). For instance, using available census data in combination with other empirical evidence from Africa, Latin America and Asia, Buvinic and Yousseff (1978) estimate that women headed households constitute between 25 and 33 per cent of all household in the world.

The data across different countries indicate that compared to married couples, more number of families headed by women live in poverty. Various UNDP studies show that women are poorer than men because more households headed by women fall below the poverty line than households headed by men. Surveys of household consumption and expenditure in many countries of North and South America, Europe and C.I.S. show the incidence of poverty to be high among female headed households. The wide range of biases in society, unequal opportunities in education, employment and asset ownership among them mean that women have fewer opportunities. Poverty accentuates gender gaps and when adversity strikes, it is the women who are most vulnerable. Women who work part-time include, in small proportion, women who are 'satisfied to have found any work at all'. If they work full time, on an average, even that is low status and low paid. Horn in *Father Facts* stated that female headed households or father's absence is a strong predictor for suicide among adult and adolescent boys.

Especially to the lower economic groups thus forcing them to give up hitherto held cultural values family ties, kinship bondage, etc. The widows are no longer absorbed in the in-laws family. Due to economic hardship, parents also discourage them to live with them and this has forced the widows to set up separate establishments. Though divorce is uncommon, separation or desertion is found to be on higher side among low income group people. Addiction of men to evil practices, low moral values, inabilities of men to support the family are found to be some of the reasons for desertion. Increasing pauperization in rural areas had led to streams of migration and polarization of wealth in the urban economy. If men migrate, then women have to take up the total responsibility for the family left behind. This results in the emergence of female headship in rural areas (Shanthi 1992). However, higher technical and professional education and new varieties of paid employment, varied opportunities for the development of new skills and wider contacts have enabled women to achieve greater equality with men, both within and outside the household in legal, social, educational, occupational, political and economic spheres of activity. They are not only becoming independent but are also taking decisions in the household and family. They are independently running the households and, thus, are assuming headship status in the households (Kumari 1989) though not often but as and when situation arise. A female headed household is one in which the woman is the head, that is she is the manager, provider and decision maker (Vardhan 1999). The women generally become head of the household in the absence of male as a result of (i) spinsterhood (ii) widowhood (iii) divorce desertion or (iv) out migration of male. Women also become head of the household in the presence of male, if the husband is invalid. Visaria and Visaria (1982) studied the census data (1961 and 1971) and consumption expenditure data of the National Sample Survey relating to Maharashtra and Gujarat for year 1972–73 and found that nearly 10 per cent of total households were headed by women. They found regional variations in the incidence of female headed households and were relatively higher in number of Southern states as also in Eastern states than in Central, Northern and Western states, though the prevalent pattern in our society as in most society is male headship. They found that women heads have little or no literacy attainment, possess little or no land, and the household headed by them have significantly lower monthly expenditure than those with male heads.

Parthasarthy (1982), based on a survey of a Community Development Block in Andhra Pradesh, found prevalence of female headed households in 20 to 50 per cent of the households and their number increasing with poverty. His finding definitely link poverty with female heads of households. The study conducted by the Institute of Social Studies Trust, New Delhi (1984) for ILO comes to conclusion that a majority of female heads of households are of elderly widows. These female headed Households suffer greater economic disadvantage than the male Headed households as most of the developmental programmes have not reached them at all and even awareness of such schemes is missing. They have little education and have few or no skills. Kumari (1987) in her study *Status of Single Women in India* has made an attempt to study spinsters, widows, divorced and separated women, both working and non-working, living in Bangalore city by using questionnaire as a tool for collecting information. Her findings reveal that economically dependent single women face economic problems to a lesser degree than those totally economically dependent or partially independent as they are expected to work the whole day in the kitchen for the sake of other family members. They are taken for granted and no effort is made by any one in the family to help them to carry out the household duties. Kumari (1989) in her study *Women-headed Households in Rural India* indicated that there has been an increase in social and economic discrimination against female headed households especially in widow's cases. She found that female as heads occurred both in the presence and absence of adult male, mainly husband. Female headed households failed to utilize the resources to the extent a male headed household could. There was a weakening support structure for females. In time of distress, they do not seem to be able to rely upon or draw support from kith and kin.

Panda (1997), in his paper 'Female Headship, Poverty and Child Welfare: A Study of Rural Orissa, India' points out that poverty and female headship are strongly linked in rural Orissa. He found that if we draw a poverty line that corresponds to 15 per cent of the population who are poor, 12 per cent of people living in male headed households are poor as compared to 33 per cent of people living in female headed households. He was of the opinion that female headship can be a better targeting indicator for poverty alleviation in rural Orissa.

Vardhan (1999), in a study conducted in Chandigarh, found the incidence of female headedness is the highest among widows (60%) followed by divorced/deserted/separated women (15%); unmarried women (13.36%) and women whose husbands were away or invalid (11.4%). He found that female headed households are not a uniform category. They belong to all socio-economic groups and their proportion is more or less the same in social hierarchy especially in an urban setting. There is a general decline in the financial position of such households after assumption of headship and they suffer from sense of deprivation and discrimination. Such women face tremendous problems and the nature of problems may be social, economical, and psychological and children related.

The various studies indicate that although women are assuming headship of the households, yet they suffer due to various problems such as economic, social, emotional, physical insecurity and having to play the role of men and women and in the process face a lot of problems like financial scarcity, lack of companionship, over-indulgence of the people, problems in job, physical insecurity, dealings in bank and day-to-day transactions, etc. Their economic problems are reflected in their low wages, dependence on welfare and difficulties surrounding child support. Single mothers who were formerly married and economically dependent on their husbands during the married life, found themselves unable to compete in job market. These 'displaced homemakers' who once believed in 'cut of domesticity', are now its victims, since their jobs as homemakers are defined as obsolete.

Need for Public Policy

The above analysis clearly provides the case for formulation of special policies for single parents. There is need for intervention of the government for helping these needy households. It can be done by pushing through a welfare reform package that provided for structural programmes and support to allow welfare. Dependent mothers need to be given training and work. With scarcity of job opportunities in government sector and more availability of jobs in private sector, there is need to formulate policy to give priority to such families.

In single parent families, single mothers need to be supported. With the current welfare-to-work hegemony the 'male breadwinner' model has covertly reinstated and the needs and desires of lone mothers have been effectively left out of policy legislation. Social scientists propose the softer option or 'rights to time to care' which allows women to attend to their care giving responsibilities of conjunction with employment and suggests that policies should be directed at enabling them to reconcile these activities.

There is a need to design a special programme for giving aid to families with dependent children. There is a need to provide assistance to needy families with children and to reduce 'dependency' by promoting job preparation, work and marriage, cash incentives, food and other things can be given under various programmes. Special health care benefits can be extended to such families. There is a need to develop a larger anti-poverty programme that provides jobs, education and child care that poor families need in order to move towards self-sufficiency.

While designing a programme for single parents, special attention needs to be paid to those single parents who have children. It can be on the lines of Child Benefit Increase Programme of Britain and Complement Familial of France. Each country provides access to welfare, based on financial need. Welfare of single parents needs to be the centre of our policies. On the pattern of the US Policy, in India, Earned Income Tax Credit (EITC) policy can be formulated. The government has policy for widows and destitute women which can be extended to single parents.

It is good to see that the Government of India has made provisions to cover Female Headed Households as a specific target group in some of their programmes but to what extent these targets are being met needs to be explored. It should be noted that no specific guidelines for identification of these target groups have been given and related programmes have not been attuned to the specific problems of female headed households (Kemp 1988). There is an urgent need to publish census data of 1991 and 2001 which has collected information on sex of the head of the household. There is a need for change in the societal attitude towards such households. Women of such households should be given opportunities to improve their education and professional competence to enable them to take up remunerative work. It is necessary to reserve a certain percentage of jobs for them and their children. Children of such households should be given certain concessions in education.

Lone mothers, who are raising a significant proportion of the next generation, are the creators and nurturers of human capital. Their 'work' should be recognized and valued. In an era of economic countdown, 'care-giving allowance' is one way to make an investment in human capital that is essential for a nation's continued health and prosperity, just as investment in factories, equipment infrastructure. The policies for single mothers may also include single father families. To conclude, it can be said that single parents are now a reality in the contemporary society and special policies need to be formulated for such families of future, which are emerging as viable alternatives to nuclear families.

References

Aggarwal, Bina, 1988, *Structure, State, Community and Household in Modernizing Asia*, Vol. II, New Delhi: Kali for Women.

Amato, P.R. and A. Booth, 1996, 'A Prospective Study of Divorce and Parent-child Relationship', *Journal of Family and Marriage*, 58: 356–365.

Barros, Ricardo, Louise Fox and Rosane Mendonca, 1997, 'Female Headed Households, Poverty and the Welfare of Children in Urban Brazil', *Economic Development and Cultural Change*, 45(2): 231–259.

Bharat, S., 1988, 'Single Parent Families', *Journal of Social Work*, 49: 227–236.

Buvinic, M. and N.H. Youssef, 1978, *Women-Headed Households: The Ignored Factor in Development Planning*, Washington, D.C.: ICRW.

Buvinic, M. and G.R. Gupta, 1997, 'Female Headed Households and Female maintained Families: Are they Worth Targething to Reduce Poverty in Developing Countries?', *Economic Development and Cultural Change*, 45(2): 259–280.

Federal Interagency Forum on Child and Family Statistics, 1999, *America's Children: Key National Indicators of Well-Being*, Washington, D.C.: US Government Printing Office.

Fields, J. and L.M. Casper, 2001, *America's Families and Living Arrangements*, Current Population Report, Washington, D.C.: US Census Bureau.

Garfinkle, I. and S.S. Mclanahan, 1986, *Single Mothers and Their Children*, Washington, D.C.: Urban Institute Press.

Goode, W.J., 1963, *World Revolution and Family Pattern*, New York: The Free Press.

Harlombos, M. and R.M. Heald, 1998, *Sociology: Themes and Perspectives*, Calcutta: Oxford University Press.

Hilton, J.M., S. Desrochers and E.L. Devall, 2001, 'Comparison of Role Demands, Relationships and Child Functioning in Single Mother, Single Father and Intact Families', *Journal of Divorce and Remarriage*, 35 (1): 29–56.

Kemp, Sandra, 1988, *Kipling's Hidden Narratives*, Oxford: Blackwell.

India's Commitment to Family Well-Being: An Overview and Agenda for Action, 1994, Draft Document, Bombay: Tata Institute of Social Sciences.

Institute of Social Studies Trust, 1984, *India's Female Headed Households*, Geneva: ILO.

Jones, E., 1983, *Raising Your Child in a Fatherless Home*, London: The Free Press of Glencoe Collier, Macmillan Ltd.

Krein, S.F., 1986, 'Growing Up in a Single Parent Family: The Effect of Education and Earnings on Young Men', *Family Relations*, XXXVI: 161–168.

Kumari, Krishna, N.S., 1987, *Status of Single Women in India*, New Delhi: Uppal Publishing House.

Kumari, R., 1989, *Women-Headed Households in Rural India*, New Delhi: Radiant Publishers.

Mclanahan, G. and K. Booth, 1989, Single Mothers and Their Children: Problems, Reproduction and Politics', *Journal of Marriage and the Family*, 51: 557–580.

Marsden, D., 1969, *Mothers Alone*, Allen Lane, London: Penguin Press.

Murdock, G.P., 1949, *Social Structure of the Family: Its Functions and Destiny*, R.N. Anshen (ed.), New York: Harper & Row.

Panda, P.K., 1997, 'Female Headship, Poverty and Child Welfare: A Study of Rural Orissa, India', *Economic and Political Weekly*, October 25: 73–82.

Parsons, Talcott, 1959, The Social Structure of Family' in R.N. Anshen, *The Family, Its Functions and Destiny*, New York: Harper.

Parthasarthy, V., 1982, Land Reforms and Changing Agrarian Structure', in C.H. Shah (ed), *Agrarian Development in India – Policy and Problems*.

Shanthi, K., 1992, 'Economics of Female Headed Households: Incidence, Characteristics and Level of Living in Kerala and Tamil Nadu: Comparative Study', Project Submitted to Department of Women and Child Development, Government of India.

Sugarman, S.D., 2003, 'Single Parent Families', in Mason A. Skolnick and S.D. Sugarman (eds), *All Our Families: New Policies for a New Century*, New York: Oxford University Press.

Thorne, Barrie, 1982, *Rethinking the Family: Some Feminist Questions*, New York: Longman.

Vardhan, R., 1999, *Female Headed Households in Patriarchal Society: A Sociological Study*, New Delhi: Indian Publishers & Distributors.

Visaria, Praveen and Leela Visaria, 1983, 'Indian Households with Female Heads: Incidence, Characteristics and Level of Living', in D. Jain and N. Banerjee (ed.) *Tyranny of Household*, New Dehli: Shakthi.

Yousseff, N.H. and C.S. Hetler, 1984, *Rural Households Headed by Women, a Priority Issue for Development*, Geneva: ILO.

Index